RETHINKING POVERTY

RETHINKING

POVERTY

ASSETS, SOCIAL
EXCLUSION,
RESILIENCE AND
HUMAN RIGHTS
IN BARBADOS

CORIN BAILEY

JONATHAN LASHLEY

CHRISTINE BARROW

The University of the West Indies Press
Jamaica • Barbados • Trinidad and Tobago

The University of the West Indies Press
7A Gibraltar Hall Road, Mona
Kingston 7, Jamaica
www.uwipress.com

A catalogue record of this book is available from the
National Library of Jamaica.

ISBN: 978-976-640-732-2 (paper)
978-976-640-733-9 (Kindle)
978-976-640-734-6 (ePub)

Cover image © Caribbean News Service.
Cover design by Robert Harris.

Printed in the United States of America

In memory of Rebecca Louise (Bex) Lashley
and Wilma Rosalind Bailey

CONTENTS

TABLES

FIGURES

ACKNOWLEDGEMENTS

This study would not have been possible without the permission granted by the Barbados Ministry of Social Care, Constituency Empowerment and Community Development for the use of data from the 2010 Barbados Country Assessment of Living Conditions, as well as the time and resources afforded by the Sir Arthur Lewis institute of Social and Economic Studies, the University of the West Indies, Cave Hill.

The contributions of Professor Andrew Downes and Dr Patricia Ellis were integral to the data collection exercise as was the research assistance provided by Dr Jan Obermuller and Ms Rean Gibson.

Special thanks goes to the men and women who voluntarily gave of their time and shared their experiences in order to provide us with the necessary information. This study is based on their testimonies.

ABBREVIATIONS

AMKA	Municipal Department of Multicultural Affairs
BOP	balance of payments
CALC	country assessment of living conditions
CARICOM	Caribbean Community
CDB	Caribbean Development Bank
CLTs	community land trusts
CPA	country poverty assessment
CRC	Convention on the Rights of the Child
DESA	Department of Economic and Social Affairs
DFID	Department for International Development
FAO	Food and Agriculture Organization
GM	gay men
IDB	Inter-American Development Bank
ILO	International Labour Organization
IM	immigrants
IMF	International Monetary Fund
IPV	indigent, poor and vulnerable
JSIF	Jamaica Social Investment Fund
LMRU	Lady Meade Reference Unit
MSEA	macro social and economic assessment
MSM	men who have sex with men
MUD	moral underclass discourse
NEET	education, employment or training
PES	public employment services
PLHIV	person living with HIV
PPA	participatory poverty assessment
RDC	Rural Development Commission
RED	redistributionist

ABBREVIATIONS

SDGs	sustainable development goals
SID	social integrationist discourse
SLC	survey of living conditions
SLF	Sustainable Livelihoods Framework
SW	sex workers
UNDP	United Nations Development Programme
UDC	Urban Development Commission
UY	unattached youth
WHH	women who head households

CHAPTER 1

A LOCAL APPROACH TO POVERTY MEASUREMENT

SOCIAL SCIENCE STUDIES OF POVERTY AND SOCIAL INEQUALITY proliferate across the globe and have provided a central focus of interest among Caribbean scholars, particularly since the 1990s. Although local researchers initially followed the trend by privileging an economic approach and indicators that measured income against consumption in order to define those above and below a poverty line, recent approaches have challenged this narrow focus by highlighting social, psychological, political and environmental determinants. New indicators have been added, for example, in health and education, social capital and participation, environmental degradation and citizenship rights in law, policy and practice. Our research and analysis seek to further that trajectory with a conceptual frame that foregrounds and maps the intersections among four key concepts: *asset-deprivation, social exclusion, resilience* and *human rights.*

As a small island developing state in the Caribbean, Barbados presents unique perspectives and challenges for research. At the same time, the context offers opportunities for analysis and policymaking that resonate with other countries of the region and around the world and that share a heritage of colonialism and plantation slavery, contemporary economic problems of low productivity and growth, export concentration, high dependence on imports and mounting indebtedness, compounded by the shocks of the recent global crisis that has plunged them into the recession from which they struggle to recover. Colour-class social hierarchies, unemployment and poverty also persist.

Our framework is multidisciplinary as it integrates economic, social, political and environmental perspectives and multi-level as it combines macroeconomic and -social analysis with that at the individual and household

1

levels. We investigate the circumstances of the three social groups that are most prone to indigence, poverty and vulnerability, namely the working poor, the unemployed and retirees. And, by highlighting their voices, we interrogate in depth the experiences and resilience of persons socially excluded by asset-deprivation, stigma and discrimination, namely gay men, sex workers, persons living with HIV, immigrants, women who head households and unemployed youth.

For this research, we used the concept of social exclusion, which is, in turn, rooted in the dearth of a wide range of assets – human, social, physical and environmental, as well as financial. We ask how asset-deprivation and the absence of asset-building mechanisms make individuals and social groups vulnerable to social exclusion and how certain persons might demonstrate the resilience to survive, recover and even improve the quality of their lives. Recognizing that resilience is a function of individuals' efforts to enhance their asset base but is also dependent on context – on whether the economic, social, political and environmental context offers opportunities or constraints to self-improvement – the central question for development policy is: What needs to be done to ensure access to assets and asset-building mechanisms to promote social inclusion and human rights?

Barbados shares with other Caribbean countries an economy and society that emerged from colonialism and slavery and a plantation system that was established shortly after European settlement and continued well after emancipation. Evidence of this legacy persists in contemporary structural and environmental vulnerabilities, including low economic productivity and growth, export concentration and high dependence on imports, including energy, food and industrial inputs. Small domestic markets and the openness of economies provide limited scope for diversification and constrain competitive advantage, though some advantage has been realized in tourism and, more recently, in cultural industries. These characteristics have combined to trigger mounting indebtedness and severe balance of payments deficits, exacerbated by the recent global financial crisis. The plantation system also generated rigid social hierarchies of race and class, social exclusion and persistent poverty. Unemployment levels continue to be unacceptably high, especially among women and youth.

Caribbean economic and social problems are compounded by environmental vulnerability as a result of geographical location in a hurricane belt and a zone of earthquakes and volcanic activity. Significant proportions of populations live in low-lying coastal areas and are highly susceptible to new threats related to climate change. Land resources are limited, and, in some countries, mountainous interiors and other physical barriers complicate the provision of water, sanitation, utilities and communication to outlying areas. Countries have, nevertheless, done well to conserve and develop their respective ecosystems. Recently, too, many have adopted Green Economy initiatives in recognition of the importance of the environment to the economic mainstays of tourism, agriculture and fisheries.

Despite challenges, Caribbean countries have, since independence, achieved a good record of economic, social and environmental development, though not all to the same degree or with sustainable outcomes. Positive records in health are evident in basic indicators of child and maternal mortality and longevity. As a result of immunization coverage and public health outreach, epidemics of infectious diseases are a problem of the past. But Caribbean governments now confront the challenge of chronic, non-communicable illness, especially cardiovascular disease and diabetes. These illnesses take their toll on human well-being and on the public purse. It is also estimated that 280,000 persons across the region are living with HIV, but a rapid and effective response has reduced the rate of transmission by 50 per cent (UNAIDS 2015). Investments in education are also evident in high levels of literacy, universal primary education, efforts to expand the provision of secondary and tertiary education and, more recently, the availability of early childhood education and vocational and technical training. National insurance schemes offer pensions and unemployment benefits, while social assistance provides a range of benefits to those in need, including food security; legal aid; educational provisions in the form of schoolbooks, uniforms and transport; skills training and small business development; and day care and shelters for survivors of violence. Social protection schemes focus on supports for vulnerable groups, especially children and youth, the elderly and persons with disabilities. The majority of people have access to basic utilities, though there are still weaknesses and inadequacies in provision. Social unrest is rare and temporary in Caribbean countries and is generally associated with periods of political electioneering. But crime and violence, with evidence of street gangs, gun violence, drug trafficking and organized crime, especially in urban areas, have escalated to the extent that many countries of the region have had to divert resources from economic and social development to security.

The expansion of education in tandem with economic diversification softened the rigid social hierarchies based on race and class and promoted social mobility and a heightened degree of social equality. Not all, however, have benefited and not all equally. Gender inequalities persist and are evident in the under-representation of women in political systems and in higher female unemployment levels, along with lower-paid jobs and job insecurity – this despite their higher performances in education. Women are also held back by teen pregnancy, the burden of social care and household headship, as well as exposure to domestic violence. Also vulnerable are Caribbean youth, the so-called unattached males in particular whose educational underperformance, school attrition and high unemployment are perceived to drive them towards deviance and crime, drug abuse and violence. A concern for all Caribbean governments, too, is the demographic phenomenon of ageing populations and the burden of care for the elderly, complicated by chronic disease, poverty and social isolation. Though pension provisions are in place, they are inadequate in coverage and value and increasingly under strain. Persons with disabilities continue to be excluded from care, support, education and employment despite the efforts of governments and NGOs (non-governmental organizations) to promote social inclusion. The quality of life of other vulnerable social groups who are targets of stigma and discrimination has only recently begun to emerge in research and in NGO outreach, and these groups continue to be marginalized and invisible in government policy. Among them are migrants, ex-prisoners, the homeless, persons living with HIV, sex workers and LGBTQ persons, gay men in particular. Some, such as sex workers, gay men and undocumented migrants, are also criminalized. For most of these vulnerable groups, state social protection schemes, NGOs and families provide essential care and support, though to varying degrees. In addition, the resources of many of these agencies, even those of extended families, are overstretched, and, for some stigmatized peoples, they may also be sources of discrimination and abuse.

Official statistical rankings of GDP, per capita income and compliance with millennial and sustainable development goals mask the existence of inequality and poverty. Across the Caribbean, high proportions of populations continue to live in poverty, with rates ranging from 9.9 per cent in the Bahamas in 2001 to 47.2 per cent in Suriname in 2012. Persistent poverty is heavily concentrated among vulnerable social groups. State initiatives to address poverty and inequality across the Caribbean have their genesis in the Moyne Commission Report of 1945, which was established as a response to the riots of the late 1930s that spread across the region. The commission's report pointed to poverty and appalling living conditions as the cause of social unrest and recommended, among other things, interventions in education, health and social welfare but no fundamental economic transformation or reduction in social inequality. To address poverty – and to ensure social stability – poor relief was implemented in the form of a palliative stipend for basic survival rather than promoting any escape from poverty. Since then, poverty reduction programmes have undergone marked changes. Basic needs schemes that expanded deliverables to include health and education for social advancement were transformed with the addition of rights-based, people-centred, asset-based approaches that challenged structural barriers to poverty alleviation in legal, economic and social systems, with particular focus on stigmatized identities. With this came the recognition that income alone is an insufficient measure of poverty and that the benefits of economic growth do not automatically "trickle down" to the poor. But, despite this reconceptualization, implementation continues to fail many people. Poverty persists and demands a continuous rethink of approaches, policies and programmes.

The global crisis has had a profound, far-reaching and prolonged impact on Caribbean economies. Up to 2008, many countries of the region had made significant progress in GDP per capita and in the achievement of millennium development goals (MDGs), but there is evidence that these gains are being reversed. Some countries even succeeded in lowering poverty levels during the period 1995–2004, but since then, levels have increased, and there are reports of under-nutrition and food insecurity (Caribbean Development Bank 2016, 24; FAO 2015). The capacity to achieve poverty reduction, the first of 17 sustainable development goals (SDGs), is in jeopardy. Rising burdens of debt, current account deficits and the need for financial stringency have forced governments across the region to implement austerity measures and to cut back on public capital and social service expenditures. School enrolment, which increased between 2004 and 2008, has since been on a downward trend in most Caribbean countries, disproportionately affecting children from poor households (United Nations Development Programme [UNDP] 2016, 66). There are also reports of the degradation of eco-systems, which not only undermines tourism, agriculture and fisheries but also reduces resistance to natural disasters.

Caribbean states struggle, as they have in the past, to promote economic growth, protect human development goals and strengthen gains in education, health, gender equality and poverty reduction. The contemporary economic crisis demands a critical re-examination of economic, social and environmental development paradigms and responses to poverty; yet governments across the region, along with private sector partners, have been slow to respond to the crisis with innovative ideas and policies.

THE BARBADOS MODEL OF DEVELOPMENT

The so-called Barbados model of development is rooted in the realities of a Caribbean small island developing state, only 432 square kilometres in area with limited natural resources and one of the highest population densities worldwide. Key to the country's success are consistent social investment and the harnessing of human resources for development. Social investments have generated a literate, educated, healthy population to drive economic growth, which has, in turn, enabled successive administrations to reinvest in institutional development; physical infrastructure; access to water, sanitation, utilities and road network; public health; education and welfare; and environmental conservation. Economic diversification has kept unemployment levels generally low and has reduced the burden of social protection on the state. Steady development and progress are rooted in an underlying strategy of integrating economic with social development – in combination with sound economic management, accountability and good governance; a strong partnership between government, the private sector and labour unions; careful environmental planning; and social mobility and stability. Poverty levels have remained low, and social inclusion has been promoted through policies that promote equality and universalism. The legal, political and social framework generally ensures that the human rights of the majority are respected. Barbadians enjoy freedom of speech, religion, movement and association. There are no politically motivated disappearances or political prisoners. Child labour laws are in place and are effectively enforced, and there are no official reports of forced labour, though anecdotal evidence suggests this occurs among immigrants in domestic service (United States Department of State 2016, 13–14). However, a recent report spotlights violence against women, child abuse, discrimination against LGBTQ persons and non-professional conduct by the police, including intimidation and assault, as issues of serious concern (United States Department of State 2016, 1–2, 8–9, 12).

As a small open economy and society, vulnerable to external shocks, Barbados has shown some resilience during periods of economic crisis. The country has earned international acclaim for its record of economic management, good governance and political stability, human and social capital development and a well managed environment that facilitates economic investment. During the 1980s, the Barbados model was promoted as a developmental paradigm for other developing countries, providing clear evidence that small size and scarce resources need not preclude a positive record of social and economic modernization.

Barbados has experienced significant economic and social gains despite the deep-seated and long-term impact of the plantation heritage. By the turn of the 20th century, little change was evident in the system in which virtually all arable land was consolidated into plantation sugar production for export and basic food staples were imported. By contrast, in neighbouring Caribbean countries, the available land in mountainous interiors facilitated the establishment of viable peasantries producing food for local consumption. Plantation sugar in Barbados generated great wealth for the country and the planter elite, but this occurred at the expense of severe malnutrition, high mortality, overcrowding, dispossession and poverty for the black majority of the population. Some relief was provided by mass migration to Panama for the construction of the canal and by the remittances sent home during the period 1904–14, but the plantation system remained firmly entrenched.

It was not until mid-century, with the collapse of sugar, that evidence of economic diversification became apparent. Initial opportunities, mainly in services and the informal sector, were concentrated in and around the capital of Bridgetown, triggering rapid urbanization. Fuelled by the push of rural poverty and the absence of land for small farming, as well as the subdivision and sale of marginal, urban estates into small residential lots or house spots, Barbados, in common with other Caribbean countries, became heavily

urbanized around one major city. In recent years, the urban flow has
stabilized. In 1990, the most urban parish of St Michael was home to 37.4 per
cent of the population, but by 2010 this proportion had been reduced to 31.9
per cent. Some ease in congestion has been provided by the spread of
urbanization to the suburbs and along adjacent coastal areas where tourism
is concentrated. An estimated 66 per cent of the population lives in this urban
corridor (Government of Barbados 2015, 26).

Most recently, the economic base of Barbados was transformed from
agriculture to services, with the addition of high-end tourism, supplemented
by international business and financial services. A small sugar production
sector for export persists, and, although there has been no major land reform
project, local food production is evident in an effort to stimulate some self-
sufficiency and reduce the escalating food import bill. Nevertheless, Barbados
is among the majority of Caribbean countries that import more than 80 per
cent of their food requirements. This amounts to over US$4 billion annually,
with the Barbados proportion at US$312 million (FAO 2015, 9–10).

Economic diversification, in combination with enlightened social policy,
has generated the social transformation of Barbadian society from a rigid
class-colour hierarchy, with mass poverty and almost non-existent
opportunities for social advancement, to a social system characterized by
greater social mobility and overall equality. The service economy has provided
employment for women more on par with men and at higher levels than
agricultural labour. The expansion of education, especially with the
introduction of free secondary education and a gender balance in enrolment,
has also made a significant contribution. In this regard, government
investment has ensured that public education became a critical agent for
social transformation. Educational enrolment is high in Barbados at all levels,
and the 61 per cent rate at the tertiary level positions the country among the
highest in the region (UNDP 2016, 117). Consistent investment in public
health is evident in basic indicators. While child, maternal and adult
mortality has fluctuated across the region with some evidence of increase, in
Barbados they have declined consistently (UNDP 2016, 120). The infant
mortality rate (IMR), for example, plummeted from a high of 125 per 1,000
in 1950 to 10.1 today, and life expectancy, at a low of 28.6 years in 1921, has
risen to 77.7. The multi-pronged response to HIV and AIDS in the Caribbean
effectively combined counselling and testing, antiretroviral treatment, and

public educational and awareness campaigns to lower the rate of new infections by 43 per cent in adults and to reduce AIDS-related mortality by 59 per cent between 2000 and 2014. Key populations, however, continue to be hard to reach. In Jamaica, for example, the HIV prevalence among men who have sex with men (MSM) is estimated to be 33 per cent (UNAIDS 2015). The Caribbean response, in general, has been less successful in challenging and eliminating the structural drivers of HIV, including stigma and discrimination, gender-based violence (GBV) and human rights violations along with punitive laws and social policies.

One of the more significant and essential investments made by successive Barbadian governments has been that of birth control. By the turn of the nineteenth century, the population had climbed to 186,000, giving a high density of 1,120 persons per square mile, and a crisis of overcrowding threatened. In comparison with other Caribbean countries, Barbados had the greatest need for fertility control and, arguably, the greatest success. The birth control programme, in combination with emigration, rescued the country from widespread poverty, disease and mortality. Less well recognized is the dramatic impact of fertility reduction on the status of women. With the capacity to control and space births, women completed their education, benefited from occupational opportunities, reduced their burden of childcare and raised their standard of living and that of their families. Across the Caribbean, adolescent motherhood has generally declined, though there continue to be fluctuations, and, in some countries, the figures are unacceptably high. Between 2005 and 2010, in St Lucia, St Vincent and the Grenadines and Guyana, births to girls aged up to 19 years constituted 20 per cent or more of the total births (Nam 2016, 44). In Barbados, teenage births were reduced to 11.1 per cent of total births during the same period. This, in combination with the legalization of abortions as a result of the passage of the Medical Termination of Pregnancy Act of 1983, has mitigated the inter-generational cycle of poverty. Within the Caribbean, however, only Barbados and Guyana have liberal abortion laws. In addition, for Barbados, gender inequality, girls' social vulnerabilities and sexual risk behaviours are evident in high rates of HIV infection, where adolescent girls (aged 10–19) outnumber boys by a ratio of 2.3 to 1 (Barrow 2009).

Sustained reformist policies to promote social development and improve the quality of life for all sectors of the Barbadian population, combined with focused poverty alleviation through social insurance and social protection schemes, have also facilitated social participation and cohesion and has kept crime rates relatively low. Since 2000, the homicide rate has fluctuated from a high of 12.7 per 100,000 population to 8.4 in 2013. This compares favourably with some other Caribbean countries with significantly higher rates in 2013 – Jamaica at 39.3, the Bahamas at 31.5, and Trinidad and Tobago at 28.3 (Bailey 2016). In Barbados, too, stable parliamentary democracy, along with regular elections under universal suffrage and community participation, has engendered social stability and investor confidence for economic development. The relative absence of natural hazards, in combination with sound environmental planning and infrastructural development in communications, utilities, sanitation and public transport, has also facilitated a continuous record of sustainable development.

Aggregated data for Barbados reflect progress in comparison with Caribbean neighbours but also troubling regression. Barbados's ranking on the Human Development Index (HDI) of the UNDP has fallen from twenty-nine in 2004 to thirty-seven in 2009 and to fifty-six in 2014. Though remaining in the High Human Development category, Barbados has not been keeping up relative to other countries. In addition, the Barbados poverty level was at 19 per cent of population in 2010. This reflects an increase from 13.9 per cent in 1996–97, though it remains below the 24 per cent average for the Caribbean. Income inequality is high, with a Gini coefficient of 0.47 that places Barbados among the top three in the region for inequality (UNDP 2016, 114). Unemployment rates in 2015 varied across the region from a high of 25 per cent in St Lucia to a low of 3.2 per cent in Trinidad and Tobago, with Barbados at 12 per cent (UNDP 2016). Migration continues to have a significant impact in terms of both the economic and social costs of losing younger, skilled persons but also of the receipt of remittances that reached US$275 million in 2014 in Barbados. Remittances provide significant alleviation of financial strain at household levels, but most funds supplement household incomes and are spent on immediate basic needs of home repairs and consumer durables (UNDP 2016, 136) rather than being invested in education, training and business development for a more sustainable alleviation of poverty.

In common with other Caribbean countries, Barbados confronts a range of social problems. With birth and death rates under control, the country has reached the final stage of demographic transition with declining rates of natural increase and the burden on the state and families of an ageing population. Despite pension reform initiatives in an effort to ensure financial sustainability, Barbados is expected to eventually reach the point where NIS (National Insurance Scheme) fund expenditure on rising benefits exceeds contributions. In the event that economic growth continues to be low and unemployment high, Barbados may be forced to draw on investment reserves to meet payments, a course of action that is predicted to deplete assets in the next few decades (International Monetary Fund 2016). Health concerns increasingly focus on chronic lifestyle diseases, including hypertension, diabetes and cardiovascular disease, as well as HIV and AIDS. Across the region, obesity among women is estimated at between 29 and 42 per cent, with Barbados at 38.2 per cent (UNDP 2016, 121–23). Rampant diabetes, among the highest worldwide, has earned Barbados a reputation as the "amputation capital" of the Caribbean. These health problems have been linked to poor diets, in particular the dependence on imported food, much of it described as "calorie-dense, high-fat, high-sweetener" in content and more prevalent in the diets of poor households (FAO 2015, 18). Though education is compulsory by law to the age of sixteen in many countries, levels of attrition and the proportions of school-leavers without certification, especially boys, are a source of concern. Gender disparity in education has become increasingly evident. At the tertiary level, Barbados has the highest imbalance for the region, with a ratio of 88.1 per cent of females enrolled as against 35.9 per cent of males in 2013 (UNDP 2016, 118). The educational underperformance of male youth is perceived to fuel unemployment, drug and alcohol abuse, delinquency and crime. Family and community fragmentation, conflict and violence are said to have increased in recent generations, though research, albeit limited, suggests that these perceptions may be exaggerated (Barrow 2001).

Problems associated with urbanization are evident even though, as suggested, there is no sharp distinction between urban and rural zones. Urban population density is high, at 2,270 persons per square kilometre in St Michael, although overcrowding in households is very low with little urban–rural distinction. Urbanization has put pressure on housing, employment, and social, health, educational, transport and leisure services, but it has also triggered the concentration of these in urban areas with consequent rural neglect. Although these problems are mitigated in Barbados by small size, a well-established road network and regular public transport that enable daily travel to and from the city, this has resulted in severe traffic congestion and threatened air quality (Government of Barbados 2015, 52–53). Urban areas in Barbados are also prone to flooding and under threat of sea level rise.

Towns and cities on the periphery of global capitalism also act as gateways to external influences, and, as a small, open, dependent economy, Barbados is no exception. The exposure to modern Western consumerism, most recently facilitated by the information technology revolution and driven by aggressive media promotion and advertising, is evident in the Americanization of tastes and lifestyles. Tourism has added an extra layer of demand for luxury goods. This has exacerbated the already high import bill for food, consumer durables and status symbols, and conspicuous consumption polarizes the population.

More than any other issue, that of crime and violence associated with urban areas is preoccupying governments, businesses and the general public. Across the globe, violence in towns and cities seems to be becoming part of the daily reality, generating mounting alarm. As a tourist destination, the consequences for Barbados's international reputation are of particular concern. Given this focus of attention, urban violence is surprisingly under-researched, and the response, in terms of both official policy and of programming, and the public panic and fear are based largely on anecdotal evidence and exaggerated media reports.

What evidence there is points to an urban concentration of violence in that, for example, the majority of murders were reported for the area around Bridgetown. But, although particular urban areas are stigmatized as undesirable ghettos by association in the public mind with crime and violence and, according to anecdotal evidence, avoided by women and girls for fear of harassment, there is little indication of stigmatized "no-go" areas in Barbados. Neither is there evidence, as in some other Caribbean countries, of residents locked into politically linked and labelled communities, afraid to venture from home and therefore constrained in terms of access to employment, schooling and other opportunities. However, those in Barbados with the wherewithal to leave undesirable urban areas have been relocating to more salubrious suburbs (Government of Barbados 2015, 4) and separating themselves in gated communities with high walls, alarms, bars and security guards. With people reluctant to invest in their own neighbourhoods and motivated to escape, community cohesion is eroded.

What research there is confirms the association of crime and violence with male youth; both the perpetrators and the victims of murder and assault in Barbados are predominantly adult males under the age of thirty-five years (Bailey 2016, 14–17). There is also an alarming increase in the use of firearms, linked to international trade in gun trafficking. Information on gangs is severely limited. For example, the police have no estimate of the number of youths involved (Bailey 2016, 37), and, although their existence is not in doubt, there seems to be some denial of their potential impact and a reluctance to address it. They are assumed to be mainly urban based, their territorial claims centred on high-rise buildings and government-provided housing areas, so-called blocks, and they are composed of young, "unattached" men driven onto the streets by unemployment, family conflict, home overcrowding and educational attrition. Though organized with leadership, codes of conduct and initiation, police claim that gangs are more informal in Barbados (Bailey 2016, 36–37). There is little evidence, for example, as there is elsewhere in the Caribbean, that members of the public, disaffected with the police and other official legal agencies, are turning towards the gangs for protection. Gangs do, however, tend to protect their own at the expense of wider social cohesion.

The response to crime and violence has been centred on crackdown strategies focusing on the arrest and incarceration of individual perpetrators rather than on investigating and addressing the structural drivers embedded in the urban economic and social environment, including youth culture and unemployment, poverty and social exclusion. There is some evidence of outreach in the form of six community policing outposts established in urban areas and in partnerships with community organizations that protect women, the elderly and other vulnerable persons, but much dependence is still on already overextended family support. Without a shift to evidence-based, prevention strategies that tackle the underlying causes, violence continues to escalate, reinforcing a climate of fear among urban dwellers.

Social policy and programming have been designed in accordance with principles of universalism and equality, but specific key populations continue to be socially excluded and vulnerable to poverty. Gender inequality also persists. The educational achievements of girls are yet to be translated into social and political mobility. In 2013, 59.3 per cent of women in the region were employed as compared with 78.7 per cent of men. Women were also concentrated in lower-level, less well-paid jobs (UNDP 2016, 58). In only three countries of the Caribbean, namely Antigua and Barbuda, Grenada and Guyana, are 25 per cent or more parliamentary seats held by women (UNDP 2016, 65). Domestic and interpersonal issues also impact women's life chances. As indicated, teenage motherhood persists and is well known to initiate a cycle of negative consequences, including school dropout, menial employment, physical and psychological health problems and social exclusion, all of which combine to perpetuate intergenerational poverty. Gender-based violence has similar social and health consequences, and, although estimates are problematic as a result of under-reporting and woefully inadequate data collection, rates are generally assumed to be high. In Barbados, homicides as a result of domestic violence climbed to 33 per cent in 2013 (Bailey 2016, 25). Women continue to bear the burden of caring labour and to head households. The high proportions of female-headed households, at 47.5 per cent in Barbados, have been directly linked with poverty. The overlapping impact of female household headship, teen pregnancy and domestic violence constrain women's employment and are major social drivers of poverty. Indeed, the fact that studies elsewhere have revealed female-headed households to be particularly vulnerable (Safa 1999) has been fuelling the debate over the feminization of poverty – the growing gap between the men and women in society who live in poverty. Safa found that women were likely to be living alone (with their children) as opposed to living within an extended family unit and that they therefore suffered from the absence of additional income. Their relatively low labour force participation also meant that they were more likely to have no one employed in the household (45 per cent) when compared to households headed by men (22 per cent).

Young persons are also disproportionately vulnerable to poverty. Youth unemployment is high, between 18 and 47 per cent across the region, with Trinidad and Tobago the exception at 10 per cent. This amounts to between two and three times that of adults (UNDP 2016, 72). The link with juvenile offending has also been reported. In Barbados, 44 per cent of all individuals under eighteen self-report as having been involved in crime, with males twice as prevalent as females. This compares with 54 per cent and 53 per cent in St Lucia and Dominica, respectively (UNDP 2016, 69).

Children bear the brunt of poverty, exploitation and abuse in the Caribbean as they do elsewhere. Child labour rates among those aged between five and fourteen years varied from 0.7 per cent in Trinidad and Tobago to 16.4 per cent in Guyana in 2006. In Barbados, the figure was 2.3 per cent (UNDP 2016, 87). Children work in domestic service, agriculture, vending and begging, with those most at risk in sex work and drug trafficking (UNDP 2016). Child labour has been directly associated with low school attendance and attrition, but there is also evidence that Caribbean children work to pay for their schooling. Violence against children includes emotional, physical and sexual abuse and neglect and is also a cause for deep concern (Bailey 2016). In most countries of the region, the corporal punishment of children is legally sanctioned and culturally acceptable in homes and schools.

Women, children, the elderly and persons living with disabilities have been afforded special protection by law and by social policy and programming, but other social groups continue to be marginalized. Among them are immigrants, ex-prisoners, the homeless, persons living with HIV (PLHIV), men who have sex with men (MSM) and sex workers (SW), who continue to be targets of discrimination. The sexual activities of MSM and SW are also criminalized by law, though infractions are rarely pursued. Socially excluded from employment and housing, stigmatized by health services providers and scorned by the public and by their families, members of these groups are at high risk of poverty, violence and human rights abuses.

The contemporary global economic crisis continues to present severe challenges to the future development of Barbados and the wider Caribbean. While economic growth throughout the region was positive up to 2007, this trend has been reversed. Signs of fragility are manifest in weak growth, escalating public debt burdens and deficits, continued dependence on a narrow economic base of tourism and financial services, growing unemployment and austerity, and signs of social discontent and decay. By 2014, the total public sector debt-to-GDP ratio had soared to 108.5 per cent, way above the recommended 60 per cent benchmark (UNDP 2016). With low economic growth, traditional productivity and a limited competitive edge, there is little flexibility in relation to solutions. In terms of fiscal policy, while there are indications of some potential in the Caribbean for raising the personal income tax, this may be more limited in Barbados where the rate of revenue collection rose to 32.4 per cent of GDP by 2015, the highest in the region. There is also evidence of tax and value-added tax (VAT) evasion, especially as regards corporate taxes (UNDP 2016, 138). While there are signs of recovery in some Caribbean countries, in Barbados, along with Trinidad and Tobago and Jamaica, such signs have been described as "weak and uncertain" (UNDP 2016, 139). It remains to be seen whether the Barbados model of neo-liberal development, which has over the years proved to be resilient to external shocks and has ensured economic and social modernization, will weather the present crisis and ensure sustainability. It is more than likely, though, that Barbados has reached a point where future growth and development necessitate fundamental rethinking and remodelling.

RETHINKING CARIBBEAN POVERTY

Since the nineteenth century, researchers have been struggling to find an adequate means of defining poverty; yet no universal consensus exists today. Much of the debate has been concerned with whether poverty should be defined in absolute or relative terms. Based on the concept of absolute poverty, there is a level below which individuals and households are at risk of starvation. In order to determine that level, it became necessary to identify what was necessary for survival. Defining absolute poverty therefore involves a determination of the resources necessary to maintain health and physical well-being. That usually involves pricing these basic necessities, drawing a poverty line based on them and defining the poor as those whose income falls below this line.

Studies done in the Caribbean have generally defined poverty in absolute terms. Poverty and the importance of improving the economic status and overall living conditions of poor and vulnerable citizens of the British Caribbean were first firmly placed on the agenda following the deployment of the West India Royal Commission in August 1938.[1] The commission was charged with investigating the socio-economic conditions of the region that had incited a series of labour unrests throughout the 1930s and submitting recommendations for their improvement. The report of the commission provided extensive details on the poverty and powerlessness experienced by persons living in the British Caribbean colonies. It revealed the dire living conditions in which persons were living, which included a host of incivilities such as poor housing, poor environmental conditions and poor labour conditions, as well as extremely limited access to education and health care (Potter et al. 2014). The work of the commission was one of the first extensive research studies on poverty in the region. It analysed the causes and effects of poverty in purely economic terms and resulted in the rise of the social welfare system. Poverty in this case was understood in absolute terms as the absence of basic daily requirements such as adequate housing, sanitation, education, health care and food (Girvan 1997).

The 1990s saw a considerable increase in research that examined poverty in the Caribbean. During this period, a number of countries commenced the conduct of surveys of living conditions (SLC) and labour force surveys, or both, to measure poverty and identify vulnerable groups (Barker 1997). During the 1990s, over half a century after the Moyne Commission Report, papers produced throughout the region continued to study poverty, using a similar method, one based solely on the economic measurement of income.

In 1989, Henry and Melville sought to shed light on the state of poverty in Trinidad and Tobago through an assessment of previous studies conducted in the country. They noted that "poverty can be defined as a state in which individuals in a population are living below the minimum standard of living and are constrained in their access to basic goods and services when compared to their counterparts" (Henry and Melville 2001, 224). To determine the reality of poverty at the time, the researchers calculated the minimum income necessary to afford food and drink, lighting and fuel, clothing, transport and education and used this to establish a poverty line to estimate the proportion of the total population living in poverty. Similarly, within the same period, Thomas (1993) conducted a study of the state of poverty in Guyana. The results of this study were also based exclusively on economic measures since the indicators used to determine the incidence of poverty were total income and on the ability of a household to utilize this income to purchase the basic necessities.[2] Research on poverty in the Caribbean at this juncture was primarily through the conduct and analysis of quantitative surveys on population income and expenditure levels. Poverty was therefore narrowly conceptualized based on consumption measures, which are aggregates of total expenditure on basic needs (Barker 1997).

Meanwhile, international research on poverty was experiencing a paradigm shift, characterized by the release of the inaugural Human Development Report (HDR), published by the United Nations Development

Programme (UNDP). It can be argued that this was the culmination of ideas that first emerged as early as the 1960s in the scholarly works of researchers such as Dudley Seers, who was highly critical of the exclusive use of economic indicators to measure poverty and social development. He called for the "dethroning" of measures such as GDP and encouraged his contemporaries to consider more multidimensional social indicators of development such as the education, health and quality of life of individuals and the extreme inequality in access to social resources (Seers 1969). Considerable research has now demonstrated that human deprivation cannot be accurately portrayed purely as a lack of financial resources. Indeed, this has been the main criticism of the concept of absolute poverty. It assumes that there are minimum basic financial needs for everyone, everywhere. This is particularly problematic when one considers the manner in which cultural needs vary with place and time (Bailey 2004). Financial indicators can also be somewhat misleading, as evidenced by the example of India, in which economic growth has been occurring alongside high levels of child malnutrition for years. Indeed, participatory exercises in India and other developing economies have revealed that the poor themselves describe their own poverty in multidimensional terms (OPHI 2017).

Townsend (1979) argued that poverty can be defined objectively and applied consistently only in terms of the concept of relative deprivation. This view was based on his belief that it is society that determines the needs of individuals. Relative deprivation should be based on the resources available to individuals, as well as on the standard of living, which is determined by how those resources are used. Income is therefore not enough to determine a household's material situation. Standard measures of poverty have proved inadequate in the face of a variety of factors, including violations of human rights, increased migration, weakening of family ties, environmental inequalities and reduced social and political participation (Devicienti and Poggi 2011). Townsend argued that what was important was how resources affected one's ability to participate fully in society. So, in this vein, individuals, families and groups in a population can be said to live in poverty when they lack the resources necessary to enjoy the standard of living that is deemed acceptable in their society. Their resources are so seriously below those commanded by the average individual or family that they are, in effect, excluded from ordinary living patterns, customs and activities (Townsend 1979).

Following the advancement of development ideas, such as those proposed by Seers (1969) and Townsend (1979), it became generally recognized internationally that income-based indicators alone were inadequate for the measurement of the levels and severity of poverty experienced globally. This led to the watershed moment in 1990 when the UNDP published its Human Development Report and the Human Development Index as a measure of poverty. These assessments factored in social, environmental and political indicators, including social exclusion, to the definition of poverty. Since then, a number of scholars have attempted to apply multidimensional concepts to the measurement of poverty. Bourguignon and Chakravarty (2003) provided a framework for this that included a means of identifying the number of dimensions in which an individual or household is deficient, as well as a statistical summary component for overall poverty. This represented an extension of the ideas of Foster, Greer and Thorbecke (1984). Although there is now general agreement that deprivation is multidimensional, Dhongde and Haveman (2017) argued that the United States has been lagging behind some of its more developed counterparts in providing adequate measurements of this phenomenon. In response, they compiled individual-level data on a variety of indicators of well-being, such as education, security, social connections, housing quality and the like, in order to develop a Multidimensional Deprivation Index. Similarly, Whelan, Nolan and Maitre (2014) applied the Adjusted Headcount Approach to the measurement of poverty in response to the need for a more multidimensional approach to studying poverty in the European Union. Much of the focus of multidimensional approaches has been on identifying appropriate means of measuring poverty (see Deutsch and Silber [2005] for a review) rather than on means of identifying who is poor. Atkinson (2003) discusses two approaches to achieving the latter: the union approach and the intersection approach. The *union approach* considers anyone who is deprived in any dimension of poverty to be poor, while the *intersection approach* requires those considered to be poor to be deprived of all dimensions. While both approaches be useful, they can, however, reveal dramatically different results.

In 1997, seven years after the introduction of the HDR and the accompanying expansion of the concepts of poverty and human development, the first national poverty study was conducted in Barbados. This study aimed to provide an explanation of poverty and, in turn, facilitate the implementation of informed policy measures to address poverty reduction and improve the overall socio-economic conditions of the population.[3] Despite the shift in focus beyond basic economic measures encouraged by the UNDP report, however, this study approached poverty utilizing per capita income as the main indicator to establish poverty levels. Based on this income measure, the poverty line was calculated at Bds$5,503 per annum, and this resulted in a poverty estimate of 13.9 per cent of the total population (Diez de Medina 1998).

The basic premise of an income measure of poverty rests on three main assumptions: (1) that money can be utilized to buy items that will make persons feel less destitute; (2) that money is an adequate estimate of welfare/ utility and (3) that one year's income can be used to estimate future income (Haveman and Mullikin 1999). Such measures, however, do not adequately include and examine factors that expand capabilities, such as individuals' social and political participation in society, their access to capacity building programmes in formal education and skills training, the state of their living environment or the state of their health and access to proper health care. Further, annual income is a poor indicator of an individual's "command over resources" since it does very little to explain consumption patterns (Nam, Huang and Sherraden 2008). Individuals' access to income may in fact be cyclical, since they may experience periods of employment and unemployment. This is particularly applicable within the Caribbean context where most economies depend on tourism and agriculture, which are seasonal in nature. An individual may be employed for six months of the year and then experience hardship for the remaining six months.

Since 1995, the Caribbean Development Bank (CDB) has commissioned a series of country poverty assessments (CPA)/country assessments of living conditions (CALC) throughout Caribbean member states. The main objective has been to establish the level, severity and characteristics of poverty in the Caribbean in order to facilitate the development of strategies and policies that would effectively reduce poverty. All CPAs/CALC have key components such as participatory poverty assessments (PPAs), institutional assessments and surveys of living conditions (SLC).[4] In addition to examining the consumption levels of the poor, the CPA/CALC also gathers first-hand reports from poor and vulnerable members of society on their living conditions in an attempt to foster the development of evidence-based policy to address poverty. The CPA/CALC also assesses the contribution of institutions to overall socio-economic conditions. Although these studies represent an improvement on earlier poverty research studies conducted in the region, they still continue to premise the definition of poverty in individuals' access to income.[5]

As indicated, traditional poverty measures are proxies for the numerous forms of disadvantage experienced by the poor. This has been recognized by Caribbean scholars, who have been calling for the inclusion of non-economic variables in the definitions of poverty. Alcock (1997, 85–86) insisted: A full picture of poverty involves the recognition of the many forms that deprivation can take in complex societies, a recognition of the extent to which it is a relative experience. . . . This involves a focus not just on monetary poverty and on comparisons between income levels but also an analysis of the social and economic situation of individuals and families".

We therefore, propose the use of a more comprehensive conceptualization of deprivation, which takes into consideration the range of resources or assets necessary to maintain an acceptable standard of living as well as access to asset-building mechanisms. We argue that the absence of critical financial, physical, human, social and environmental assets leaves individuals and groups vulnerable to social exclusion. Given that, we use the concept of social exclusion rather than more traditional measures of poverty and offer a more holistic framework against which future discussions of Caribbean poverty should take place. Using quantitative and qualitative data from Barbados, the following questions are explored:

1. What is the nature of access to and utilization of physical, human, social and environmental assets within Barbadian society?
2. How does the absence of these assets and of access to asset-building mechanisms render individuals and groups vulnerable to social exclusion?
3. How do certain individuals and groups demonstrate the resilience necessary to survive and cope in conditions of social exclusion?
4. Going forward, what needs to be done on a policy level to both identify those groups susceptible to exclusion and to ensure adequate access to the assets and asset-building mechanisms necessary to promote social inclusion?

METHODOLOGY

The historical context of poverty and the complex interplay of the causes, consequences and feedback mechanisms that perpetuate it require multiple methods of collection and analysis of data. Consequently, we adopt a series of approaches to seek to understand poverty in all of its dimensions, including data collection through interviews (elite, stakeholder and individuals living in and vulnerable to social exclusion); reviews of existing research, both qualitative and quantitative; and data analysis using both qualitative and quantitative techniques. While noting that available quantitative data is mostly cross-sectional in nature, the analysis attempts to understand changes over time, extracting underlying causal mechanisms and highlighting the importance of placing the analysis of social exclusion within a systems framework.

Chapter 2 draws on reviews of current critical thinking in the area of social exclusion and poverty in order to develop a comprehensive conceptual framework of the causes, consequences and representation of social exclusion.

Chapter 3 seeks to provide a general description of social exclusion in Barbados by utilizing quantitative data from the CALC conducted in 2010.

In chapter 4, the analysis shifts from simple description to a more in-depth qualitative understanding of social exclusion. This chapter presents the voices of the excluded by drawing on testimonies from vulnerable groups and communities.

Chapter 5 looks specifically at the issue of resilience within the context of the findings to emerge from the preceding chapters. The chapter details the responses at the institutional and individual levels to address social exclusion.

Chapter 6 concludes and presents recommendations to address social exclusion in Barbados.

CHAPTER 2

CONCEPTS AND CONTEXT

AN ASSET-BASED APPROACH

The use of *assets* as a means of determining levels of poverty is not new. An asset-based approach in research on poverty emerged in the 1990s in response to the growing concerns over the inadequacies of traditional conceptualizations. As part of the ongoing debate, Oliver and Shapiro (1997) asserted that wealth, which was necessary to secure a sustained desired standard of living, must encompass more than simply measures of income. Whereas traditional social policy focused almost entirely on access to and level of income to identify the poor in society, the ideas proposed by Oliver and Shapiro were demanding a more robust measure that also accounted for the assets that individuals and families had accrued over their lifetime. It was argued that income and consumption were not adequate drivers to propel individuals out of poverty, although the ideal pathway could be established through savings and accumulation (Sherraden 2001).

These ideas were later refined by Haveman and Wolff (2001), who defined households in which available "wealth type" resources prevented individuals from meeting their basic needs even for a limited period of time as being asset poor. The premise was that whereas income was immediate and used to support daily existence for the acquisition of food, shelter and clothing, assets were those "resources which provide a buffer against income loss, enable greater financial security and have transformative effects in helping people to proactively take control of their future" (Shapiro, Oliver and Meschede 2009, 1).[1] The availability of assets therefore provided families with economic security in times of hardship and with investment opportunities such as education, a business or a home, which are income generating and promote social and economic advancement, thus encouraging upward mobility (Bynner and Paxton 2001; Caner and Wolff 2004; Nam, Huang and Sherraden 2008). As such, when combined with income, assets provide an opportunity to secure a decent standard of living through education, business, training, health, home ownership, comfort and leisure (Shapiro 2001; Caner and Wolff 2004). Following this, households are categorized as poor when they do not earn income in excess of the poverty line or possess enough assets to ensure a minimum standard of living for a short period of time generally determined to be three months (Haveman and Wolff 2004).

Like traditional conceptualizations of poverty, however, Haveman and Wolff (2004) saw financial resources as most important, producing definitions that manifested in strict monetary terms. Although more inclusive, this presents similar limitations to the use of absolute measures of poverty. Indeed, to date, the relationship between assets and poverty has been generally explored against the background of one of three different models: the consumption model, which views assets as investments to be utilized for future consumption; the social stratification model, which analyses how assets perpetuate social inequality through inter-generational transfers; and the social development model, which purports that asset accumulation fosters socio-economic development through the expansion of capacity (Nam, Huang and Sherraden 2008). Towards the reduction of poverty, the social development model is most useful, as the overall aim of poverty reduction strategies is to expand the capabilities of poor individuals with the goal of improving their overall socio-economic situation. However, there is a flaw in the concept of asset poverty as just discussed. Despite the notable expansion that asset poverty represents over income poverty, its primary focus is limited to income, and it does not adequately consider the social and environmental assets that contribute to human development and poverty reduction or indeed the underdevelopment and increases in poverty. Beckford (1972) adopted this theme of underdevelopment in his articulation of *persistent poverty*, which he saw as being associated with the underachievement of human dignity. Beckford believed Caribbean countries to be trapped in a cycle of underdevelopment fuelled by regional economic, social and political realities. Although external forces were critical, he did not believe these to be enough to provide an explanation for the persistence of poverty. He argued that poverty alleviation required not only an increase in income but the eradication of what he saw as other forms of poverty, such as nutritional poverty, nutritional poverty and non-income poverty (health and education) (Osei 2001).

The reliance of such definitions on financial resources impedes a comprehensive understanding of poverty and reduces the ability to develop the necessary strategies for poverty reduction. We argue that assets are critical to the discussion but seek to broaden its conceptualization beyond a focus on the financial assets necessary to provide for basic consumption needs, towards the physical, human, social and environmental assets that determine an individual's level of social inclusion. The broadening of the scope of assets used in poverty analysis to include both tangible and intangible resources, therefore, produces a more comprehensive definition, which sees assets as a stock, which can be accumulated, developed and transferred across generations (Ford Foundation 2004). In addition, access to the mechanisms that allow for asset accumulation is also critical in understanding the dynamic nature of changes in levels of poverty.

The monetization of assets to assess poverty levels is understandable at the global level in order to enable comparison between countries and develop universal strategies. However, this quantification masks specific issues at a country level that could assist in providing a greater understanding of the underlying causes of poverty and therefore the development of suitable, country-specific, evidence-based policy solutions. While quantification has enabled to some degree the identification of the correlates of poverty, the focus here is on understanding the mechanisms and causes of poverty in a single state, Barbados, rather than seeking to provide broad generalizations of poverty in small states. In essence, we seek to provide a mechanism for understanding the underlying causes of poverty that can be adopted and adapted for other small states, rather than suggesting that the findings neatly fit with the contingent circumstances in other small states.

While poverty, as traditionally defined, refers to the chronic deficiency of the basics necessary for survival, a more holistic definition, by contrast, draws attention to the process by which individuals and communities are denied access to these necessities, rendering them unable to adequately function, integrate within society and build assets. This takes into consideration material and financial needs but only as one aspect of a broad and dynamic range of issues (Vrooman and Hoff 2013). Assets at the individual level relate to physical and financial assets, human capital assets, social assets and environmental assets.

The centrality of assets in the framework employed is similar to that of the United Kingdom Department for International Development's (DFID) Sustainable Livelihoods Framework (SLF), where the presence of asset stocks, through transforming structures and processes and livelihood strategies, achieves positive livelihood outcomes within specific vulnerability contexts (shocks, trends and seasonality). However, our framework, while appreciative of the feedback mechanisms in the SLF, focuses to a greater degree on access to asset-building mechanisms as determined by an individual's latent characteristics and asset stocks and on the role played by a variety of intervening factors such as politics, institutions, economic conditions, social and cultural factors and environmental conditions. This framework is described in greater detail at the end of the chapter. But first we review the core concepts and constructs related to assets, poverty, social exclusion and human rights.

Physical and Financial Assets

Physical and financial assets are those assets that have a direct monetary value, whatever their level of liquidity. These assets are utilized for consumption, investment and protection in the case of stresses and shocks to livelihoods. The actual physical and financial assets that individuals and households possess include savings, land, buildings, stocks and shares, pension funds, insurance policies, livestock and personal possessions. The available level of such assets enables households to access other means of asset accumulation such as credit, which can be utilized for productive purposes such as investment in an enterprise or education.

Due to their immediate effect on everyday life, physical and financial assets are regularly utilized as measures of poverty. The accumulation of these assets is facilitated by income from employment and self-employment, returns on investments, transfers from government, remittances from abroad, inheritances, pension payments and the disposal of other assets at a profit, including gambling. Given the means through which assets are accumulated, the inability to access or the absence of these mechanisms would increase the likelihood of not being able to provide for basic nutritional needs or cope in the event of external stresses or shocks. For example, limited employment opportunities, either through the general state of the economy or, at the individual level, through the lack of relevant skills or the absence of a social safety net, can all retard the ability to accumulate physical or financial assets.

Human Capital Assets

Human assets are those skills and benefits that afford individuals the ability to generate goods and services. These include education, health and nutrition. Garfinkel and Haveman (1977) used the concept of "earnings capacity" to describe poverty in terms of the capabilities of an individual or household rather than monetary income. This is the income stream that would be generated if each individual or household was able to utilize its human assets to the maximum (see also Haveman and Buron [1993]). While education is still the most effective means of upward mobility in the Caribbean and is generally the aspect of human assets that is easiest to measure in terms of years of schooling and qualifications, health and nutrition also affect an individual's ability to engage in productive labour. As such, the absence of one or more of these can significantly affect the ability to participate effectively in society. Indeed, many view health and education as central to the discourse on poverty and as such, see the achievement of both as primary objectives for individual well-being (Department for International Development [DFID] 1999).

Social Assets

Social assets are intangible and unique, in that, unlike other assets, they relate to the social relations between and among individuals and so are very difficult to measure or quantify. They are the social relationships that are utilized by individuals in order to maintain or improve their living standards. In the Caribbean, extended and transnational family networks are critical sources of care and support, as are community- and faith-based social relationships and patronage contacts across class, ethnicity and race lines. Putnam's definition of social capital (1993) also highlights the rules, norms, obligations and trust that facilitate collective action among individuals. Social assets are differentiated from most other forms also in that their generation does not depend solely on individual decisions (Attanasio and Székely 1999).

Environmental Assets

Environmental assets are the naturally produced raw materials that are critical to human existence. These include plant and animal life, the land on which we live and use to produce food, the atmosphere, the air from which we obtain oxygen and the water we drink and use to irrigate crops. These assets are also used for the disposal of waste. Environmental assets are critical to the survival of individuals in rural areas but also to those in urban areas where issues such as access to transportation and open spaces are very important in determining the quality of life of individuals and communities.

SOCIAL EXCLUSION AND ASSETS

The following discussion expands upon the preceding basic definitions and provides context for an understanding of the manner in which each asset operates to determine social exclusion.

Shaffer (2002) insisted that the analysis of poverty must continue its transition from a model of deprivation that has focused primarily on material needs towards a social model of deprivation that, in addition to material needs, takes into consideration a wider range of issues, including a lack of autonomy and self-respect. Within the last few decades, work on poverty has indeed been proceeding in this direction; that is, it has been extended to include a recognition of social exclusion. The social exclusion approach to the conceptualization of poverty places, as paramount, the inability of groups within society to access the range of resources that are necessary to effectively participate in activities and to enjoy an accepted standard of living. Rather than focusing solely on material resources, social exclusion is a multidimensional concept encompassing a range of social, political and environmental, as well as economic indicators. The multidimensional nature of the concept is illustrated by its four theoretical dimensions as articulated by Jehoel-Gijsbers (2004): *limited social participation*, which relates to the inability to take part in social networks and a general lack of social contact; *lack of normative integration*, or a failure to follow the typical norms and values present in one's community; *material deprivation*, which relates to a lack, due to financial hardships, of the goods and services that are critical to survival; and *inadequate access to basic social rights*, which occurs when individuals are unable to secure adequate health care, education and living conditions. The simultaneous absence of any or all of these dimensions renders an individual socially excluded.

The idea of social exclusion, first put forward by the Child Poverty Action Group in Britain (Alcock 1997), has been promoted by the European Union's Social Charter as the means of broadening the discourse on poverty and deprivation to include both those who are excluded and those who exclude. It was therefore designed to encompass the reactions to poverty by individuals and social agencies. It was seen as a way to turn the spotlight on the gap between those who play an active role in society (the included) and those who occupy the fringe (the excluded). In other words, social exclusion was conceptualized as a process involving all.

Social exclusion refers to the process by which individuals are unable to take part in critical societal activities. It is seen as an extension of the ideas behind the concept of relative deprivation in that it does not concentrate solely on income to measure material condition but assesses how resources could affect individuals' participation in the lifestyle of their community. Thus, for individuals to be socially excluded means they are shut out of those systems, which are integral to community integration (Bailey 2004).

Social exclusion deprives individuals and communities of access to social services, political representation and productive employment. Since the lack of assets disproportionately affects socially excluded groups, interventions must be aimed at reversing structural inequalities and, by extension, enabling individuals to claim their rights and entitlements. What follows is an explanation of the manner in which the absence of assets, as outlined previously, can serve to render individuals excluded from society.

As mentioned, physical and financial assets relate to the possession of an asset stock and to the availability of mechanisms to accumulate assets. While the possession of an asset stock will to some degree determine access to asset accumulation mechanisms, such as the case of access to credit being determined by possession of collateral, broader social provisions also influence access to physical and financial asset accumulation such as education, health, property rights and social safety nets. One crucial issue here is the relationship between human assets and physical and financial asset accumulation due to the impact of health and education on access to productive employment opportunities; without the appropriate skills or ability to under-take paid employment or self-employment, the unemployed are unable to provide for their basic nutritional needs, in addition to being barred from accessing asset accumulation mechanisms such as investments or credit. Therefore, access to opportunities to build human assets through access to education and health care has a direct effect on opportunities to build phys-ical and financial assets, although the mechanisms through which assets are built are more than just from income.

Therefore, unemployment poses one of the biggest challenges to physical and financial asset accumulation. However, unemployment is more than just a bar to physical and financial asset accumulation. Gallie and Vogler (1994), in looking at the labour market in Britain, documented the kind of sacrifices that the unemployed are forced to make in order to make ends meet, such as the reduction of spending on necessary clothing and eventually on food. However, people lose more than money when they lose their jobs, for work provides more than a salary, even for those who find their jobs uninteresting or unlikable. Work fills the day and allows time to pass. Time hangs heavily on the hands of the unemployed. They also have a sense of not belonging, of being isolated from others, for, when work places people into different group-ings, it gives them an identification tag, providing recognition and a sense of security and status. Fagin and Little (1984) related the isolation and alien-ation that accompany unemployment. The unemployed, they said, believe that their role is not a part of the system of goals of the society, so they become removed from the wider mainstream social order. Since what they are doing is not contributing positively to their personal identity, they become self-estranged, feel powerless and see themselves as victims of an impersonal, distant system. Their exclusion from the job market leads to the creation of an alienated group of people who feel that they occupy no stratum in the society.

This is not merely a compartmentalized consequence of unemployment but a factor contributing to further alienation and reduced probability of reconnecting with mainstream society, hence further constraining the ability to accumulate the required assets. It can lead to environmental degradation and to the unsustainable exploitation of environmental assets.

The steadily increasing rates of unemployment in the Caribbean raise a range of issues for regional scholars, particularly in light of the recent global economic downturn. One such issue is the unemployment gender gap. Early international attention came in the form of the seminal works of Marston (1975) and Clark and Summers (1979), which explored gender differences in unemployment in the United States. More recent empirical work has produced mixed results. While some have utilized microdata to demonstrate a widening of the gap between male and female unemployment in the United States and European cities (Azmat, Guell and Manning 2006), others have found that, in light of the manner in which the economic recession has negatively affected males in particular, the gender unemployment gap has been shrinking (Sahin, Song and Hobijn 2010; Theodossiou and Zangelidis 2009). As is the case in much of the developing world, unemployment among women in the Caribbean is far higher than among men (International Labour Organization [ILO] 2014). Indeed, this is a long-standing issue as evidenced by a 1999 Jamaican survey revealing that, at the time, women comprised 45 per cent of the labour force (Planning Institute of Jamaica 1999). The number of unemployed women was twice that of unemployed men (Planning Institute of Jamaica 1999). In addition, the fall in employment was weighted heavily towards women. In 1999, 6,800 women lost their jobs, compared with 2,600 men. More recently, data have shown that among the major economies of Trinidad and Tobago, Jamaica, and Barbados, the higher propensity for women to be jobless remains evident (Seguino 2003). Seguino noted that this situation is exacerbated by the fact that the job status of women in these countries is more insecure than for men, with females showing consistently higher levels of unemployment rate volatility.

While data have shown that, overall today, Caribbean women are approximately 30 per cent more likely to be unemployed than men (ILO 2014), the gender disparity for youth unemployment is also cause for concern. Lashley et al. (2015), for example, reported that 34 per cent of young females were employed in Barbados, as opposed to 37 per cent of young males. Similarly, the Planning Institute of Jamaica (2013) found that in Jamaica as many as 57 per cent of all unemployed youth were female.

These arguments on the role of employment give the impression that what is important in the creation of an identity is paid work and that any type of work will perform this function. Young (1999), however, pointed to the largely repetitive and demeaning aspects of work that the majority of the employed have to endure. The use of the word "work" by the so-called contented classes in reference to their highly paid, fulfilling activities, he wrote, was an insult to the low-paid, oppressive chores of the working poor. The notion of work as fulfilling, something for children to aspire to and a liberation of the self, was a further cause for concern. For those of the elite – the famous, the sportsmen and -women – and for the majority of the contented upper classes, the workday was never long enough. These were the individuals for whom work may give a sense of identity, and it was for them that work defined who they were. For the rest of society, work definitely defined who they were not (Young 1999).

Following this line of argument, this issue is not so much another dichotomy of employed/unemployed but a spectrum of economic engagement, from chronic unemployment and total exclusion to full engagement and work satisfaction.

Feelings of inadequacy are, however, exacerbated in situations of chronic unemployment, as a result of which people become used to unemployment and detached from the labour force (Warr, Banks and Ullah 1985) and from mainstream society. Chronic unemployment causes a degeneration of individuals' work ability, thereby affecting their ability to work in the future. Research has shown that the longer individuals are unemployed, the less likely they are to find gainful employment in the future (Nilsen and Reiso 2011). Similarly, engagement in unskilled, low-paying, low-quality employment also constrains the individual's ability to break out of a cycle of poverty, and with this come feelings of inadequacy.

McNeil and Townley (1988) made the very important observation that education is a political activity in that it can be used to influence and change people and society. Political decisions are made about the type of education that is to be provided, the manner in which the system is to be organized, and ultimately who is to be provided with education. These decisions are influenced by the views held about the type of society that is wanted, and, as a result, education becomes a powerful tool of social engineering (McNeil and Townley 1988). With this in mind, sociologists have had widely differing views of the role of education in the society. Two issues, however, emerge clearly from the discussions. One concerns the role of education in the transmission of values and to some extent its transformative nature, while the other revolves around the question of inequality in access and in achievement. Insofar as the transmission of values is concerned, some classic sociologists focused on what the education system can do for society (Durkheim 1961; Parsons 1961). Schools, they believed, taught conformity. Individuals who were not related learned to work together in the school environment, and therefore schools in modern industrial society could be seen as society in miniature: "[E]ducation perpetuates and reinforces . . . homogeneity by fixing in the child from the beginning the essential similarities which collective life demands" (Durkheim 1961, 87–88).

Some have looked at the role of education from a slightly different standpoint, that is, its ability to transform individuals by developing their full intellectual, physical and emotional abilities (Dewey 1953). With good teaching methods, children acquired skills, allowing them to solve problems and to think critically about issues affecting them and society. Education has also been seen as an important vehicle with which to rise out of poverty.

Research both in Britain and in the United States has demonstrated that the children of the middle classes had a greater probability of obtaining educational success than those of the working class. Bowles and Gintis (1976), using sophisticated statistical techniques, demonstrated that socio-economic background was a better predictor of educational and occupational success in the United States than intelligence, for the education system did not function as a meritocracy. Halsey, Floud and Anderson (1961) showed that, although educational reform in Britain had allowed more children of all classes to achieve higher qualifications, and although the rate of increase was the same for all classes, the middle class retained an overall advantage. In the Caribbean also, while education has the potential to open doors to higher-level employment and social mobility, the reality among the poor reveals an absence of qualifications and vocational skills, in addition to unemployment or casual, menial labour in "odd jobs", workplace exploitation, and a hand-to-mouth existence with no savings put aside for emergencies (Bailey 2004; Henry-Lee and Le Franc 2002).

While it is generally agreed that within the Caribbean, socio-economic status provides the best predictor of educational attainment, it is important to note, too, the effect of gender across socio-economic categories. In contrast to the reality in much of Africa and Asia, Caribbean countries have largely succeeded in improving access to educational opportunities for girls and women. So much so that there now exists a reverse gender gap in education across much of the region (Duryea et al. 2007; Elliott 2006). Indeed, there is a general trend in most Caribbean countries that sees widening enrolment disparities, in favour of females, at the upper secondary and tertiary levels (Bailey and Charles 2010), as well as higher average years of schooling than males (Duryea et al. 2007).

Also critical to human capital assets is health. The World Health Organization (WHO) suggests that the highest possible level of health must be recognized as a basic right of every human being. This is primarily a question of access and includes access to affordable, timely care of appropriate quality (WHO 2008). Peters et al. (2008) articulated four main aspects of access as it relates to health care. *Geographic accessibility* relates to the length of travel time between the service provider and the user. *Availability* relates to the adequate type of care being available to those who are in need of it; examples include hours of operation or waiting times. *Financial accessibility* relates to the relationship between the cost of a given service and the ability of the potential user to afford that cost. *Acceptability* relates to the sensitivity of service providers to the social and cultural needs of individual users.

Of particular importance to the present framework is the manner in which accessibility is negatively impacted by socio-economic status (see Peters et al. [2008] for a review). Generally, the poor have considerably less access to adequate health care than other social groups within society. Victoria et al. (2005), for example, examined maternal and child health care provisions across several countries and found the poor to be consistently disadvantaged. This is in keeping with results obtained elsewhere (James et al. 2006; Peters et al. 2008), including the Caribbean (Bailey 1981). Stigmatizing and judgemental attitudes have also been reported in Caribbean public health centres, especially towards persons living with HIV, along with the degree to which they are deterred from seeking these services (Figueroa 2008).

Gender differences in access to health care also have the propensity to exacerbate socio-economic disparities. While recent years have seen considerable improvements in access to health care for girls and women, particularly in developing countries, in many cultures still, there is the belief that women are negatively impacted by gender imbalances that affect their level of health. This is often viewed as something of a paradox, since while life expectancy for women is longer, when health indicators such as chronic illness, disability and mental health are considered, the health status of women compared to men is notably poorer (Case and Paxson 2005; Verbrugge 1985).

Establishing gender as a determinant of poor health has, however, been met with mixed results. While a number of studies have found female gender to be a significant risk factor for insufficient health care (Lavesque, Harris and Russell 2013; Bryant, Leaver and Dunn 2009; Denton, Prus and Walters 2004), others have been unable to reach such conclusions (Chen and Hou 2002). Considering the global gender disparities in employment previously discussed, this lack of consensus is believed to be due to the difficulty in establishing the extent to which socio-economic factors explain disparate access to health care, as opposed to gender (Socias, Koehoorn and Shoveller 2016).

There is a dual nature to the effects of the relationship between access to health care and poverty. On the one hand, financial restrictions create a major obstacle among the poor to utilize health services, which in turn can lead to ill health. On the other hand, however, ill health exacerbates conditions of poverty due to an inability to work, as well as the high cost of health care.

Wilkinson (1996) believed that poverty can lead to a "cycle of poor health" and an inability of individuals to be in total control of their lives. He felt that, from the time of childhood, poor nutrition and the absence of a stimulating, positive environment can lead to health problems from which the child may never completely recover. Generally, poor conditions, he felt, lead to poor health. As adults, the poor are more vulnerable to health risks for a variety of reasons, including occupational hazards associated with undesirable jobs, as well as the consumption of cheap, non-nutritious food (Begum and Sen 2003). These factors make access to adequate health care particularly important for those of low socio-economic status. Among the many different aspects of accessibility previously mentioned, it is perhaps financial accessibility that has the most detrimental impact on the health status of the poor. Because of the high cost of health care, poor households either have to make the decision to forgo medical treatment or seek cheaper, less effective alternatives, both of which increase the likelihood of advanced disease or complications (Ruthven and Kumar 2003). Though Caribbean data on the subject are limited, Bourne (2009) illustrated a significant association between not seeking medical care and poverty in Jamaica.

Despite the general recognition that access to affordable health care is a basic human right, large numbers of persons descend into poverty annually as a result of the high cost of health care (Peters et al. 2008). Indeed, from a human capital standpoint, poor health and its related expenses are claimed to be the factors most likely to cause an individual or household to become poor (Krishna 2006). Cohen (2006) referred to the "double impact" of poor health, due to the propensity for a decrease in income along with an increase in health costs. Evidence suggests that of critical importance is the health of the primary income earner. WHO (2008) illustrated the manner in which a major sickness suffered by the breadwinner of vulnerable households results in a sudden halt in income, along with the incurring of debt and the sale of assets in order to pay for medical treatment. Such coping strategies are termed erosive by De la Fuente (2007). This sets in motion a rapid descent into or a worsening of conditions of poverty, leaving family members susceptible to conditions such as malnutrition as a result of the inability to purchase food.

Putnam (1993) focused on forms of social capital relating to civic engagement, that is, people's connection with the life of their community. Social capital, he said, was closely related to civic virtue, which was most powerful when embedded in a dense network of reciprocal social relations (Putnam 2000). There has been a great deal of research around Putnam's view of social capital and civil society (Cox 1995; Fukuyama 1995; Halpern 1999). Some have demonstrated its importance to physical and psychological health (Kawachi, Kennedy and Glass 1999). Others have assessed its importance in combating poverty (Warren, Thompson and Saegert 2001) and in promoting economic well-being. Fernandez-Kelly (1995), for example, tried to illustrate the effect that low social capital has on the decision of young girls in urban ghetto communities in Baltimore to leave school and have babies. Indeed, social relations can operate in such a manner that exacerbates gender inequalities, reducing female participation in social activities (Healy, Haynes and Hampshire 2007; Bennett and Daly 2014). When compared to their male counterparts, women tend to be members of more informal networks and involved in domestic responsibilities and caregiving activities as opposed to more formal civic and political activities that are likely to generate greater amounts of social capital (Cagatay 1998). Women's access to socio-economic resources is generally more limited than that of men, placing poor females at a distinct disadvantage in the generation of the vital social capital necessary to gain access to material and social assets in order to improve their living conditions (Lavesque, Harris and Russell 2013). As a result of these factors, therefore, women and men tend to experience poverty very differently (Cagatay 1998).

There is evidence to suggest, too, that social capital has significant effects on the economic status of different racial and ethnic groups. Light and Kara-georgis (1994), Portes (1995), and Knack and Keefer (1997) compared the economic statuses of different immigrant communities in the United States and found that those groups with strong social capital, such as Koreans and Chinese, fared better than other groups that were low in social capital, such as Mexicans.

It is important to note that the resources that individuals can draw upon to implement strategies of social mobility are those they have access to by virtue of being socially integrated into groups and organizations, that is, social capital. Residents of poor communities have ties of less social worth and suffer from extreme levels of social and economic marginalization. For these members of society, the socio-economic forces are cumulative and have structurally entrapped extremely large segments of urban and rural society.

Communities are the outcome of internal social relations and are held together by networks without which survival would not be possible. But communities are also shaped by their relations with the rest of the society, and some of these relations are also contentious and power laden. Communities are the products of very complicated social, political, economic and cultural relationships, and the outcome of relationships affects the choices that are open to their members. They are the products of the internal attributes of their members, as well as of the power relations within the community. These critical networks of support are missing within many communities, and, for this reason only, the quality of the relationship with external forces assumes great importance. DeFilippis (2001), in his critique of the social capital thesis, questioned the view of communities that focuses only on these internal characteristics, while ignoring the relationship between the communities and the rest of the society.

Social relations between communities and wider societies are particularly important within the context of disadvantaged Caribbean communities. Earlier, we discussed the importance of employment to the accumulation of financial assets, and, from this perspective, it is important to note that large segments of society are excluded from productive enterprises, relegating them to some of the most undesirable locations of society. Many are the recipients of a level of stigmatization from the wider society that directly or indirectly denies them job opportunities. Even their places of residence can be the focus of stigma. Bailey (2004), for example, described the manner in which participants among his Jamaican sample were denied employment as a result of where they lived. Indeed, there is anecdotal evidence from across the Caribbean suggesting that residents of poor communities employ strategies such as the use of false addresses or even leaving poor communities to live with relatives in "better" areas in the hope that a change of address would improve their chances of finding employment. The response to this type of disadvantage is an intense form of alienation of young males in particular, since place of residence for young men becomes seen as a proxy for poverty but also, more importantly, a resulting proneness to criminality. In such instances, the individual is accurately labelled as socially disadvantaged but in turn inaccurately associated with dangerousness and a perceived alternate value system (Harriott 2003).

In this study, we explore the intersectionalities of stigma, discrimination, social exclusion and poverty. How, for example, does HIV status and disability or being a sex worker, an immigrant, an ex-prisoner or a gay/bisexual/transgender person exclude individuals from employment, education, housing and health services, even family care and support – all essential to poverty alleviation? Stigmatized populations are excluded from legal and police protection at the same time as they may be targets of police harassment, in both instances without recourse. Stigma is compounded as layered stigma and self-stigma, the latter characterized by shame, self-blame and self-isolation from services and society (Barrow and Aggleton 2013). Ultimately, then, stigma and discrimination violate human rights and the entitlement of individuals to dignity and self-respect.

In the Caribbean, the disruption of family and community life is attributed to the plantation heritage of slavery and colonialism. Patterns of out-migration and urbanization, together with insecure land tenure arrangements among the poor, generate a high turnover of community populations. Social atomism and the evaporation of community spirit are evident in the decline in traditional self-help schemes to build, repair and clean up public areas, in the sharing of food and basic needs, in communal childcare and protection of the elderly and vulnerable, and in informal social control of deviant behaviours. Community decay, therefore, is often accompanied by insecurity, crime and violence. While the wealthy have the means to protect themselves behind bars in gated communities, the poor may become increasingly shut in and fearful, even of their own neighbours.

Despite a history of family fragmentation, households and kinship networks are a long-term source of care and support that is multifaceted – economic, social, protective and psychological – thereby acting as a buffer against destitution for many among the poor. But their families generally ensure little more than survival, not an escape from poverty. In conditions of economic crisis, even survival is threatened as families are stretched beyond capacity in providing for dependent members. Family poverty, therefore, tends to be chronic and inter-generational – linked with a downward spiral from teenage pregnancy, leaving school early, multiple children, unstable conjugality, absentee fathers and single parenting by mothers. Children in large households headed by women, who struggle with the double burden of income generation and caregiving, are especially vulnerable. While family care and support are critical to the quality of life among the poor, there is also evidence of high levels of family conflict and violence targeted against powerless women, children, persons with disabilities and stigmatized family members.

It has been argued that the ability to accumulate environmental assets is just as unequal as other forms of wealth, and it is in this regard that environmental assets are particularly relevant to contemporary discourses on poverty. Low-income groups have limited access to important environmental assets and often occupy undesirable residential locations that may be on or adjacent to land used for waste and other environmental hazards (Boyce and Pastor 2001). The Barbados Office of the Auditor General (2014, 137) notes that squatting in Barbados "is quite extensive and is expanding" and cites several locations associated with poor living conditions or on lands where building is prohibited due to the proximity to the water table. Squatting locations include The Belle; the area of My Lord's Hill/The Ivy/Howells; Bath Tenantry; Six Men's and Licorish Village. Recent squatting activity has also been seen at a former garbage dump site adjacent to the country's international airport at Rock Hall.[2] Not only is this site providing accommodation for low-income persons, it has also evolved into a money-generating activity where "Land is being sold and leased and houses rented to the ever expanding squatters' village" (para. 1).

Environmental assets have considerable relevance to well-being both at the personal and at the macro levels. At the personal level, within the Caribbean, the accumulation of natural assets may, for example, include the ability to provide adequate resistance to natural disasters and exposure to dangerous environments as well as the ability to exploit valuable natural resources. At the macro level, there are natural resources that represent economic assets, such as oil and gas, or assets that can be indirectly exploited such as beaches, which benefit the tourism industry, or land/soil that is suitable for agriculture. Also at the macro level, the ability to mitigate the effects of natural disasters and climate change processes, such as increases in sea level, is also critical.

Access to environmental assets is important to the overall well-being of individuals since the sustainable management of commodities such as water, soil and the atmosphere affect the livelihoods of people, regardless of place and time. Bass et al. (2006) estimated that environmental assets represent approximately 26 per cent of the wealth of low-income countries as a result of the economic and social benefits of industries such as fishery, agriculture, tourism and mining.

At an individual level, the immediate environment in which people live greatly affects the way in which they view their own lives. According to Frey and Stutzer (2002), the value that people place on their surroundings is directly related to its traditional, or cultural, aspects. Life satisfaction, therefore, is a function of the assessments individuals make of their own living conditions. Within the Caribbean, low-income residents are typically relegated to communities beset by a range of conditions that are indicative of neighbourhood decay. The work of the Chicago School attempted to explain the spatial segregation of urban residents through their depiction of the city as a super organism containing a variety of natural areas – different residential areas, shopping districts, industrial areas. This model was taken from plant ecology and put forward the notion that the ecological processes of invasion, competition and succession led to changing patterns of urban land use. Human beings, it said, were like plants in that they have a natural inclination to compete for space and scarce goods, and this competition or struggle by groups in the ecological order led to the division of the city into subareas inhabited by people and activities that are broadly similar. The most desirable locations were seized by big business and rich residents, while those with low competitive abilities were excluded from the mainstream and had to be content with less desirable environments. Such areas received the most recently arrived, poor migrants from rural or overseas territories who could not compete with the more affluent (Cresswell 2000). As a result, large numbers of poor urban residents reside in neighbourhoods characterized by environmental incivilities, such as derelict and unoccupied buildings and the presence of young men, gang members, loitering on street corners. Clemente and Kleiman (1977) referred to this phenomenon as indirect victimization, and it signifies a serious erosion in the quality of life.

Exclusion also affects the vulnerability of individuals as it relates to the exposure to risk and to the ability to survive environmental changes and events such as natural disasters. Indeed, research has demonstrated that the impact of disasters is affected by the same exclusionary forces that affect particular groups in non-disaster periods. Factors such as wealth and poverty are strongly related to the ability to survive natural hazards (Bolin and Standford 1998). This intrinsic association between poverty and climate change can be attributed to the fact that the poor tend to depend most on occupations that are heavily vulnerable to climatic shifts. They generally have limited access to the mechanisms that could best mitigate the effects of these shifts, thus increasing their level of vulnerability (United Nations Development Programme [UNDP] 2013). Even among the poor, however, the extent of the impact of changes in the environment is affected by other variables such as gender. Women comprise the majority of the world's poor and, in much of the developing world, are considerably reliant on local natural resources for their incomes (Dankelman 2010). Women are generally responsible for the nutritional needs of their families. Indeed, despite the advancements of Caribbean women, research shows that the expectation among men and children is that a woman's primary responsibility is still domestic (Bailey 2013). Despite this, women have limited autonomy over the mechanisms and resources necessary to maintain these responsibilities if agricultural conditions become unsustainable. Women also typically have limited access to the ownership of land and the means of production, as well information and training in disaster management. These factors render women, particularly in rural areas, considerably susceptible to the effects of climatic change with some studies reporting that women are as much as 14 per cent more likely than men to lose their lives during or in the aftermath of a natural disaster (Araujo et al. 2007).

Climate change, as a continued manifestation of global warming, has meant that across the globe there has been and will continue to be an increase in extreme weather events (Parry et al. 2007). As noted by Field et al. (2012, 111): "changing climate leads to changes in the frequency, intensity, spatial extent, duration, and timing of weather and climate extremes".

One of the most detrimental effects of natural disasters is the reduction in access to valuable environmental resources. This reduction in access is particularly prominent in low-income countries such as those of the Caribbean and applies to low-income residents in all countries (Parry et al. 2007). For example, low-income residents were severely affected during the approach of Hurricane Katrina in 2005 as a result of the failure of the state to provide the necessary assistance for the poor, mainly black majority residents (Cutter 2005). Similarly, the Indian Ocean tsunami in 2004 claimed the lives of a disproportionate number of impoverished residents (Nishikiori et al. 2006).

In the Caribbean, there have been many recent examples of the increase in extreme weather events. In Jamaica, between 2002 and 2007, there were five hurricanes, two storms and a seven-month drought (Campbell and Beckford 2009); St Lucia and Grenada were also affected by hurricane Ivan in 2004, while Grenada also suffered from hurricane Emily in 2005 during the recovery period after Ivan. The effect of Emily after Ivan was pronounced on Grenada. While Ivan damaged 90 per cent of the housing stock in the country, only a small fraction had been repaired by the time Emily landed (Organization of American States 2005). Ivan had a distinct effect on poverty in Grenada, with an increase in the number of persons on welfare and the destruction of housing, leading to homelessness and unemployment as jobs were lost in the agricultural and tourism sectors (Kairi Consultants Limited 2008).

The main direct costs of extreme weather in the Caribbean relate to destruction of farmlands, replanting costs, loss of livestock and property and loss of employment (Lashley 2012). In addition to these direct monetary costs, it should also be noted that in the post-disaster period, "informal safety nets (family and friends) tend to break down" (Mechler, Linnerooth-Bayer and Peppiatt 2006, 6) due to the covariate nature of extreme weather. These results suggest that not only does the environment provide a number of assets from which low-income groups can build livelihoods, specific environmental "liabilities" are also present that can reduce resilience. While these liabilities are ever present, any increase in frequency or intensity of extreme weather events will have a significant effect on low-income groups. This effect manifests not only in the actual magnitude of potential asset loss but also in the ability to regain pre-disaster asset levels; as extreme weather events increase in frequency, the time available to recoup larger losses is reduced, overall leading to a reduced asset base and a degradation of livelihoods over time.

However, the negative effect of the environment on the poor is not unidirectional, as the poor can also have detrimental effects on the environment. The accumulation of environmental assets is essential to the material needs of, in particular, the rural poor, since their livelihoods are disproportionately dependent on natural resources and agricultural activities. The World Resources Institute (2005), for example, estimated that approximately 90 per cent of the world's poor are at least partially dependent on forests for their income. The ability to effectively harness these assets is, however, severely limited by the lack of financial resources at the disposal of the poor (International Fund for Agricultural Development 2011). As a result, they engage in detrimental activities such as overfishing, over-hunting and over-farming in an attempt to meet short-term objectives, which further exacerbates their precarious position (Oliver and Shapiro 1997). Added to this is the fact that the dependence of the poor on environmental assets means that, unlike the affluent who can employ the use of physical, social or human capital as a substitute for natural resources, the rural poor, bereft of alternatives, are particularly vulnerable to the effects of events that may disturb these ecosystems (Ellis and Allison 2004). The ability of the rural poor to satisfy their material needs is, therefore, directly related to the preservation of natural ecosystems. Although the use of agricultural conservation techniques, irrigation systems and other management strategies can mitigate the effects of environmental shocks, the poor typically lack the means to access these mitigation measures. The failure of state mechanisms in many developing countries to assist in providing this access leaves large groups of rural residents acutely vulnerable to extreme conditions of poverty.

RESILIENCE

Poverty renders many individuals incapable of achieving or obtaining the resources and assets that make daily living more amenable. As such, they are forced to devise diverse mechanisms or strategies aimed at minimizing adversity or managing their situation in order to deal effectively with the obstacles faced in acquiring the goods and services necessary for their survival (Monroe et al. 2007).

It is important here to make a clear distinction between two similar but distinct concepts – coping and resilience – as they relate to poverty. Whereas coping refers to actions taken that sustain, resilience addresses those measures implemented that lead to adaptation and an overall improvement of living conditions (Tchombe et al. 2012). Resilience, therefore, is exemplified by the ability of poor individuals and households to anticipate, absorb, accommodate/adapt, recover and improve living conditions following the effects of a shock or stress (Bene et al. 2014; Mitchell and Harris 2012; Sanders, Sungwoo and Woosung 2008), through the resourceful utilization of the assets and social capital available (Pemberton, Sutton and Fahmy 2013). Coping and resilience are, nevertheless, not mutually exclusive, as the ability to implement and expand upon effective coping strategies to deal with the incidence of poverty should contribute to an improvement of socio-economic conditions in the long term.

An analysis of the strategies that help foster resilience is essential, since determining good practice can prevent permanent negative effects that make it difficult for families to break free of the cycle of poverty (Amendah, Buigut and Mohamed 2014; Garba 2011). Positive/active strategies require resourcefulness and empower families, providing them with a firm foundation to rise out of poverty. They are implemented when individuals living in situations of poverty seek to increase the income and resources available to them through measures such as increased home production, acquiring an additional job or borrowing from a bank. Comparatively, negative or weak strategies can lead to the destruction of production capital within the household and also to negative behavioural changes. These include the sale of assets, the removal of children from school in order to introduce them to the workforce, a reduction in consumption and the neglect of health care (Garba 2011). Moser (1998) explained that key factors, such as the level of education of household members, the size of the household and the welfare level of the household before poverty occurred, have a significant influence on the type of strategy that is adopted.

Another distinction to be made is between that of pre-emptive/precautionary and "ex post" strategies. Pre-emptive/precautionary strategies include the accumulation of mechanisms of formal or informal financial savings and assets (such as food stocks, gold and jewellery) or insurances secured in anticipation of an income shock (Farchamps 2003; Amendah, Buigut and Mohamed 2014; Dercon 2000). Alternatively, ex post strategies are implemented after the financial shock has occurred in order to reduce its negative impact (Amendah, Buigut and Mohamed 2014; Dercon 2000). Oftentimes, many of the strategies adopted are short term in nature, as persons prioritize their most essential daily needs (Pemberton, Sutton and Fahmy 2013).

Given limited income and resources, individuals and households living in poverty are often faced with the choice of either "making ends meet" or budgeting/minimizing income and "going without" (Clark 2007; Farchamps 2003; Garba 2011; Pemberton, Sutton and Fahmy 2013).[3] Households will carefully prioritize and manipulate their budget to align their monthly income against expenses to ensure that bills are paid on time and that the basic necessities for daily survival can be purchased. Often, budgeting results in reduced expenditure wherever possible, and this often means reducing expenditure on basic goods and services that others often take for granted (Flint 2010).[4] However, despite careful financial planning and budgeting many find that, faced with unanticipated events, they have to make the difficult decision to cut back even further on already reduced consumption or default on the payment of bills (Kempson, Bryson and Rowlingson 1994).

Pemberton, Sutton and Fahmy (2013) advanced the view that material and emotional hardships that result from "going without" would appear to be mitigated by the presence of kinship and community networks. Where there are cohesion and collaboration between households and individuals in the community, informal arrangements are introduced to develop and share networks of financial and emotional support; this appears to "soften the harsh reality of poverty" (Pemberton, Sutton and Fahmy 2013, 19) and to assist with coping on a limited income (Dercon 2000; Farchamps 2003; Sherman 2006). Laguerre's (1990) work on the urban poor in Martinique has highlighted the manner in which the *sousou* operates successfully in order to mitigate the effects of poverty. It does not exclude those that make use of formal banks, thus giving individuals the opportunity to utilize both formal and informal saving mechanisms. In doing so, persons are able to access both short- and long-term strategies with the formal bank offering long-term safety and a credit line, while the *sousou* offers a relatively rapid solution to emergencies. Other examples of rotating credit mechanisms exists throughout the region. Clark (2007) also offers another mechanism that allows poverty-stricken individuals to cope with their conditions. He notes that the cultural and religious ideas into which individuals have been conditioned may allow poor persons to accept and justify their conditions of poverty.

When legitimate means of survival prove unsuccessful, there are segments of the poor, often characterized by stigma, trans-generational unemployment and alienation as a result of their exclusion from the labour market, who may turn to illegitimate activities as a means of improving their situation. Indeed, this can be interpreted as a direct result of material deprivation and the need to survive under conditions of structural inequality (Caribbean Development Bank 2012a; Berkham 2007; Craine 1997). Such illegitimate activity may take the form of illegal actions aimed at securing the income or goods necessary for daily existence (Berkham 2007) or of violent activity as a result of feelings of frustration. In the Jamaica Social Investment Fund (JSIF), participatory study of five poor communities in the Kingston Metropolitan Area (Moser and Holland 1997), participants articulated a perceived linear relationship between poverty and violence. In their view, poverty included aspects of the wider conceptualization of deprivation associated with social exclusion, such as the lack of education. The participants explained that violent activity outside of the communities increased when men were out of work and that, when opportunities were limited, communities were more likely to become embroiled in physical conflict.

The capacity of the poor to successfully manage their socio-economic reality and to make changes to improve their living conditions is directly related to the likelihood that they will be able to rise out of poverty. While studies have focused primarily on the social problems associated with poverty, relatively little attention has been given to an interrogation of the factors that cause some but not others to improve their situation. This is indeed the essence of resilience (Narayan and Petesch 2007). An analysis of CPAs conducted throughout the Caribbean suggests a similar focus.

Narayan, Pritchett and Kapoor (2009), in their study of five hundred communities across fifteen countries, investigated how people are able to emerge from poverty in Africa, South Asia, Latin America and East Asia.[5] The evidence revealed that resilience is most heavily influenced by two factors: first, the characteristics of the poverty-stricken individual or collective household members and, second, the nature of the initiatives they undertake to improve their situation. Studies have shown that high levels of agency and personal or group initiative are essential for upward social mobility (Narayan and Petesch 2007). The strongest indicator of individuals' ability to improve their social situation is the initiative that they take to find a job or start a new business in order to increase their flow of income (Narayan, Pritchett and Kapoor 2009). The likelihood that individuals will exhibit this initiative is, however, dependent upon their level of self-confidence, sense of autonomy, agency and outlook on life (Perlman 2007; Secombe 2002; World Bank 2013). This is further influenced by other individual characteristics such as physical and mental well-being, level of educational attainment/ intelligence and mental well-being (Gordon-Rouse 1998; Secombe 2002). At the community level, the network of relationships that individuals have also positively influences their resilience. Participation in community activities and interaction with community members extends social capital development, providing employment opportunities, supportive networks, and also lends to the development of important life skills (Bene et al. 2014; Perlman 2007; Secombe 2002). The work of Oscar Lewis, seen as a response to the urban crisis in the 1960s, spoke to the individual characteristics of those living in poverty. Lewis conducted studies on the lives of the poor in several countries, including Puerto Rico and Cuba, and everywhere, he said, he found similarities in family structure and interpersonal relationships that developed both as an adaptation and as a reaction to their marginal position in capitalist societies (Lewis 1965). Many of the characteristics of this culture, he said, could be linked to attempts to find local solutions to problems that existing institutions and agencies could not solve. These families developed the art of suppressing the expectation of long-term employment and wealth, focusing on day-to-day strategies to survive without affluence in an affluent society.

Lewis had very little faith, however, in the ability of the poor to be resilient. One important characteristic, Lewis felt, of this "culture of poverty" was the lack of effective participation and integration of the poor in major institutions. They developed a hatred of the police and a mistrust of government. Chronic unemployment, low wages, no savings, little or no property – all effectively eliminated the chances of the poor to participate legitimately in society. Family life within the culture of poverty was characterized by an absence of childhood, early sex, wife beating and the use of violence in the training of children. The general idea was that poor people in an affluent society developed a separate culture, a subculture, that prevented them from acquiring the wealth that was available to others. On an individual level, Lewis felt that feelings of helplessness, dependence and inferiority pervaded the lives of the poor within the culture. They had a weak ego structure and lacked the ability to plan for the future.

While the work of Lewis was important in that it drew attention to the manner in which individual characteristics can affect one's ability to emerge from poverty, it has been heavily criticized on a number of grounds. First, it has been said that he paid no attention to the forces of the wider society, choosing to focus solely on the individual or family. He also showed bias in using middle-class values to determine the culture. Another criticism was the ambiguity of his work. Lewis distinguished in his writing between those who were a part of the culture and those who were just poor. By doing this, he "disarmed the critic", as any criticism could be said to apply just to those who were just poor (Townsend 1979). Most importantly, it is felt that Lewis's culture of poverty lacked consistency. Central to his thesis was the idea that these values are passed down from generation to generation. However, if the culture consists of a system of values, beliefs and institutions different from those of the majority, then this needed to be clearly shown in order to claim further that it was transmitted from generation to generation. The characteristics put forward by Lewis are neither approved nor perpetuated, and a culture of poverty cannot be upheld if its very values are not accepted by those who are supposedly upholding it (Townsend 1979).

The second factor that influences resilience is the creation of a local social, political and economic environment that provides the necessary opportunities to adapt and innovate. The existence of sound and effective macroeconomic and social policy at the level of government is indispensable in enabling individuals to significantly improve their living conditions. Indeed, without sound policy, the individual characteristics just discussed will have a limited effect. In reality, government policy should create an effective union between social policy and economic goals, providing individuals with the best opportunity to meet their social, economic, health and educational needs (World Bank 2013). The opportunities and tools that individuals require to improve their lives can be provided only through sound government policy (Narayan, Pritchett and Kapoor 2009).

Similarly, the *multidimensional approach* to understanding poverty and resilience put forward by the Caribbean Human Development Report (UNDP 2016) stressed the need to take into account resilience at the individual level. The report argued that, in addition to the responsibility of the state, resilience and ultimately escape from poverty are heavily influenced also by actions taken at the individual and household levels. Critical to the process of resilience is human agency: "Human resilience is about removing the barriers that hold people back in their freedom to act. It is also about enabling the disadvantaged and excluded groups to express their concerns, to be heard and to be active agents in shaping their destinies" (UNDP 2016, 36).

SOCIAL INCLUSION

Understanding the role of social inclusion in the process of fostering resilience is not without its challenges. Although we are advancing the concept as a means of addressing poverty and the resulting vulnerability of individuals and groups, it is important to resist the propensity to view social inclusion merely as a response to social exclusion since it has value in and of itself both as a process and as a goal (Mitchell and Shillington 2002). It has been defined as a process whereby those vulnerable to poverty and social exclusion are afforded the resources necessary to improve their situation and become fully participating members of society (Frazer and Marlier 2013). Whereas income and employment have typically been seen as the most effective ways of addressing poverty and exclusion, social inclusion also places emphasis on improving the opportunities for vulnerable groups to gain access to a more comprehensive range of assets.

Mitchell and Shillington (2002) identified five critical dimensions, or cornerstones, of social inclusion. (1) *Valued recognition* refers to the respect afforded to individuals and groups through sensitivity to developmental, cultural and gender differences. Here universal programmes such as health care are particularly relevant. (2) *Human development* refers to the fostering of capabilities and talents to allow individuals to make worthy contributions to society. Learning and developmental opportunities here are critical. (3) *Involvement and engagement* refers to having the right as well as the opportunity to participate in decision making. Citizen engagement and political participation are important here. (4) *Proximity* refers to the sharing of physical and social spaces in order to encourage interaction. Such spaces may include parks, libraries, integrated schools as well as mixed income neighbourhoods. Finally (5) *Material well-being* refers to being equipped with the material resources that enable individuals to effectively participate in community life. Housing and income assume particular relevance here.

Others have cautioned that when using the concept of social inclusion, one has to be cognisant of the dynamic and multilayered nature of the term. The inclusion of whom (social groups or communities), of what (goods, services, resources), into what (labour market, welfare system, physical space, political space, cultural space, social space), how (equally, voluntarily, involuntarily) and for what purpose are all variables that can have significant effects on the success of inclusion efforts (Dugarova 2015). Inclusion may not always be beneficial to vulnerable groups, for example, if it occurs on highly adverse terms (Hospes and Clancy 2011).

Whether policy should address deficiencies in social and economic structures or seek to provide pathways for marginalized groups into fair and adequate structures is the difference between creating inclusion and preventing exclusion. Novick (2001) referred to this as the critical dilemma confronting social policy throughout history. The manner in which social inclusion is approached is affected by one's philosophical assumptions as regards the root causes of exclusion (Mitchell and Shillington 2002).

Levitas (1998) provided a useful illustration of this. Many feel that the sole reason for the existence of social exclusion is unemployment. Levitas referred to this as the social integrationist discourse (SID), which sees exclusion as exclusion from paid work rather than exclusion from social participation, and sees integration through paid work as the answer. The SID discourse links exclusion to poor housing conditions, low levels of education and opportunities, discrimination and poor integration in the local community. It treats the absence of skills such as linguistic, scientific and other knowledge (which is referred to as basic knowledge), as well as technological skills, placing the emphasis on information technologies, as the reason behind social exclusion. The idea is that the basic skills that are needed for integration into a society are the same as those needed for employment. A lack of this leads to what "European social policy" refers to as exclusion from the "cycle of opportunities". The danger here is that it ignores the possibility that those engaged in work may nonetheless experience poverty. Wage inequalities could create a "working poor unable to survive decently on their wages and thus lead to a form of exclusion just as damaging as unemployment" (Levitas 1996, 11). The SID discourse also places no value on unpaid work and its role in maintaining social life and human relationships (Levitas 1998).

Similarly, under the redistributionist (RED) notion of exclusion, unemployment is seen as a major cause of poverty. The main concern of RED is the impact of exclusion on the lives of excluded people, as well as the resulting poverty and inequality. RED sees the burden of responsibility for creating inclusion to rest on the wider society. The absolute and relative living conditions under which the poor live are key indicators here (Mitchell and Shillington 2002). The adoption of this restricted interpretation of social exclusion could encourage the view that a redistribution of resources would ensure full participation in all areas of economic, social and political life. Alcock (1997) argued that, in Britain and the United States, social exclusion is increasing because of family breakdown, hardened racial cleavages, racism among the less privileged, and gender inequalities. Poverty does not necessarily lead to social exclusion, as other factors such as good social contacts and good health can mitigate the effects (Walker 1997). The concept, Alcock (1997) felt, should focus on the relations between people and not on the distribution of resources.

Levitas also saw social exclusion embedded in the moral underclass discourse (MUD). Young (1999) argued that in Europe the welfare state was seen as the main instrument of the state to *include* citizens. It ensured that the marginal had the minimal benefits of economic citizenship. However, there was a complete reversal in the 1980s and 1990s, and there was an acceptance of the view that the welfare state created a culture of dependency, creating a group of people who excluded themselves. Initially, there was the idea that benefits were good for the deserving but not the undeserving poor (Levitas 1998). However, this feeling soon changed. Benefits were seen as a disincentive to entering the world of work, and those permanently on benefits would eventually be unable to function in the world of work. MUD argues that the boundary between the included and excluded is defined by the moral and behavioural inadequacies of the excluded. Here, an important function of work is the avoidance of dependence. Inclusion therefore occurs by reducing the number of persons on social assistance through greater employment.

Policies inspired by SID and MUD, as with the New Labour's "New Deal" in Great Britain, can have the effect of reinforcing exclusion by portraying the poor as distinct from hard-working citizens. Fostering resilience through social inclusion, therefore, requires more than simply the provision of paid employment. As mentioned earlier, resilience requires intervention in the local (economic, social, political) environment as well as at the individual and household levels. Success therefore depends on the extent to which assets are made accessible to meet these goals.

HUMAN RIGHTS

The concept of human rights was traditionally understood as the rights of citizenship in the context of the nation state. Within this framework, rights were essentially political and defined in terms of political participation with an emphasis on the right to vote. Nationals were distinguished from "aliens", who had no such rights. Much changed after World War II as the United Nations (UN) spearheaded an international agenda of principles and practices that encoded the universality of human rights. Its landmark treaty, the 1948 UN Declaration on Human Rights, also encompassed a comprehensive range of rights – economic, social, cultural and civil, as well as political. The notion of economic and social rights as integral to human rights gave priority to the right to work in favourable conditions, the right to an adequate standard of living and the right to social security. From the 1990s onwards, attention turned towards poverty. Indeed, the mitigation of poverty has become the central focus of human rights for countries worldwide (Davy 2014). Initial generalized social welfare provisions became more targeted towards specific vulnerable groups, particularly those highlighted in subsequent UN conventions, such as women, children, indigenous peoples and persons with disabilities. Human rights, as promoted by the United Nations and other global agencies, were presented as a set of legal and social guarantees that emerged from the fundamental principles of liberty, equality and dignity shared by all persons. They provided global signposts for human and social development.

This reconceptualization, in turn, triggered a transformation in social policy thinking and poverty alleviation programmes. While not denying the centrality of employment and social protection, policy attention shifted from the provision of welfare benefits to a consideration of all-round well-being. Basic needs interventions became rights-based, and asset-based approaches adopted a holistic view by broadening the range of assets essential to human rights from specifically financial to include physical, human, social and environmental assets. Ferguson (2006), more specifically, illustrated the manner in which human rights and assets intersect – with physical assets tied to property rights, human assets to rights to education, and social assets to citizenship rights. The multidimensional character of poverty was revealed in the demonstration of human rights violations as both a cause and consequence of poverty (Donald and Mothershaw 2009). Thus, poverty as a result of asset deprivation was perceived as a breach of human rights; conversely, the denial of human rights by social exclusion or discrimination was seen to constrain access to assets.

Recently, research on social development and poverty and the recommendations arising therefrom have also been rights based. Centred in this approach are the voices of the poor as they speak of poverty in terms of their lived experiences that deny not only their basic needs but also their fundamental dignity and justice (Narayan et al. 2000). Recent analyses of poverty include PPAs that use qualitative research and adopt an "emic" point of view to articulate human rights perspectives expressed in the views and experiences of the poor themselves (Renard and Wint 2007). PPAs, then, as Shaffer (2002, 197) points out, are more about who defines poverty than they are an analytical redefinition of poverty. In this respect, an interesting finding from the PPAs conducted in the Caribbean and elsewhere is the denial by the poor that they live in "poverty" (Frank 2007, 29–31; Narayan et al. 2000) and an emphasis on quality of life, independence and self-respect, as much as on income poverty (Chambers 1995). As the perspectives, local knowledge and capacities of the poor were highlighted, they also became more active participants in poverty research and assessments and in policy formulation and implementation, and they were empowered to make changes in their quality of life and claim their human rights.

Human rights, by definition, are universal, not discretionary or context specific. All persons, whatever their age, gender, nationality or sexual orientation, have equal rights to life and freedom, protection from harm and violence, social inclusion and participation and a life without discrimination and poverty. Moreover, these rights are inherent and inalienable – they cannot be given up or taken away by others or by the state. Human rights operate both at a personal level to challenge and reduce personal suffering and marginalization and at broader institutional and societal levels to create more inclusive legal and social environments. As well as addressing individual and household asset deprivation, the trajectory points to underlying structural inequalities of gender, ethnicity and class, nationality, disability and sexuality that drive social exclusion and deny social justice and human rights. Human rights are also intended to trump cultural relativism. The right of the child to a life free of violence, as enshrined in the UN Convention on the Rights of the Child (CRC), takes priority over the legal and cultural acceptance of the corporal punishment of children; the right of gay men to live without stigma and discrimination should override culturally embedded homophobia. These and other examples point to the need to recognize the inherent human rights of marginalized populations in particular. Human rights discourse also does more than provide practical guidelines. By operating hand in hand with social justice, gender equality and social participation, human rights lift these principles to a higher plane by adding the weight of legal obligation and political authority.

Repositioning poverty within a human rights context deepens understandings and provides a more holistic frame for poverty alleviation. The intersection of poverty, social exclusion and rights takes the analysis beyond narrow economic conceptions of poverty based on the gap between household income and consumption and the assessment of who falls below the "breadline". Within this traditional frame, policies and programmes to alleviate poverty concentrate on the provision of employment, micro credit for small business development and basic needs welfare. As the analysis moves upstream to ask why individuals and social groups are poor – why they are unemployed, uneducated, unhealthy and homeless – attention focuses on the politics of social exclusion as a result of systemic unequal treatment, stigma, discrimination and violence and meted out to specific social groups.

Initial distrust and resistance to UN declarations of human rights on the part of nation states have generally given way to greater acceptance (Davy 2014, 247). Nevertheless, some rights are considered more acceptable than others. Most countries across the world are in full agreement with the rights of their populations to the basics of food, clothing and shelter, as well as to health, education and welfare, and often the only stumbling block to implementation is the lack of state resources. But other human rights provoke legal, cultural and moral resistance. The 1989 Convention on the Rights of the Child provides a case in point. The Caribbean response was overwhelmingly positive – all CARICOM (Caribbean Community) countries had signed and ratified it by 1993 and implementation in terms of child "provision" and "protection" generally ensued to the extent that resource capacity allowed. But the path has been less smooth in relation to the right to "participation", which redefines children as subjects with rights to be heard and to be involved in decisions affecting them rather than as objects of adult authority. There has also been opposition to banning corporal punishment of children, which is deeply entrenched in Caribbean culture and viewed as a parental right of "ownership". Still other human rights, sexual rights in particular, cross the boundary between social acceptability and moral abhorrence. Any move towards the decriminalization of sex work and homosexuality provokes strong resistance from faith-based organizations, governments and the general publics across the Caribbean. Their mission, vehemently stated, is to protect and preserve "traditional moral values" by depicting a mythical past founded on Christian family morality. Modern liberal secularism is denounced as Western imperialism seeking to impose a deviant and immoral sexual agenda. In terms of human rights acceptance and implementation, there is a point beyond which they will not go. This resistance has been echoed by scholars sceptical about the implementation of the "lofty goals" of human rights (Davy 2014, 261). And, while UN conventions set out specific obligations for states parties, sanctions for non-compliance are weak, and many states do little more than conduct regular reviews and submit reports, often belatedly.

Caribbean contextual analyses highlight social and legal inequalities that act as barriers to the realization of human rights for all. All societies are characterized to a greater or lesser degree by inequalities, but in the Caribbean these are perhaps more entrenched as a result of the legacy of slavery and colonialism. Unequal power relations persist between men and women, rich and poor, adults and children, nationals and migrants, heterosexuals and "others". In Caribbean societies, these social distinctions are compounded by racial and ethnic inequalities. In addition, specific social groups such as women, children and the elderly, along with stigmatized populations including persons with disabilities or living with HIV, and those who are also criminalized such as sex workers (SW) and men who have sex with men (MSM) are all denied human rights, though to different degrees and in different ways. Infringements of their human rights intersect with social exclusion promoted by discriminatory practices that deny access to assets in a variety of contexts – including employment, housing, education and health – to generate poverty. Regarding health, for example, poverty results not only from health care that is inaccessible due to high cost, distance and unaffordable transportation but also because the stigma and discrimination, real or expected, from health service providers in clinics and hospitals keep vulnerable populations away. In other words, human rights violations, including stigma, criminalization and the fear and threat of violence constitute an obstacle to poverty alleviation.

The contemporary language and centrality of human rights has also triggered a focus on agency and advocacy among marginalized populations, on efforts to empower themselves to act on their own behalf. PPAs have acknowledged the resourcefulness of the poor and their capacity to articulate problems and act for self-improvement. In contrast to the rhetoric of charity and welfare, the human rights response encourages socially excluded groups and individuals to secure their entitlements, removing the notion of personal shame by recognizing both socio-economic and citizenship rights (Lister 2004). Mobilization and public pressure, in turn, build stronger cultures of political participation and civil society action to ensure transparency and accountability in governance structures.

In the Caribbean, articulation and agency for the realization of human rights are evident in community engagement and mobilization by non-governmental organizations (NGOs) and coalitions of interest groups representing the rights of specific vulnerable groups. Such advocacy is increasingly viewed as the pathway to human rights and poverty reduction, but it is still somewhat nascent and weak, and there is a lack of clarity as to what community mobilization entails and how it may be effected. Another element for successful advocacy that is clearly lacking is knowledge of the law and social rights and how to ensure them. The majority of Caribbean persons remain unaware of their rights or where to turn for redress in cases of discrimination.

In summary, the UN-driven agenda for human rights mandated all nation states across the globe to redesign social policy from "poor relief" and welfare benefits to rights-based poverty alleviation programmes that entitled all persons to a range of financial, physical, human, social and environmental assets. But Caribbean countries continue to fall short in translation. The reality reveals resources that are stretched and inadequate, and significant sectors of populations remain socially excluded by stigma, discrimination and criminalization and are still vulnerable to poverty and violations of human rights. Among the most affected are gay men and sex workers, who are perceived to flout heteronormative codes and local "traditional moral values". Across the Caribbean, persistent resistance to universal human rights in law and culture, the lack of social protection and recourse against violations and the low-key advocacy for rights on the part of vulnerable groups act as deterrents to the full implementation of human rights.

ANALYTICAL FRAMEWORK

Jehoel-Gijsbers and Vrooman (2004, 4) illustrated the multidimensional nature of social exclusion by indicating its operation at two levels: socio-cultural and economic/structural. The components were defined as follows:

A. Socio-cultural exclusion:

1. Insufficient social participation: A lack of participation in formal and informal social networks, including leisure activities; inadequate social support; social isolation.
2. Insufficient cultural/ normative integration: A lack of compliance with core norms and values associated with active social citizenship. This is reflected in a weak work ethic; low willingness to become educated; abuse of social security system or delinquent behaviour; deviating views on children's education; deviating views on the rights and duties of men and women.

B. Economic/structural exclusion:

3. Material deprivation: Shortages in relation to basic needs and material goods; "lifestyle deprivation"; problematic debts; payment arrears (in particular housing costs).
4. Inadequate access to government and semi-government provisions ("social rights"): Waiting lists and/or financial and other obstacles to health care, education (especially of children), housing, legal aid, social services, debt assistance, employment agencies and social security, but also to commercial services such as banking and insurance; insufficient safety.

It is proposed here that the underlying causes of social exclusion, which are manifested in the manner just highlighted, are based on individuals' characteristics and their stock of assets, as well as their level of access to asset-building mechanisms. The earlier discussion highlighted the complex interplay between these factors and the manner in which institutions, economic conditions, social and cultural norms and the environment all permit or deny access to these asset-building mechanisms. In order to understand this complex interplay, we draw on the issues just examined to develop our conceptual framework. An explanation of this framework is given next, along with the implications for the analysis that follows in subsequent chapters.

Understanding the role of assets and access to asset-building mechanisms is critical in any analysis of poverty. Conceptually, an individual possesses assets drawn from wider society, as well as personal assets to transfer back to society in the form of labour, trade, taxes, participation in social networks and the democratic process, and environmentally in the exploitation, preservation and/or degradation of a country's natural and human-made resources. The individual's assets are used to maintain livelihoods, build further assets, build resilience by coping with shocks and stresses (resilience) and meet obligations to wider society such as taxes, community participation and the provision of labour.

An individual's assets are, however, not separate and distinct from one another, as they interact for in mutual support of one another to build an asset base. Assets also possess substitution qualities, whereby the lack of one type of asset can be compensated for by the surplus of another. In this sense, a lack of physical and/or financial capital can be compensated for by a high level of assets, where, for example, an individual's inability to access labour markets due to a lack of certification (tangible assets) may still be able to access these labour markets through personal, community, family or political contacts. Individuals may also be able to avoid social exclusion in the form of material deprivation, even if they lack physical, financial, human or social capital, through the exploitation of the natural environment, such as fishing. These substitution qualities of assets can be complex, and the manner in which the system of access to asset-building mechanisms is navigated is discussed in chapter 4 in relation to the results of interviews with individuals in vulnerable groups.

The interaction and dependence between assets can be illustrated through a farmer's use of skills (human assets) and fertile land (environmental asset) to produce goods in exchange for financial assets or through the use of a social network to obtain training opportunities to build human assets. An individual builds assets by utilizing current assets to effect a transfer from the country's assets through specific mechanisms. The individual may, for example, transfer a specific asset to accumulate either more of the same asset (for example, financial investment) or a different asset (for example, the use of human capital to accumulate financial assets), in addition to transferring to the state such assets as taxes. However, for these transactions to occur efficiently, transfer mechanisms are required.

The mechanisms that exist to access a country's assets are comprised of a number of markets, systems and networks that interact to provide and grow the overall asset base. These *asset-building mechanisms* include the manipulation of market mechanisms involving the exchange of goods, services and labour; human resource development systems, that is, education and training and health; social networks and their facilitation of the *exchange* of social assets; and the character of natural ecosystems. At the same time, however, an individual's access to these mechanisms is determined by a number of *intervening external factors* including the actions of the state as it relates to politics, legislation and regulations; the state of the national economy, which is itself dependent on exogenous factors; social and cultural conditions and values; and environmental conditions and climate change. These external factors affect an individual's access based on interaction with a number of *latent conditions,* including the individual's current asset stock and personal characteristics such as age, gender, marital status, ethnicity, race, nationality, religion, employment status, health status and sexual orientation. While an individual's current asset stock and latent characteristics are internal and a relic of previous access to asset-building mechanisms, if any, other factors are external to individuals and determine their current and future ability to build assets; we conceptualize that the effect of these external factors on individuals' access is what determines their level of vulnerability to social exclusion, while their current level of assets determines their level of resilience and whether such resilience is sustainable or not over the long term. In such a situation, individuals may be vulnerable because of external conditions that preclude their access to asset-building mechanisms, but they may be resilient if their asset base is sufficiently large to enable them to cope with shocks and stresses over the longer term.

As figure 2.1 illustrates, individuals' access to the mechanisms to access assets is critical to determining their level of inclusion or exclusion. A lack of access to these mechanisms is deemed a violation of an individual's human rights, as by socially excluding them, it neglects to provide them with the necessary means to cope effectively and sustainably with external shocks to and stressors on their livelihoods.

If the level of access to asset-building mechanisms is low due to constraints imposed on individuals through various intervening factors, then their level of social inclusion will be low. In such a situation, the feedback effect is directly to their asset stock, where in order to maintain their livelihood, they would need to exploit their current asset stock, leading to its degradation. At a broad conceptual level, these relationships seem logical. However, the manner in which specific assets are degraded needs to be made clear. It is clear that an individual's property – physical and financial assets – can be degraded/lost as they are utilized for coping in the short term, for example, by the sale of physical assets to provide for consumption, by using savings as pseudo insurance or by letting physical assets decline in value due to neglect. Degradation of the natural environment can occur in a similar manner, through over-exploitation to meet basic needs. However, understanding

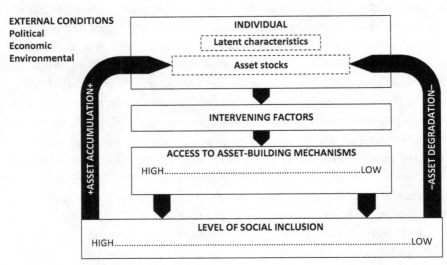

Figure 2.1. A framework of social exclusion

the degradation of elements of social and human capital assets is somewhat more complex.

Social assets are comprised of social ties at various levels, including the household and community in which one resides, works and generally interacts with, both physically and virtually. As noted by Attanasio and Székely (1999), social assets do not depend solely on an individual's decisions and are therefore somewhat differentiated from physical, financial and human assets. In this sense, one may possess social assets that are directly *accumulated* through individual action, *inherited* or drawn from other individuals in a network to which one has access. Social assets can therefore be degraded by both the individual and others within the network. From an individual's perspective, the focus of the analysis here, social assets can be utilized to access asset-building mechanisms through network contacts and as a substitute in the event of a lack of other supporting assets; access to employment due to political patronage or through birth by nepotism are two examples. However, these assets can be degraded due to the breakdown in networks as a result of overuse or to the contraction of networks due to the covariate nature of natural disasters or a change in government. The greatest threat to the degradation of social assets is the lack of power due to the lack of position in a network obtained from other assets such as physical, financial or human capital assets. These assets can, conversely, place persons in positions of power through which their place in the network is assured. Individuals with limited power due to a lack of other assets can see their positions in a social network, from which they obtain social assets, become marginalized. A lack of power in this sense limits the utilization of social assets. Moreover, the overuse of contacts and connections to compensate for a lack of *power* can lead to further marginalization and eventual disconnection from social networks.

While an individual's health, one element of human assets, can degrade due to a lack of adequate nutrition or living in an unsafe environment, the degradation of human assets gained from education, training and experience is somewhat more difficult to understand. In this sense, the degradation is understood from a perspective of devaluation, where through the lack of use, skills and abilities become outdated, and future earning potential is also constrained through a *scarring* effect. Whereas other assets can be degraded through overuse, the degradation of this element of human capital is degraded through underuse.

Overall, the analysis is undertaken within a human rights framework, where the constraining factors are deemed breaches of human rights and occur through the intervening factors identified in table 2.1. For ease of reference, the other factors included in the model are also listed in the table.

Table 2.1. Components of the Framework of Social Exclusion

Individual	
Latent Characteristics	*Asset Stocks*
Age	Physical
Gender	Human
Marital status	Social
Sexual orientation	Environmental
Ethnicity/race/nationality	

Intervening Factors
Politics
Institutions, legislation and regulations
Macroeconomic conditions
Social and cultural conditions and values
Environmental conditions (natural and human-made)

Asset-Building Mechanisms
Trade in goods and services
Labour markets
Health systems
Educational systems
Welfare systems
Social networks
Political networks
Natural ecosystems
Infrastructural systems

Social Inclusion
Social participation
Cultural/normative integration
Access to state/non-state provisions
Material endowments

CHAPTER 3

SOCIAL EXCLUSION IN BARBADOS

THIS CHAPTER SEEKS TO ANALYSE ECONOMIC AND structural exclusion in Barbados utilizing the data from a 2010 survey of living conditions (SLC), a component of the wider country assessment of living conditions (CALC) (Caribbean Development Bank 2012a).[1] The other component of social exclusion, sociocultural exclusion, is examined in greater depth in the chapters that follow.

The economic/structural component of social exclusion, as proposed by Jehoel-Gijsbers and Vrooman (2004), includes a number of potential measures in relation to material deprivation and inadequate access to "social rights". To operationalize the analysis, we review issues related to the stocks of physical, financial and human capital assets, as well as access to the main related asset-building mechanisms, that is, trade in goods, services and labour, education, health care and social safety nets. While we are appreciative of the complex interplay of all of the various components of the system of asset accumulation or degradation, the structure of the SLC only allows for a cross-sectional analysis of certain variables.

In seeking to highlight the main correlates of social exclusion, asset stocks and access to asset-building mechanisms are analysed based on individual (age, gender, marital status, nationality and religion) and household characteristics. The analysis in this sense seeks to reveal "tendencies" or general regularities in the relationships seen rather than seeking to understand underlying causes; this element of the exercise is undertaken in the chapters that follow, where a deeper investigation is presented.

MATERIAL DEPRIVATION, HUMAN CAPITAL DEFICITS AND ACCESS TO THE REAL ECONOMY

The SLC component of the CALC provided estimates of consumption poverty using an indigence line, a poverty line and a vulnerability line. Indigence relates to a lack of resources to provide for basic nutritional levels, that is, food poverty, while those in "poverty" are considered able to meet basic nutritional needs but are unable to meet other needs such as housing. The issue of vulnerability relates to those at risk of falling into poverty and includes those within 25 per cent of the poverty line. In seeking to assess material deprivation, we include all individuals and households below the vulnerability line in our assessment of economic and structural exclusion. From the SLC results, this group of indigent, poor and vulnerable, referred to here as IPV, comprised 26.6 per cent of the sample; overall, 7.8 per cent were indigent, 8.7 per cent poor, and 10.1 per cent were vulnerable. The following analysis highlights the main demographic characteristics of IPV, followed by a discussion of their access to physical and financial asset-building mechanisms.

Characteristics and Correlates of Poverty and Vulnerability

With reference to the analytical framework, where the issues of asset accumulation and degradation are core, table 3.1 highlights the increased experiences between 2007 and 2010 between IPV and non-IPV. The table

Table 3.1. Asset Accumulation, Switching and Degradation by IPV Status 2007–2010 (%)

Increases In . . .	IPV (%)	Non-IPV (%)
Personal income (financial assets – accumulation)	31.2	41.5
Personal expenditure (financial assets – degradation)	57.0	62.6
Consumption of food and services (financial assets – degradation)	42.9	48.7
Hours worked (financial assets – accumulation)	9.3	15.3
Purchase of new household durables (physical asset stock accumulation/asset switching)	12.1	21.2
Spending on education (human capital asset accumulation/asset switching)	23.5	25.3

indicates that personal income, expenditure and consumption had increased for a greater proportion of non-IPV than IPV, suggesting both asset accumulation and degradation for both groups. However, the cohort that experienced financial asset degradation (those that experienced decreases or no change in income but experienced increases in expenditure) accounted for 35.6 per cent of IPV and 31.2 per cent of non-IPV. This suggests that a greater proportion of those identified in 2010 as vulnerable have suffered asset degradation over the period and are in a worse position than they were in 2007. While the difference between the two groups is marginal, it highlights the continued worsening of the situation for the most vulnerable.

At a more qualitative level, nearly 25 per cent of IPV rated their household standard of living as "low" or "very low" as opposed to 9 per cent of non-IPV; this undefined "standard of living" variable suggests a disconnect between the monetized aspect of social exclusion and general "well-being", that is, even though IPV lack financial assets, over 75 per cent do not consider their general "standard of living" as low. Although by no means definitive, it appears that households consider standard of living to be more than just the possession and ability to accumulate financial assets.

While there is limited difference between the cohorts with respect to residing in a separate house (87 per cent) or owning the dwelling (75 per cent), land ownership and access to utilities are more of an issue for IPV: 55 per cent of IPV versus 66 per cent of non-IPV own the land on which they live, 6 per cent of IPV toilet facilities are pit latrines as opposed to 2 per cent of non-IPV and only 94 per cent of IPV have water piped into the dwelling versus 99 per cent of non-IPV. With respect to housing conditions, the materials of the outer walls were wooden for 30 per cent of IPV versus 18 per cent of non-IPV; the related percentages for concrete walls were 37 per cent for IPV versus 56 per cent of non-IPV. These housing issues demonstrate a relationship with income poverty and indicate that the poor and vulnerable suffer from both material deprivation with respect to asset ownership (land) and asset quality (wooden housing), as well as inadequate access to sanitary facilities.

With respect to other assets and access to asset-building mechanisms, the starting point in the analysis of economic and structural exclusion drew on two main demographic variables – age and sex – and sought to determine the cohorts that were over-represented in the IPV group. While the IPV rate for the entire sample was 27 per cent, the youth rate was 34 per cent as opposed

Table 3.2. IPV Rates by Age Group and Sex (%)

Age Group	Male	Female	Total
Youth	30.9	37.1	34.2
Middle-aged	22.4	26.3	24.6
Elderly	24.4	27.3	26.0
Total	24.5	28.3	26.6

to 25 per cent for the middle-aged and 27 per cent for the elderly.[2] The IPV rates for these age groups by sex are shown in table 3.2.

Table 3.2 demonstrates that young females suffer the highest IPV rates followed by young males and elderly females. Overall females have a significantly higher IPV rate than males.[3] With an understanding that correlation does not mean causation, information on union status for the IPV does highlight a couple of associations of interest (see table 3.3); first, that divorcees not currently in a union and the legally married have the *lowest* IPV rates, 15.2 per cent and 19.6 per cent, respectively. In addition, the *highest* IPV rates were seen with those in a visiting partner relationship (35.4 per cent), single persons (30.9 per cent) and widows (30.5 per cent). While single females or females in a visiting relationship exhibit the highest IPV rates, widowers have a marginally higher IPV rate than widows. Of interest is that male divorcees have the lowest IPV rates of all subgroups (10 per cent), with female divorcees

Table 3.3. IPV Rates by Union Status and Sex (%)

Union Status	Male	Female	Total
Single (never married)	28.2	33.0	30.9
Legally married	19.0	20.1	19.6
Common-law union	27.6	28.0	27.8
Visiting partner	32.3	37.3	35.4
Married (not in a union)	25.0	25.0	25.0
Widowed (not in a union)	32.8	29.6	30.5
Divorced (not in a union)	10.2	18.1	15.2
Total	24.5	28.3	26.6

having the second lowest IPV rate (18 per cent). This particular result notwithstanding, the general relationship here between poverty and vulnerability and union status, where "couples" in formal unions (marriage or common law) have lower IPV rates than single persons or those in a visiting union, would be expected due to income pooling and expenditure sharing. This relationship finds support in Kenney (2004), who suggests that the more formalized the relationship is (marriage/children together), the greater the likelihood is of income pooling.

Barbados promotes itself as a "Christian" society, and 76 per cent of the population are affiliated to a Christian denomination (Barbados Statistical Service 2013). Analysing the CALC results by religious affiliation demonstrates some clear differences within the sample, with Rastafarians having the highest IPV rate at 36 per cent, particularly among male Rastafarians (38 per cent) rather than female Rastafarians (17 per cent). The highest IPV rate is seen among females with no religious affiliation (40 per cent). The lowest IPV rate is seen among Wesleyan Holiness at 13 per cent with limited difference between males and females. (See table 3.4.)

Table 3.4. IPV Rates by Religion and Sex (%)

Religion	Male	Female	Total
Anglican	21.4	25.9	23.9
Baptist	27.3	32.9	30.7
Jehovah Witness	24.2	14.2	18.1
Methodist	19.0	22.0	20.9
Moravian	20.0	25.0	23.4
Nazarene	13.6	20.0	17.7
Pentecostal	26.4	29.9	28.6
Rastafarian	38.3	16.7	35.8
Roman Catholic	22.4	26.3	24.7
Seventh-Day Adventist	28.0	27.4	27.6
Wesleyan Holiness	13.1	12.9	13.0
None	29.2	39.6	33.5
Other	25.0	33.9	29.7
Total	24.5	28.3	26.6

Table 3.5. IPV Rates by Nationality and Sex (%)

Nationality	Male	Female	Total
Barbadian	25.3	28.5	27.1
Non-Barbadian	17.0	30.2	24.7
Total	24.5	28.3	26.6

With respect to nationality, the lowest IPV rates are seen among non-Barbadian males at 17 per cent, as opposed to 30 per cent among non-Barbadian females, the highest rate seen by nationality. (See table 3.5.)

The preceding analysis of SLC results by demographic factors suggests that income/consumption poverty is most prevalent among:

- the youth, especially young females;
- single persons and those in visiting relationships, particularly females;
- male Rastafarians and females with no religious affiliation; and
- non-Barbadian females.

These general findings suggest a complex mix of correlates of social exclusion: age, gender, marital status, religion and nationality. With the exception of male Rastafarians, there is a consistent theme of gender in relation to poverty and vulnerability.

This review of these general characteristics raises key questions. What access to group physical and financial asset-building mechanisms does the IPV group have? That is, what is their access to the real economy? Table 3.6 highlights that the highest IPV rate is seen among those not in education, employment or training (NEET), where there is limited difference between males and females. Not surprisingly, given the income/consumption basis for the definition of IPV, the lowest rate was seen for those who were working.

These results demonstrate IPV rates for the various cohorts and indicate that these rates are highest for those not in employment, education or training (NEET). In looking at the overall composition of the IPV cohort specifically by main economic activity, table 3.7 demonstrates that 51 per cent and 44 per cent of IPV males and females, respectively, are working, while 22 per cent are NEET and 18 per cent are retired.

Table 3.6. IPV Rates by Main Economic Activity and Sex (%)

Main Economic Activity	Male	Female	Total
Working	19.3	22.2	20.8
NEET	48.6	49.5	49.1
Keeping house	20.0	27.9	27.6
Education	28.3	34.3	31.7
Retired	26.6	30.3	28.7
Incapacitated	36.0	28.6	31.7
Other	41.7	26.3	32.3
Total	24.5	28.3	26.6

At the household level, a correlate of poverty and vulnerability was found in relation to dependency, that is, the number of dependent, non-working persons in the household. Measuring dependency by the percentage of dependents indicates a significant difference between IPV and non-IPV households where the share in IPV households was 48 per cent versus 34 per cent in non-IPV households.[4] This result, in addition to the results in table 3.7, highlights three important areas for analysis:

1. What is the nature of employment for the "working poor"?
2. What are the characteristics of IPV NEET?
3. What is the background of the retired IPV?

Table 3.7. Composition of IPV Cohort by Main Economic Activity and Sex (%)

Main Economic Activity	Male	Female	Total	Sample Size
Working	50.6	44.5	47.0	552
NEET	21.0	22.1	21.6	254
Retired	17.8	18.5	18.2	214
Education	7.5	8.2	7.9	93
Keeping house	0.2	4.5	2.7	32
Incapacitated	1.9	1.4	1.6	19
Other	1.0	0.7	0.9	10
Total	100.0	100.0	100.0	1,174

Cutting across these areas is also the issue of inter-household dependency levels. These areas are explored in greater detail in the sections that follow.

The Working Poor

Conceptually, the prevalence of the "working poor" in an economy is related to a variety of factors at several levels from the macroeconomic to the structure of enterprises and households; the structure of the economy in relation to sectoral composition and level of informality; educational and skill levels of the employed; age; and household dependency levels. Frazer and Marlier (2010) highlight the explanatory factors of *in-work poverty* as shown in table 3.8.

Table 3.8. Explanatory Factors of In-work Poverty

Structure of the economy/ labour market	Low-quality employment and wages
	Highly segmented labour market and low upward mobility
	Non-standard forms of employment
	Low net wages
	High-risk occupations (agriculture, self-employment)
	Geographic location
Family/household composition and low work intensity (dependency levels)	Children
	Low work intensity
Individual/personal characteristics	Low education/qualifications
	Nationality
	Being young
Institutional factors	Regulations
	Minimum wages
	Taxation
	Lack of in-work benefits
	Lack of child income support
	Cost of essential services

Source: Frazer and Marlier (2010).

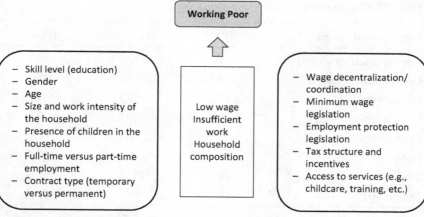

Figure 3.1. Factors influencing in-work poverty

Source: Adapted from EU Social Protection Committee (2014, 6).

The EU Social Protection Committee (2014), drawing on this and other research in the area, presents these factors diagrammatically, as shown in figure 3.1.

Analysing the data for Barbados provides initial support for some of these explanatory factors as next described.

Those IPV that are currently working demonstrate a significantly different employment profile from that of non-IPV. As shown in table 3.9, 17 per cent of IPV are not working full-time as opposed to only 9 per cent of non-IPV.

Table 3.9. Working Status by IPV Status (%)

Working Status	IPV	Non-IPV	Total
Full-time	83.1	91.2	89.5
Part-time	10.8	6.9	7.7
Seasonal	2.4	1.2	1.4
Occasional/odd jobs	3.7	0.8	1.4
Total	100.0	100.0	100.0
Sample size	539	2,060	2,599

Table 3.10. Employment Status by IPV Status (%)

Employment Status	IPV	Non-IPV	Total
Employer/self-employed	13.7	17.1	16.4
Government employee	17.2	22.9	21.7
Private employee	67.7	59.3	61.1
Unpaid family worker	0.0	0.1	0.1
Apprenticeship	0.7	0.2	0.3
Other	0.7	0.4	0.5
Total	100.0	100.0	100.0
Sample size	548	2,084	2,632

With respect to source of employment, IPV were less likely to work for themselves or in the public sector, with 68 per cent privately employed as opposed to 59 per cent of non-IPV. (See table 3.10.)

For the IPV who were self-employed, their businesses were more likely to be informal, with only 41 per cent being registered as opposed to 56 per cent for non-IPV, and 57 per cent operating from the home, an often-used indicator of informality; the related percentage for non-IPV was 47 per cent. (See table 3.11.)

Industry of employment for IPV is highly concentrated in three of the industries most vulnerable to general economic conditions: wholesale and retail trade; tourism (accommodation and food services); and construction, mining and quarrying. These three industries account for 43 per cent of IPV employment as opposed to 31 per cent for non-IPV. (See table 3.12.)

Table 3.11. Employer/Self-employed Location of Business by IPV Status (%) (Multiple Response)

Locations of Business	IPV	Non-IPV	Total
Home	57.3	47.1	48.8
Other fixed location	17.3	32.5	29.9
Mobile business	13.3	20.4	19.2
Other	17.3	5.3	7.4
Sample size	75	357	432

Table 3.12. Industry of Employment by IPV Status (%)

Industry	IPV	Non-IPV
Wholesale/retail trade	17.1	8.8
Accommodation/food services	16.1	12.3
Construction/mining/quarrying	9.8	9.9
Agriculture/fisheries	6.1	3.5
Administration	5.4	9.4
Manufacturing	5.4	3.8
Transport	4.8	4.3
Health and social work	4.1	6.6
Financial services	3.7	8.8
Education	2.2	5.9
Electricity/energy/water	2.2	2.6
Professional/technical activities	2.2	6.2
Information and communication	1.7	3.4
Other	19.3	14.5
Total	100.0	100.0

Not only are IPV in vulnerable industries, they are also in vulnerable occupations where 42 per cent are employed as service/sales workers, craft workers or clerical support workers. The related share for these occupations for non-IPV is 37 per cent. While there is only a marginal difference in these categories between the two cohorts, the starkest differences are seen at higher-rated occupational levels, where 14 per cent of non-IPV are professionals as opposed to only 5 per cent of IPV, and 9 per cent of non-IPV are managers as opposed to 2 per cent of IPV. (See table 3.13.)

Demonstrating the inadequacy of current employment among IPV to meet their basic needs, 22 per cent were seeking extra work versus 15 per cent of non-IPV.

Examining the characteristics of the working poor indicates a greater proportion of females within this group (56 per cent), while for non-IPV, the related proportion is 51 per cent. A review of the proportions of the employed that are IPV by sex and age reveals two clear trends: (1) youth, especially females, are more likely to be in the group of working poor and (2) the

Table 3.13. Occupation by IPV Status (%)

Occupation	IPV	Non-IPV
Service and sales worker	26.3	19.7
Craft and related trades worker	8.5	5.6
Clerical support worker	7.2	11.6
Plant and machine operators/assemblers	5.1	2.9
Elementary occupations	5.1	2.5
Professional	4.8	14.0
Skilled agriculture/fisheries worker	4.6	3.0
Technical/associate professional	4.2	6.3
Manager	2.5	9.4
Other	31.6	24.9
Total	100.0	100.0

employed elderly are less likely to be included in the group working poor. (See table 3.14.) Of greater concern here is that over one-quarter of young employed females are not earning enough to raise them above the vulnerability line.

In addition to the association between age and sex and IPV status for the employed, there is also a clear association between IPV status and highest level of education completed and highest qualification obtained. For the

Table 3.14. IPV (Working Poor) Rates by Sex and Age for the Employed (%)

	Age Category	IPV	Non-IPV	Total
Male	Youth	20.7	79.3	100.0
	Middle-aged	19.7	80.3	100.0
	Elderly	16.4	83.6	100.0
	Total	19.3	80.7	100.0
Female	Youth	27.0	73.0	100.0
	Middle-aged	22.4	77.6	100.0
	Elderly	18.1	81.9	100.0
	Total	22.2	77.8	100.0

working IPV, 75 per cent had completed secondary or above, while the percentage for non-IPV was 84 per cent. This difference is mostly driven by differences in levels of tertiary education where only 10 per cent of IPV had completed this level as opposed to 26 per cent of non-IPV. As expected from this result, the actual level of qualifications also differs with 42 per cent of IPV having no formal qualifications, as opposed to 22 per cent of non-IPV. Approximately 20 per cent of IPV have a post-secondary qualification as opposed to 45 per cent for non-IPV. This demonstrates a clear association between education as an element of human capital and the effective use of the labour market as an asset-building mechanism. The issue of the effective use of education in building human capital assets is discussed later in the chapter.

In an analysis of levels of household dependency (level of work intensity), that is, the percentage of dependents in the households of the working poor, the average level of dependency in these households was 29 per cent (29.3 per cent of household members were not working), while the related level of dependency in the non-working-poor households was 20 per cent. This result indicates that catering to the consumption needs of dependents would be one of the drivers of poverty and vulnerability in these households.

The general results here for the working poor fit with the general explanatory factors previously described, in that the main factors relate to low levels of human capital as it relates to education and qualifications, gender, age, share of dependents in the household and insecure employment in relation to part-time work, vulnerable sectors and low-level occupations. In general, the trend of age and gender as correlates of social exclusion is seen again.

The Unemployed

In a discussion of unemployment, there are generally two types. The first type is a broad conception of unemployment that includes those not in employment, education or training (NEET) who can be seeking or not seeking work and that excludes the retired or permanently incapacitated. This is essentially the group of persons that could be in the labour force but are not currently employed. The second type includes those not in employment, education or training (NEET) who are seeking work. This is the standard definition of unemployment that is reported by statistical agencies. As we are concerned with exclusion, we speak to the first type, which is the broader group of NEET, as this group is unable to access the labour market to build its asset stock. Here we look at the correlation between characteristics and asset stocks, as well as the lack of access to the labour market. As an indication of the difference between the broader conception of unemployment used here and official unemployment figures, the NEET unemployment rate for the entire sample from the SLC was 16 per cent as opposed to 11 per cent by the official definition.

Who Are the NEET?

The NEET cohort is evenly comprised of IPV and non-IPV. However, the IPV group overall accounts for only 27 per cent of the entire sample, suggesting a higher NEET rate for IPV, which was 32 per cent versus 11 per cent for non-IPV. While NEET are represented across all age cohorts, a greater proportion of NEET youth are IPV (54 per cent), as opposed to 47 per cent of the middle-aged and 49 per cent of the elderly. There is, however, a clear gender dimension to NEET by age group. As shown in table 3.15, NEET elderly males and young females are more likely to be IPV than other age and sex cohorts, with NEET elderly females the least likely to be IPV.

Apart from the association of NEET with being indigent, poor or vulnerable, another association seen was in relation to human capital assets, specifically education. With respect to NEET rates by highest level of education achieved, there is a clear trend of NEET rates declining as higher levels of

Table 3.15. Composition of NEET by Sex and Age (%)

	Age Category	IPV	Non-IPV	Total
Male	Youth	48.6	51.4	100.0
	Middle-aged	43.6	56.4	100.0
	Elderly	69.2	30.8	100.0
Female	Youth	58.0	42.0	100.0
	Middle-aged	48.6	51.4	100.0
	Elderly	38.3	61.7	100.0
	Total	100.0	100.0	100.0

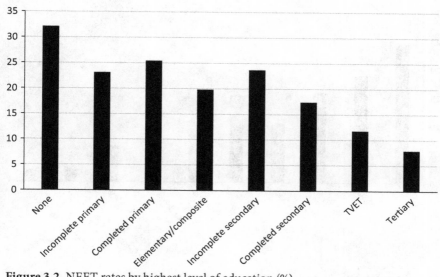

Figure 3.2. NEET rates by highest level of education (%)

education are completed. As shown in figure 3.2, those with at least a secondary education have NEET rates of nearly half of those with no education, and those with tertiary education have a NEET rate that is less than half of those with secondary education.

A similar picture is seen in relation to the highest examination passed, where the lowest NEET rates are seen for those with a postgraduate degree (2 per cent) or professional qualification (3 per cent), as opposed to 24 per cent of those with no qualifications (see figure 3.3). Also of interest in this respect is that the average age on leaving education was sixteen years for NEET as opposed to eighteen years for the employed.

These results indicate correlations between being NEET and IPV status, age, sex and education. In addition to these correlates, the SLC also enquired as to the specific reason for being NEET. Noting that the NEET cohort comprises the unemployed who are seeking work, according to the standard definition of unemployment, and the unemployed who are not actively seeking work, the following discussion focuses on those not seeking work as those seeking work would be employed if suitable work was available; 81 per cent of those actively seeking work indicated their reason for being unemployed was simply no work available.

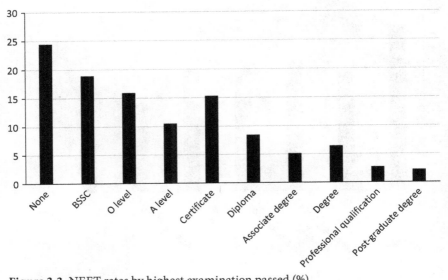

Figure 3.3. NEET rates by highest examination passed (%)

Overall, 44 per cent of NEET were not actively seeking work. The main reasons given were long-term illness (22 per cent), not wanting to work (22 per cent), providing care (12 per cent) and lack of knowledge of any vacancies (10 per cent). Overall, health issues account for 27 per cent of reasons for not working, while an element of self-exclusion from the labour market is seen with 28 per cent not wanting to work or being discouraged. While unavoidable or temporary reasons were seen for not working among 49 per cent (illness, pregnancy, waiting for responses to applications, caring for another), the level of "reversible" reasons (not wanting to work, discouraged, lack of knowledge of vacancies) accounts for over 37 per cent of those NEET not seeking work and for approximately 15 per cent of the entire NEET group. While knowledge of vacancies can be addressed through greater outreach by employment agencies, the reasons behind an apparent "aversion" to work and discouragement would need greater examination in order to develop interventions to promote greater labour market participation by this significant proportion of the unemployed. (See figure 3.4.)

The preceding discussion has addressed factors related to access to the labour market as an asset-building mechanism. Issues related to a lack of human capital assets, both health and education, appear to be related to a lack of utilization of

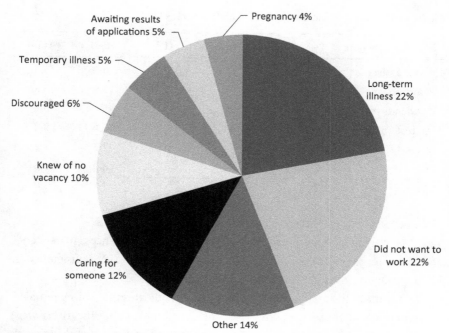

Figure 3.4. Reasons for not working among NEET not seeking work

the labour market to build individuals' overall asset stocks. Overall, the stock of human capital assets appears to be related to both the suboptimal exploitation of the labour market for the working poor and the ability to access the labour market, as just demonstrated, in relation to the NEET.

The question arises as to how unemployed persons manage to meet their basic needs. In general, it would be expected that NEETs meet their basic needs through intra-household transfers, relying on others in the household who work. However, NEETs appear to live in households with high levels of dependency, where others in the household are also not working and therefore unable to provide income support. In an analysis of levels of household dependency, that is, the percentage of dependents in the households with NEETs, the average level of dependency in IPV households was 50 per cent (half of household members in NEET IPV households were not working), while the related level of dependency in the non-IPV households with NEETs was 51.0 per cent. This level of dependency is higher than in the households of the working poor, which was 48 per cent and 34 per cent for working poor households that were

Table 3.16. Sources of Income for NEET by IPV Status (%)

Source of Income	IPV	Non-IPV	Total
Public assistance	7.2	6.0	6.6
Remittances	4.5	13.8	9.6
Dividends from local and foreign investments	0.0	5.7	3.1
Interest on bank deposits	0.9	5.1	3.2
Interest from stocks/shares	0.0	2.2	1.2
Other income	6.2	5.0	5.6

IPV and non-IPV, respectively. So how do NEETs survive? Table 3.16 demonstrates that the largest source of income for NEETs is remittances (10 per cent), and this is more prevalent in non-IPV households than in IPV households. In IPV households, the largest source is public assistance.

The results of the analysis of the unemployed indicates that young females, older males and those with low levels of education or qualifications were more likely to be NEET, while the main reasons given for not seeking work were health issues, caring duties, discouragement with the labour market and lack of knowledge of jobs. Of concern is that the unemployed, in both IPV and non-IPV households, are living in households comprised of other unemployed persons, placing further stress on those who are employed. In this sense, we see a link between the working poor and the unemployed, where even though an employed person may earn a suitable income, this income is subject to the needs of dependents in the household.

The Retired

The retired cohort was comprised of 43 per cent males and 57 per cent females, with 27 per cent of males being IPV and 30 per cent of females being IPV; that is, between a quarter and a third of retirees are indigent, poor or vulnerable. With respect to current union status, 46 per cent were legally married, 22 per cent were single and never married, and 21 per cent were widowed. Of interest in this respect is that the IPV rate for single retirees was 40 per cent, while the related rate for widows was 34 per cent, and for those legally married, it was 22 per cent. As with the analysis of the entire sample, the effect of income pooling and expenditure sharing among those in cohabiting relationships is to reduce the level of poverty.

Approximately 79 per cent of the retired suffered from some medical condition; this is nearly twice the national average of 40 per cent. The IPV rate for those with a medical condition was 30 per cent as opposed to 22 per cent without a medical condition. In addition, 21 per cent of the retired had a disability compared with a national average of 8 per cent. The retirees with a disability suffered a higher IPV rate than those without, 35 per cent versus 27 per cent. Of concern is that, while 26 per cent of the SLC sample were covered by private health insurance, the related figure for the retired was only 16 per cent. Of interest is that the IPV rate for retirees with health insurance was 8 per cent as opposed to 33 per cent for those without. This is not surprising given the manner in which IPV status is determined and non-IPV having greater financial resources to cover insurance premiums.

Apart from health issues, again of interest is the other component of human capital, education. While nearly 99 per cent of retirees had attended school in their lifetime, information on the highest qualification obtained shows some clear differences between poor and vulnerable retirees and those considered non-IPV. Table 3.17 shows that over 80 per cent of retirees who are

Table 3.17. Highest Qualification by IPV Status for Retirees (%)

Highest Qualification	IPV	Non-IPV
None	81.1	55.3
BSSC	4.0	5.1
O level/CXC general	5.7	6.6
A level/CAPE	0.0	1.6
Certificate	2.9	10.3
Diploma	1.7	5.3
Associate degree	0.0	1.4
Degree	1.7	4.9
Postgraduate degree	0.6	2.3
Professional qualification	0.6	5.1
Other	1.7	1.9
Total	100.0	100.0

IPV have no qualifications, while the related share for non-IPV is 55 per cent. This is a stark difference and again suggests a strong correlation between human capital assets and financial asset accumulation as seen with the working poor and the NEET.

In the absence of employment income, the income sources for the retired are mainly comprised of pensions. Of interest is that the issue of physical capital accumulation is present among the non-IPV, where 12 per cent earn rental income as opposed to only 2 per cent for the IPV. In contrasting other differences between the two groups, non-IPV's pension income was to a greater degree from employment as a public servant (26 per cent versus 15 per cent for the IPV), or as an employee of a foreign company (19 per cent versus 6 per cent for the IPV). For the IPV, a greater proportion obtained income from a non-contributory pension (18 per cent versus 8 per cent for the non-IPV), while only a small proportion obtained income from dividends or interest payments (approximately 2 per cent), unlike non-IPV where over 9 per cent obtained income from these sources. (See table 3.18.) The information here on pensions suggests that a proportion of retiree poverty is due to unemployment in earlier years where nearly one-fifth were receiving non-contributory pensions.

Table 3.18. Sources of Income for Pensioners by IPV Status (%) (Multiple Response)

Source of Income	IPV	Non-IPV	Total
Rental income	1.7	11.9	9.1
Government pension for former public servant	15.1	25.7	22.8
Pension from former *local* employer	2.4	7.5	6.1
Pension from former foreign employer	6.5	19.2	15.6
Contributory pension from NIS	35.4	34.4	34.7
Non-contributory pension from NIS	18.5	8.1	11.0
Public assistance	2.3	0.4	1.0
Remittances	8.7	6.8	7.4
Dividends from local and foreign investments	2.3	9.7	7.6
Interest on bank deposits	2.4	9.2	7.3
Insurance annuities	0.0	2.9	2.1
Interest from stocks/shares	1.2	5.9	4.5
Other income	2.3	3.6	3.2

In an analysis of levels of household dependency, the average dependency in IPV households with retirees was 75 per cent (75 per cent of household members were not working in households with retired persons), while the related level of dependency in non-IPV households with retirees was 71 per cent. While this difference is only marginal, it does suggest that IPV retirees are particularly vulnerable to remaining in poverty as there are limited mechanisms through which to enhance their resilience, especially given that they had limited physical and financial assets on which to build (assets on which to earn returns or pensions), compounded by the fact that they have exited the labour market. Given the lack of income sources for retirees, there will be a greater reliance on accumulated savings to fund normal household consumption, leading to asset degradation.

SUMMARY

The preceding description of the situation of the working poor, the unemployed and retirees – groups that form the largest proportion of the indigent, poor and vulnerable – highlights a number of correlates of social exclusion. Recurring themes throughout the analysis are gender and age, as well as the explanatory variables of education, health, caring duties and household dependency levels.

Explaining the situation of the working poor draws on three main factors: (1) general macroeconomic issues relating to the structure of the economy and industry, suggesting that the actual asset-building mechanisms themselves are deficient; (2) low levels of human capital as these relate to education and skills and hence of the ability to secure "decent work" and (3) high levels of household dependency, where even if an individual may have the ability to secure "decent work" and wages, household obligations dilute earned income to the level where the individual and the household live in poverty.

Examining the situation of the unemployed draws on similar issues – lack of employment opportunities, low levels of education and skills and the "burden of care" – constraining entry into the labour market. There is also a lack of participation in the labour market due to discouragement and lack of knowledge of opportunities available. In addition to household dependency contributing to the burden of care, disillusionment with the labour market may also be due to a demonstration effect, where the negative experiences of the unemployed in the household cause others to exclude themselves from the labour market. Undoubtedly these issues are complex, with broad economic structures contributing to negative experiences and negative experiences reinforcing and perpetuating poverty and vulnerability within the household.

The situation of the retired serves as a warning for future generations. Poor and vulnerable retirees have limited means by which to access asset-building or asset-preserving mechanisms, especially as they have exited the labour market. In this situation, the only means available to build or preserve assets lies with earnings drawn from physical and financial assets such as rent from buildings, interest on savings and dividends from investments, as well as income from pensions, both state and private. However, poor and vulnerable retirees lack access to such mechanisms as they have not invested in physical and financial assets, and due to their employment history (unemployment, low-paying employment), they lack access to suitable pensions; nearly one-fifth of IPV retirees survive on a non-contributory state pension, suggesting they were not sufficiently employed to receive a contributory pension. In addition, retirees are for the most part living in households with few income earners and hence have limited access to intra-household support. Such a situation results in the inevitable degradation of physical and financial assets that currently exist through selling possessions and using savings for consumption and pseudo insurance, which inevitably has consequences for human, social and environmental degradation, exacerbating retirees' social exclusion.

The lack of ability to build assets is most prevalent among the youth, especially young females, and among the elderly. At a *general economy level*, the main explanatory variables lie on both the demand and supply sides, where there is a lack of jobs due to the state of economy and the structure of industry, as well as a lack of education, skills and experience. At a *household level*, high levels of dependency constrain income pooling and expenditure sharing, as well as participation in the labour market due to care duties. The longer-term effect of this lack of utilization of asset-building mechanisms is demonstrated by the situation of poor and vulnerable retirees who lack physical and financial assets with which to further build or preserve them.

Institutional responses to these issues are documented in chapter 5, following a more qualitative analysis drawing on the lived experiences of the socially excluded in chapter 4.

CHAPTER 4

VOICES OF THE POOR AND SOCIALLY EXCLUDED

THIS CHAPTER PRESENTS THE LIVED REALITIES, EXPERIENCES AND opinions of poor persons in Barbados as expressed in their own words. The analysis of their testimonies provides an in-depth understanding of how the dearth of assets – environmental and physical, human, social and financial, as described in previous chapters – leads to and reinforces poverty and social exclusion. Respondents also shared their views on the impact of liabilities, such as poor health and illness or stigma and discrimination, on their capacity to deploy assets to get by on a daily basis and cope during emergencies.

A total of six vulnerable groups was identified as representing persons most exposed to poverty and social exclusion. Included were women who head households (WHH), sex workers (SW), persons living with HIV (PLHIV), immigrants (IM), unattached youth (UY) and gay men (GM). Two representatives from each vulnerable group were randomly selected and interviewed, making a total of twelve respondents.[1]

RESPONDENT PROFILES

The focus of the research on social exclusion directed attention to social groups that were most vulnerable. After much discussion with experts in the field, particularly in social services, these vulnerable groups were selected, and two representatives were chosen from each group. Not only were these groups and individuals considered asset poor in terms of their lack of physical and financial resources (see table 4.1), their low levels of health, education and vocational training (see table 4.2) and their narrow social support network, they were also among the most socially excluded. Stigma and discrimination due to public perceptions of and responses to, for example,

Table 4.1. Asset Ownership

Name	WHH1	WHH2	SW1	SW2	PLHIV1	PLHIV2	IM1	IM2	UY1	UY2	GM1	GM2
	Pearl	Gloria	Monica	Pauline	Karen	Ann	Joan	Rose mary	Dwayne	Sonia	Ryan	Tony
Land	X	X	X	X	X	X	X	X	X	X	X	X
Home	√	X	X	X	X	X	X	X	X	X	X	X
Other prop.	X	X	X	X	X	X	X	X	X	X	X	X
Home condit.	p	p		g	g	p	g	p		g		p
Other assets:	X	X	X	X	X	X	X	X	X	X	X	X
Car/m												
Fridge	√	√	X	√	√	√	X	√	X	X	X	X
TV	√	X	X	√	√	X	√	√	X	√	√	√
Comp.	X	X	X	√	X	X	X	√	X	X	X	√
Mob.	X	√	√	√	X	X	√	X	X	√	√	X
Other:	√	√	X	X	√	X	X	√	X	X	X	X

Notes:

Land – Land on which home is situated

Home – Home in which respondent lives

Other prop. – Other land or houses that the respondent owns

Home condit. – Home condition: Good (g), Dilapidated/Poor (p)

Other assets: Car/m – Car/motorbike, Comp. – computer/laptop, Mob. – mobile phone. Codes: Yes (√), No (X)

Other: blenders, radios, microwave, sewing machine

Table 4.2. Respondent Profiles

	WHH1	WHH2	SW1	SW2	PLHIV1	PLHIV2	IM1	IM2	UY1	UY2	GM1	GM2
Name	Pearl	Gloria	Monica	Pauline	Karen	Ann	Joan	Rose	Dwayne	Sonia	Ryan	Tony
Age	41	45	29	34	60	47	55	46	17	22	30	23
Sex	F	F	F	F	M	F	F	F	M	F	M	M
Rel.	Chrs	Chrs	JW	Chrs	No	Pent	Pent	7dy	Chrs	Chrs	No	No
Church Att.	>w	irr.	nt.	nt.	nt.	<w	>w	>w	irr.	irr.	nt.	nt.
Educ.	Prim	Sec	Prim	Prim	Prim	Prim	Prim	Prim	Prim	Prim	Prim	Prim
Voc.	√	X	X	X	√	X	√	X	X	√	X	√
Empl.	X	X	√	√	X	X	X	X	X	X	X	√

Notes:

Age – Age in years

Sex – Male (M), Female (F)

Rel. – Religion – Christian (Chrs), Pentecostal (Pent), Seventh day Adventist (7dy), Jehovah's Witness (JW), None (No)

Church att. – Church Attendance: Weekly or more (>w), Less than weekly (<w), Irregularly (irr.), Not at all (nt.)

Educ. – Education (highest level): Primary (Prim), Secondary (Sec)

Voc. – Vocational Training: Yes (√), No (X).

Empl. – Employed (√), Unemployed (X)

their non-national status in the case of IM, their sexuality for GM or their sexually transmitted infection for PLHIV further reinforced social isolation and poverty. Although members of all these groups have experienced negative reactions from others, the extent and level vary. At one extreme were reports of abuse and eviction from family homes, while for others, discrimination took the form of public taunting and "scorning" or the refusal of employment. Whatever the case, consequences in terms of psychological health and the reinforcement of poverty were clear.

Although all have minimal assets and poverty and social exclusion in common, the following brief profiles summarizing their living conditions also reveal differences, particularly as regards the key underlying variables that have caused their poor quality of life. Following these profiles, the analysis presents more detail on the respondents' possession of and access to assets – environmental and physical, human, social and financial – and their capacity to deploy these to improve their living conditions and cope during emergencies.

Women Who Head Households (WHH)

So-called female-headed households correlate with matrifocal family struc-
ture in Afro-Caribbean cultural contexts. Such families have been described as "female-centred", where men play a "marginal" role, and women, as mothers and grandmothers, take on the triple burden of housework, childcare and income generation. Though this depiction has been criticized as central to a pathology of Caribbean family studies, the consequent high proportion of female-headed households is clearly evident (in Barbados, as mentioned, 47.5 per cent of all households are headed by women), as is the association with poverty. Homes headed by women are among the poorest of the poor.

The two women selected as household heads were Pearl (WHH1), aged forty-five and a mother of two children aged eleven and fourteen, one of whom, a boy, is autistic, and Gloria (WHH2), aged forty-one and the mother of nine children ranging in ages from seven to nineteen, five of whom live with her. Both have survived in conditions of poverty for many years as a result of unemployment compounded by natural disasters, in the form of fire and a heavy storm, respectively, that virtually destroyed their homes. Neither, however, is socially isolated; they have received support from family members, their

mothers in particular. However, for Pearl, the death of her mother in 2011 dealt a significant blow to her quality of life, while Gloria continues to be close to her mother, who helps with childcare and financial support. However, both claim that other interaction and assistance from family are limited and that they are regularly the target of stigma as a result of their status as poor single mothers.

Sex Workers (SW)

Sex work in Barbados continues to be criminalized, and sex workers are targets of harassment and discrimination by officials, including the police and health service providers, as well as the general public. Nevertheless, sex workers, mostly females, continue to ply their trade quite openly in certain locations such as Nelson Street in the centre of Bridgetown, close to where the two SW selected for this research live. They were both female, twenty-nine and thirty-one years of age, respectively. Both are mothers and claim that their inability to find formal employment, coupled with their responsibility to provide for their children, left them no choice but to engage in sex work. Their earnings have made them more financially self-sufficient than any of the other respondents, and only they have managed to generate savings, albeit in small amounts. Monica (SW1) is in a mutually supportive relationship with a female friend with whom she shares a home, while Pauline (SW2) receives supplementary support from her current boyfriend, though this is infrequent and irregular. Her two children, aged eight and three, live with their grandparents. She reports experiencing public stigma in the form of ridicule as a result of her chosen lifestyle, and once her life was threatened. Monica is an immigrant from Guyana, possibly exposing her to a dual stigma on account of sex work and nationality.

Persons Living with HIV (PLHIV)

Both the PLHIV are unemployed, and neither is seeking work. Karen (PLHIV1) resides with her family in a household consisting of fourteen persons. Ann (PLHIV2) is supported by her two adult children, and, although the recent death of her mother with the accompanying loss of her pension has negatively affected her financial well-being, she has no desire to become employed. This is a result of a previous experience of discrimination. Six years ago she lost her job suddenly and without explanation, she believes due to an acquaintance spreading a rumour concerning her HIV status and phoning her employer. She also avoids engagement in friendships and social organizations. The stigma posed by extended family members as a result of her HIV status causes her to stay clear of them as well.

Immigrants (IM)

As migrants, both respondents have made the journey from their homelands to Barbados in the hope of seeking employment and a better life and of escaping poverty. For neither, however, have these expectations been fulfilled, and both continue to struggle to make ends meet. Joan (IM1) is a fifty-five-year-old Vincentian mother of ten children, ranging in age from seven to twenty-six years, eight of whom live with her. Rosemary (IM2) is a forty-six-year-old Jamaican female who resides with her three children aged twenty-one, eighteen and thirteen. Both women are heads of their households.

Though Joan migrated to Barbados at the age of eight with her family and has been living there since, she has been unable to regularize her legal status, does not possess a Barbados National Identification Card and therefore continues to be excluded from formal employment. Her support has been minimal, mainly in kind from a social worker and the landlady from whom she rents her home – a concrete structure badly in need of repairs. Recently, however, she and her children have been accepted into the Bridge Programme.[2] Rosemary migrated to Barbados over twenty years ago. She indicates that she depends on her older children "for everything", including psychological support, but also receives financial assistance and food vouchers from the Welfare Department and lives in a house – a wooden structure, small but in good condition – owned by her former partner. She has been the target of stigma in the form of public comment because of her status as a "foreigner".

Unattached Youth (UY)

For the purposes of this study, an unattached youth (UY) was defined as a male or female aged sixteen to twenty-four who is neither in school nor engaged in the workforce. Two UY were selected, one male aged seventeen years and one female aged twenty-two years.

For both UY, their standard of living over the past ten years has remained stagnant, neither improved nor deteriorated. Dwayne (UY1) lives with his family and receives support from them, particularly his mother. He left school early and without certification and, though he has skills in photography, is yet to put them to use to generate employment and income. Sonia (UY2) lives with her boyfriend in two rooms attached to his parental home. She describes the relationship with her "in-laws" as close and supportive and also receives assistance from her own mother in the form of food and childcare. She has been continuously looking for work but has four children. Childcare responsibilities, therefore, limit her time for employment.

Gay Men (GM)

Homosexuality is strongly condemned in Barbados, particularly as it relates to men who have sex with men (MSM). Buggery continues to be criminalized by law and heavily stigmatized as socially and culturally deviant. Though Barbados was once considered to be the Caribbean country most tolerant of gay men, there are indications that homophobia is strengthening due largely to the impact of a recent wave of fundamentalist Christianity.

The two GM selected for this study, aged twenty-three and thirty, respectively, are both openly gay and have been subjected to severe stigma and discrimination in a variety of social situations. As a result of their sexuality, and for Ryan (GM1) also his HIV positive status, both have been alienated from their families and forced to move out of their homes. They live in rented communal apartments, which are dirty and dilapidated, with personal bedrooms and a shared shower, toilet and kitchen. Neither has taken any steps to improve his accommodation, arguing that this is the responsibility of their landlords.

Tony (GM2), though out of touch with his parents and immediate family, does maintain contact with an aunt and cousins who provide some material and social support. He is also employed sporadically at a store in town. Ryan, on the other hand, has no contact with family members and has experienced homelessness. His accommodation was sourced through the Welfare Department, which also provides financial support; he receives medication and counselling support through the LMRU (Lady Meade Reference Unit); and he occasionally does laundry work for others for which he receives payment. Often, however, he finds himself relying on the support of strangers.

ASSETS AND LIABILITIES

Environmental and Physical Assets

Most respondents reside in urban, low-income communities and have been living in the same poor environmental conditions for their lifetimes or for extended periods. Both WHH, for example, live in the neighbour-hoods in which they were raised. They expressed appreciation for the familiarity and comfort of these environments and their ties with commu-nity members. Pearl has family members living close by, and Gloria spoke of two friendly neighbours. In other cases, such as those of the SW, they had only recently moved to their area. They live in the centre of Bridgetown, in the immediate environs of Nelson Street, where they work. Though ideal for business, being heavily populated with bars and small dance halls and clubs, it is a low-income area, well known for poor living conditions and associated with prostitution and crime. However, both expressed satisfaction with their environment, despite its reputation. Monica identi-fied the centrality of her residence as its greatest asset because of the ease of access to shopping areas, the beach and other facilities without needing transportation.

Both of the PLWHIV live in urban areas. Karen lives in the heart of Bridgetown, whereas Ann lives on the fringes, in the urban corridor in Christ Church. Both locations are low income and known to have a high incidence of crime. Ann complained that the area was once peaceful, but this is no longer so as "different people come in and give it a very bad name and tend to get in trouble or bring trouble into the area". Similarly, Karen noted that in her neighbourhood, there were issues with lawlessness. Presently, there is also a problem with noise as large capacity shows and events are frequently held at a nearby venue. Other than this, she expressed general satisfaction with her neighbourhood. In contrast, Ann revealed her dissatisfaction by declaring that she likes nothing about the area, but because she is renting and it is all she can afford, she can do no better.

The IM have lived in different locations across the island, but they currently reside in the rural parish of St Lucy, though in different districts. Both high-lighted "quietness and peacefulness" as what they appreciated most. Joan has lived at her address for three years after relocating from her previous home where she said she lived in squalor. She is satisfied with her current living environment and has no significant problems living in the area.

The UY live in contrasting locations. Dwayne lives in a low-income housing area that, over the years, has acquired a reputation for high levels of crime and violence, while Sonia resides in a rural district in what is considered one of the least developed and least populated areas of Barbados. Nevertheless, they, too, expressed positive views concerning their communities, in particular their neighbours. According to Dwayne: "Well the reason I like living in the neighbourhood is that it is quiet, you don't really have any problems or anything. The most thing I like about it is that the people are nice and everybody is nice and gets along with everybody, it's a good neighbourhood." Sonia echoed these sentiments: "Well some of the people are nice. It is quiet, that's the one thing I would say."

As a result of rejection by their families on the basis of their sexuality, the GM respondents were forced to move out of their homes and communities and reside in an area marked by tightly packed homes and associated with high levels of poverty and crime. Their views of their area differed. Ryan, though living at his present address for only two weeks, described the area as "a cool place". He had no problems with safety and, like others, claimed that it was outsiders who come in and "do nonsense". In contrast, Tony, when asked what he likes about it, responded: "Nothing. I would like to move. I get trouble as a gay person down here. People like walking down here and people will say things." He indicated that the stigma affects him negatively. Though, according to him, environmental cleanliness is poor and garbage has piled up, access to transportation is good, and there are no significant negative issues related to safety and security. For him, then, problems with his immediate environment were social in the form of stigma and discrimination rather than physical.

There was great variety in the living conditions among the respondents. Sonia (UY2), for example, lives in a structure built onto the home of the parents of her boyfriend, who is also the father of the last of her four children. The home is a wall structure, recently built and in very good condition. However, it is small, consisting of only two rooms – a living area and one bedroom. While electricity and a telephone service are installed, she has access to water and facilities such as a kitchen, toilet and shower only in her in-laws' adjoining home. She, nevertheless, makes every effort to improve her surroundings: "I love to clean, I love to wash. I don't like no dirty clothes around me. I like to wash, clean, cook, clean."

Barbados is well known for its infrastructural and institutional development, and, in keeping with this, respondents reported no barriers to amenities and services such as transportation, health clinics, shops, schools and the police. Most also have no problems relating to environmental issues of garbage, flooding, rodents or pests, noise or crime. Even those living in more remote rural areas, such as the IM, stated that they have good access to basic utilities including electricity, water, telephone service and social services. Joan, however, noted transportation challenges: "The bus, that's the most problem, you get it every hour. The buses are the problem." Rosemary also highlighted a challenge with water quality. On occasion, it becomes discoloured, making cooking and laundry difficult.

Gloria (WHH2), however, lacks these utilities but accesses them at her mother's home, which is a short walking distance from her own. She stated that there was no access to water because, as the Barbados Water Authority informed her, her house is located in the water course for Zone 2, which prohibits the supply. Neither is there electricity in her home; the house is not wired.

As regards environmental health, there were numerous complaints of poor garbage collection and large numbers of mosquitoes by respondents in all locations. Gloria (WHH2) noted the presence of mosquitoes, though she saw this as an island-wide issue. Pearl (WHH1) faced a challenge with poor garbage collection as the collection service to the area had fallen off in recent months, and Sonia (UY2) reported that often two weeks pass without garbage collection. Pauline (SW2), who lives in an urban, commercial area, complained of indiscriminate garbage disposal by visitors as well as residents, which occasionally attracted rats, though there were no other complaints of pests or of flooding or other environmental problems.

Most respondents raised issues of neighbourhood insecurity and a high prevalence of crime and violence that, they stated, was perpetrated mainly by persons from outside the community. Dwayne (UY1), who lives in an area reputed to be among the most unsafe, pointed out that there are issues with crime – "[T]he police does be out here every once in a while" – and that in the previous month the murder of a community resident had occurred. Nevertheless, he claims to feel safe in his environment. Both WHH claimed that individuals from outside the community would come and "cause trouble" by bringing noise and disturbance with them. While there is no crime in her district, Rosemary (IM2) did note that crime levels are high in the neighbouring district, which has become synonymous with criminal activity in recent years. Challenges with high noise levels were also mentioned, though responses were occasionally contradictory. Both SW, for example, live in the same neighbourhood, and, while Monica indicated that what she liked the most about the area was the quiet, Pauline disclosed that she has an issue with the high noise levels. Sonia (UY2) initially said she had no feelings of insecurity within the rural location in which she lives. On reflection, though, she remarked that it is somewhat lonely and, because there are no street lights, she avoids going outside. Likewise, Ann (PLHIV2) reported feeling unsafe, on account of the high incidence of illegal activity in her area.

As might be expected, poverty was evident in the stark dispossession of any real physical assets. Of the twelve respondents interviewed, only one WHH and one IM own a house. However, both homes are in a serious state of disrepair and require major repairs. As a result, Rosemary (IM2) is unable to live in her home – it is currently under repair with government assistance. Ann (PLHIV2) also resides in a rented wooden structure that requires repairs – some of the boards are termite infested. Occasionally, as is common in Barbados and as occurs in the case of Karen (PLHIV1), the wooden physical structure of the home is owned by the individual or a family member, but the land on which it is situated is not. In her case, however, her family is endeavouring to acquire ownership, but, until that happens, their tenure is insecure.

There was also some evidence of overcrowding within homes and communities. Karen's (PLHIV1) home has seven bedrooms and accommodates fourteen individuals; Rosemary (IM2) lives in a two-bedroom house with her ex-partner, her three children, ranging in age from thirteen to twenty-one, and a grandchild; and Dwayne (UY1) lives in a low-income government housing scheme in a heavily populated area on the outskirts of the city. The homes in this area are built in blocks of adjoining units and are separated only by thin walls. The blocks are packed tightly together.

Homelessness was reported in only one case, and that was due directly to stigma and social exclusion rather than poverty per se. Until recently, homelessness and frequent changes of address characterized the life of Ryan (GM1).

He has lived at his current address for only two weeks and, despite the poor quality of his current residential arrangement, reports that it is a vast improvement to his previous state when he was squatting mainly in the nearby Queens Park. Before becoming homeless, Ryan "lived by some friends" at different places across the island. Prior to that, he lived in his family home, but, when they found out he was HIV positive in addition to his sexual orientation, they evicted him.

None of the interviewees owns land or a motor vehicle. The only tangible assets that were reported were small household and personal items such as televisions, fridges, stoves, beds and the occasional microwave, computer or mobile phone. These items are often shared within the household. This is notably the case of the GM in their communal living arrangements where basic appliances such as a fridge, a stove and a microwave are supplied. Neither possesses basic tangible household assets, though both own mobile phones, and Tony owns a tablet device. The UY have not accumulated any physical assets. They do not own homes, land, motor vehicles or any other tangible assets. Neither of them possesses devices such as a laptop or tablet, though they do possess cell phones. Of interest is the virtual total absence of assets that could be put to productive use, though Karen (PLHIV1) possesses a laptop and a sewing machine.

In summary, the evidence of poverty in terms of living conditions and low ownership of assets is clear. All respondents live in poor urban neighbourhoods, mostly urban though some rural. They nevertheless generally expressed satisfaction with their environments by pointing to peace and quiet and the convenience of location in terms of access to stores, health clinics, schools and other services. All locations were also serviced by electricity, telephone connections and potable water. However, as regards environmental health, there were several complaints of pests, mainly mosquitoes but also rats, and of the indiscriminate dumping of garbage along with the irregularity of collection. Although several expressed concern at the levels of noise and lawlessness, none reported personal experiences of burglary or personal injury attributable to their residential areas. Neither was overcrowding mentioned as an issue of concern. And only on occasions and by respondents in rural areas was the infrequency of the bus service mentioned.

Conversely, several respondents expressed great concern about the quality of their housing, and several homes were in visibly dilapidated condition in some cases virtually beyond repair as a result of destruction by storm or fire. Though many indicated that they try to keep their homes as clean and tidy as possible, there was little evidence of their involvement in structural repairs or renovations. The reason given was that either they could not afford this or, in the case of those renting their accommodation, that they felt this to be their landlords' responsibility. There was little evidence of home ownership, and none of the respondents owned land. In one case, this had resulted in tenure insecurity in that the landlord was insisting that the respondent's home be moved off the land. Neither were they in possession of motor vehicles, and the items owned were in the form of small household and personal goods. Of significance too, was the minimal ownership of material goods that could be put to productive use, only the occasional laptop or sewing machine.

Human Assets

The human assets of education and health contribute positively to self-worth and self-esteem, the quality of life and the capacity of individuals to actively participate in society. Education in particular is widely acknowledged as the major escape route from poverty and as an avenue for social mobility. And given that, in Barbados, education has been provided by government free of charge at the primary, secondary and vocational levels, and until recently at tertiary level, the question arises: Why have those living in poverty not taken advantage of educational opportunities to gain quality employment and improve their life chances?

At the time of the interviews, none of the respondents was enrolled in an educational or vocational institution. As table 4.1 shows, among all participants in each vulnerable group, there were notably low levels of educational achievement and vocational training. Despite the fact that all respondents attended school to the secondary level, in accordance with the legal stipulation of education to the age of sixteen, there was very little evidence of educational certification. Educational achievement did, however, vary among the respondents. At one extreme, Pearl (WHH1) was in possession of six secondary school CXCs in Maths, English, English Literature, Principles of Business, Science and Office Procedures; at the other, Ann (PLHIV2) had reached no higher than primary school. When asked why she has never attended secondary school, she replied: "I didn't get into any."

She also has no vocational training or skills that might prove useful in securing employment and generating income.

Similarly, there were low levels of vocational training, and only a few persons possessed a formal vocational qualification. The WHH both completed the early childhood course, which is offered by the local teacher training college. Additionally, Gloria has completed short training courses in customer care and information technology with the Welfare Department through their Welfare to Work Programme, which has since been discontinued. Karen (PLHIV1) also pursued a short course in customer relations.

Both of the IM cited family poverty, early pregnancy and the lack of parental encouragement as reasons for incomplete schooling. According to Joan: "Well, the type of family I come out of, mother didn't care. . . . And when you don't have any help or guidance from your parents . . ." A family crisis subsequently cut short her efforts to acquire vocational skills. She had registered for and commenced a training course in care for the elderly. The tragic death of her sister meant that she assumed sole responsibility for the care of her sister's children in addition to her own, which left her with limited time for study. She was unable to complete this course. Rosemary stated: "Well I didn't have a dad and my mom she tried, but being the biggest of seven I had to drop out to help her out. So I didn't have the opportunity to finish up school. . . . And then I had gotten pregnant with a child at 16 . . . so you know, everything changes."

Other respondents also mentioned teen pregnancy and early motherhood among the reasons for school attrition and the lack of certification. Monica (SW1) attributed her lack of certificates to the fact that she never wrote CXC exams because she was in hospital giving birth to her first child and has since dedicated all of her energies to her children. Pregnancy also prevented Ann (PLHIV2) from completing vocational classes in cake and pastry making and sewing. She has not since attempted to acquire any such skills.

A lack of capacity and confidence was also mentioned. Pauline (SW2), who has no educational certification or vocational training, spoke of her inability to understand the teaching in a classroom. When asked why, since leaving school, she has not attempted further education or training, she responded, "I think about it, but I don't be about the maths and English . . . the maths a little hard to do." She, however, continued by expressing a keen interest in enrolling to study CXC English and Maths at the Evening Adult Continuing

Education Programme (to be offered at a local secondary school). She has obtained the application form but not signed up. Similarly, Ann (PLHIV2) responded: "I don't really have a book head. I ain't able with no books and thing. It has to be something with my hands." Last year, she applied for a course in housekeeping but was unsuccessful and at present she is informally learning to make jewellery with members of a social group. Dwayne (UY1) also referred to his low aptitude for formal educational learning and the inability, as a result of family poverty, of his parents to finance supplementary lessons. As he put it: "Well the class that I was in, wasn't a CXC class. That's why I didn't get any. . . . It was like a class that children that really don't learn properly. It was a class that would help you with skills." Sonia (UY2) pointed to her delinquency at school: "Well I left school in fourth form. I never went to fifth. . . . I was fighting and being hard-ears." Her behaviour and an early pregnancy prevented her from completing fifth form and obtaining certification. After she left school, she worked at a number of different jobs at a bakery, clothing stores and bars. She then applied to Barbados Vocational Training Board to do cosmetology but became pregnant once more and did not start her studies. According to her: "I had got in skills training . . . to do cosmetology, but I was pregnant with my second, my first little boy, so that's why I couldn't do that kind of thing."

Similarly, Ryan (GM1) attributed his lack of educational certification to the fact that he is a "slow learner" and cannot read well. He went on to explain that a member of the local gay community provides CXC classes and skills training free of cost with trained teachers conducting the lessons. He indicated his preference for the skills training classes provided and previously started the needlework, cooking and make-up classes. However, he dropped out before completing any of the classes. When asked why, he replied: "I stop because I was going through some problems with myself. I had to put myself in order." It is his wish to restart these classes sometime in the near future.

Both GM cited their experiences with stigma and discrimination associated with their sexuality as responsible for their lack of education and training. According to Tony: "When I was at school, I was confused because I was having trouble at home with my family." He went on to say that his family's disapproval of his sexual orientation and the resulting conflict caused him to "stress" and neglect his educational studies. Since leaving school, he completed a short course at the Barbados Vocational Training Board in computer awareness. He recently started additional classes but got distracted and stopped. He is hopeful that an opportunity will present itself in the near future for him to complete social studies, English and mathematics at the CXC level.

Though none of the respondents was enrolled in an educational or vocational institution, there is evidence of desire to pursue education and training. But in many cases, as indicated, this has come to nothing, despite the opportunities available. Even the UY have failed to translate intention into action. According to Dwayne: "Well I was thinking about it. I'm trying to do English, social studies and maths. . . . I would do it at the polytechnic." He also received skills training at school in the technical stream where he successfully completed a basic-level photography course. He plans to complete an advanced digital media course but is also vague on the details of where and when. Sonia also expressed a desire to sign up for any adult continuing education programme in order to write for her English and mathematics certificates, but she has not given any thought to where she would complete these studies and also pointed out that she would first need a job to enable her to pay for the courses and maintain herself while studying.

In relation to health, respondents in all groups described their general health as "good", "fair" or "reasonable". The UY respondents, in particular, reported good general health with no conditions affecting their quality of life or negatively impacting their capacity to improve their situation. Even the two PLHIV described their health as "reasonable" and "fair". However, it became evident during the interviews that many respondents have serious health complications. The illnesses reported were mainly chronic non-communicable diseases, HIV, acute angina, cataract, diabetes, hypertension, poor circulation/edema and arterial septal defect. Also reported were Chikungunya and gastric conditions. Poor health was most apparent in the two IM, one of whom suffers from a heart condition diagnosed as unstable angina and requires a series of tests that she cannot afford. When asked to describe her health, Rosemary said: "I would say out of ten it is about eight. I will be like one two days good and then next day not good. And one minute it is like I was never sick so it is just something that is coming and going. Some days I get up and somebody got to stay home because I can't be left alone." Her response seems to reflect some denial of ill health. This was also evident in Joan's response. She was medically diagnosed with a swollen heart and arthritis, also suffers from epilepsy. Yet she stated: "My general health isn't too bad. I does try to do little things, but it isn't too bad."

Poor health was further complicated by inadequate diets as access to healthy and nutritious food was limited by lack of financial resources. For example, Karen (PLHIV1) reported that, while there is never a lack of food in her home, she consumes too much *"junk"* in her diet, and Pauline (SW2) reported having to lower her blood sugar recently as it was too high from consuming too many sweet things. Both attributed their inadequate diets to poor financial circumstances. One of the GM, Ryan, is living with the HIV virus and is required to take prescription medication and vitamins daily to maintain his health. However, for him too, financial constraint makes it difficult to acquire the vitamins and food essential for the medication to be effective and for the maintenance of his health. His daily nutrition is poor, and he often goes hungry. He stated: "I am on my medication and I ain't eat nothing for the day."

When asked to give a general description of their daily diet, the WHH revealed that they do not eat breakfast and may have "just a cup of tea". During the day, they will usually prepare a meal consisting mainly of rice and pasta, which they consume and which also serves as their children's evening meal when they return from school. At night, before bed they have more tea or some porridge. The priority for both is to feed their children. According to one: "But what does got me is my children 'cause I don't like to know I don't got nothing and then them come and say they hungry. Whatever I got, they will eat. Like if I cook just rice and butter or macaroni and butter." In like manner, the other stated: "I would make sure the kids get breakfast, that would be cereal or toast and egg. For lunch, they would say what they want . . . probably like rice or pasta." They too admitted that their own nutritiously poor one meal a day often leaves them hungry. The IM reported likewise.

No substance abuse was reported, however. The consumption of alcohol was mentioned by several, including both SW, but they claimed this was limited to occasional and generally social use. None of the respondents reported illegal drug use that would negatively impact their health, except for a GM who admitted to taking marijuana. He couples this with poor nutritional habits and alcohol use – he had consumed beer two days previously – as contributing to his overall poor health.

It would appear from the responses across all vulnerable groups that psychological health has been compromised by their poor quality of life, more so than physical. Most reported mental health problems, though not to the same degree. The SW revealed that, while they may sometimes worry about their future and their children's future, they were doing well psychologically and did not experience any feelings of loneliness or depression. The other respondents, however, indicated that they very often experience feelings of depression and sadness and worry about the future. Gloria (WHH2), for example, revealed: "When I look at how I living now and how it was before. No light, no water. Then the surroundings not secure. And then I got to be asking people for things and how the people does treat you. It is just got me feel real downhearted." She indicated that her current residential situation was the major factor negatively influencing her physical and mental health. Her counterpart Pearl (WHH1) stated: "Sometimes, when I sit and I think about my situation and the things I would like to do for my children, but you can't." Both, however, have persevered for the sake of their children. The two PLHIV expressed similar experiences. Karen stated: "Every now and then I would wonder what happen and worry, but I try not to worry too much and get depressed. Then it raises my pressure and that affects me so I try not to worry." Ann related that her biggest challenge comes from loneliness and lack of companionship because of her HIV status and stated: "Sometimes especially late at night I feel lonely because I don't have any man in my life."

The psychological well-being of the IM was especially low. They both explained that their life situations and living conditions cause them worry about their future and that of their children and to become sad and depressed. Rosemary disclosed that she was once hospitalized for high stress levels and said: "Sometimes you know, you think about where you was and then how you get to a certain stage, it bothers you. And this is the first time I was ever living at anybody house so . . . ." She also associated her state of mind with unemployment: "I plan to go back and work for sure 'cause that's the main thing for me. When I'm not working my head isn't good. I does get sick 'cause I cannot stay home." Dwayne (UY1), though in good physical health, was depressed about his lack of job prospects and ponders whether, in the future, he will be "in the same position doing nothing or still stuck the same way". He compares himself to other youth: "[O]ther people working and doing things. Like children my age working in the supermarket and doing supermarket jobs. . . . Otherwise, I'm just home doing nothing cause I have to wait until I get eighteen."

The GM also reported poor psychological health. Ryan attributes this to opposition and judgement from his family, coupled with his present living conditions. He said: "I does be sad sometimes when I think about the things I go through; life could be better but that's life. . . . When I think about my family and my life and where I am I does feel bad. I think my environment could be better." Tony, on the other hand, has found a way to cope: "You know, when I does feel lonely, when I don't have a radio and I like oldies and gospel real bad. . . . I just live and thank God I live to see another day. There are people out there badder than me . . . worse off than me."

Due to the free public health provided at polyclinics across the country, health care is readily available and easily accessed – often just a short walk away – for the majority of respondents. In addition, both PLHIV receive free specialist treatment at the LMRU. Among the respondents, only one of the IM, as a result of her legal status and lack of a National ID Card, is denied access to public health services. Neither can she afford private care. In her words: "I can't go anywhere 'cause I don't have an ID. If anything Carla [her social worker] would pay for me to go doctor. She is one in a million." She pointed out that, in the past, public health care was accessible in the absence of a national ID but that recent policy changes have barred her.

In general, access to private health care for which fees have to be paid was rare among the respondents. Sonia (UY2) had to take her daughter for special treatment for her eczema, and Pearl (WHH1) has taken her autistic son to a private clinic because he finds the loud and bustling environment of the polyclinic overbearing. The cost of treatment there, however, was low at Bds$15 per visit.

Most expressed satisfaction with the overall quality of public health services, though several complained of the extensive waiting time for treatment and one of the SW was inconvenienced when officials were unable to locate her records. Most respondents praised the attitudes and general response from doctors and nurses. According to Rosemary (IM2): "Honestly, I have been treated good. I must say so. People say 'Oh I go here and this body do this', but I never had that." The PLHIV in particular highlighted positive interaction with staff at the LMRU. There was, however, a difference of opinion between the WHH. Gloria felt that the doctors and nurses were really kind and cooperative, while Pearl, though she did not feel that their overall treatment was negative, objected to the way they addressed her: "They tend to talk at you rather than to you, talk down to you." Pauline (SW2) spoke of a challenge she faced on a recent visit where "they gave her a lot of problems" before processing her and allowing her to see the doctor. Even Tony (GM2), from perhaps the most stigmatized vulnerable group, reported no ill treatment from the doctors and nurses on his visits to the polyclinic. However, on these occasions, he has experienced stigma from members of the public. In his words: "They [doctors and nurses] treat me OK to me. Sometimes I have trouble like if people come in and see me and want to say things, I does have to curse them and stuff."

In summary, most of the respondents reached secondary school level, though few achieved formal educational certification, and there was little evidence of vocational training. Their reasons for dropping out of formal education are varied and include family poverty and lack of encouragement, as well as their own low confidence and incapacity for academic work coupled with delinquency at school. For several of the female respondents, teenage pregnancy and motherhood were the defining factors. All, however, were well aware of the importance of education and training in enhancing their employment opportunities and, in turn, their quality of life. They are also cognisant of opportunities provided in Barbados and express a desire to avail themselves of these, but none of the respondents was enrolled in further education or skills training, and often a combination of reasons deter access. Primary among these are costs and, for women in particular, their heavy and often sole responsibility for childcare. Similarly, some of the respondents stated that they had self-taught vocational skills but had not put these to use for income generation.

The respondents' testimonies also revealed that poor physical and mental health contributes to unemployment and social exclusion. Though several respondents revealed chronic health issues, they seemed to be in denial over the seriousness. They also admitted to hunger and poor diets, heavily starch-based and centred on porridge, rice and pasta. Some consumption of alcohol was mentioned, and one respondent admitted to the use of marijuana but not as abuse. In general, their responses indicated that they were planning to deal with these issues through diet and exercise, but there was little indication of action. They have, however, taken full advantage of public health services provided in nearby clinics and experienced minimal, if any, poor treatment or discrimination from health service providers. More problematic than physical health, however, were psychological issues described as sadness, loneliness, worry, stress and depression, for which they have not sought treatment other than through prayer. The deliberate desire not to do so in some cases may possibly correlate with the strong stigma against mental illness in Barbados.

Social Assets

To ascertain information on social interaction and support, respondents were asked about their daily routines and with whom they spent time. It was clear that unemployment leaves most of them with free time during the day but also that much of it was spent alone and at home. Karen (PLHIV1) stated: "Sometimes I lay in bed half day and then I get up and do whatever I feel like doing", while Monica (SW1) informed that she spends her days "quiet" and "does be online whole day", though she would *chill out* sometimes at a nearby bar. Significantly, too, although Dwayne (UY2) lives with four family members, he says that he spends much of his time home alone. Both GM are involved in a communal living arrangement. But while they share the small living space that they occupy with other people – one with ten, the other with seven – they each claim to "live on my own". Some respondents went on to say that their largely solitary existence depresses them. Gloria (WHH2), for example, sleeps for much of the day. Alternatively, she goes to sit at her mother's home because, when alone at home: "I does got a lot of foolish thoughts. So I does just got to be around people to keep my mind employed. I just does feel real depressed."

Other than relaxing, sleeping, watching television or "doing nothing", respondents are occupied with chores around the house such as cooking, cleaning and washing. Joan (IM1) stated: "Sometimes I will clean, I will cook. Sometimes I go on the step there and sit down. Put on my radio 'cause the TV break down. A little reading. That is all." With further probing, she added, "I don't go at any place. If I have to go out differently I would go out. But otherwise I would be here." Rosemary (IM2) said: "Ok, sit down and read, maybe find something to sew. If there is any little thing that somebody wants fixed, I will fix them and probably watch TV or play a game on the phone or something."

Some are also busy with childcare, in particular the two WHH, both of whom are solely responsible for this and for the day-to-day management of their homes. One has seven children ranging from ages seven to nineteen years, five of whom live with her (the other two children live with her grandmother and her mother, respectively). The other has two children, a boy aged fourteen who is autistic and a girl aged eleven.

Although unemployment and limited resources limit their ability to offer financial support to others, several mentioned providing assistance in kind. Pearl (WHH1) explained: "There are some people that I would run errands for like going town and picking up their medication and thing. If they want any cleaning done I do it." She provides such support to two older persons in the community and one friend who suffers from poor health. The two PLHIV, both female, were much engaged in providing care and support to family members and friends in other ways. Other than assisting with chores around her home, Karen, until recently, provided daily assistance to her elderly mother and uncle, both of whom were in poor health; they died within the past six months. In like manner, Ann visits the home of her blind father to assist him at least two or three days a week and she also occasionally "helps out" her friend with groceries. Rosemary (IM2) provides support to an old lady living next door who is wheelchair bound, and she or her son sometimes takes her out for a walk in the wheelchair, and her grand-daughter braids her hair. Others claim to have found it impossible to provide support for others. As Joan (IM1) put it: "Who me? No, poor me can't even do for myself. No, I don't help anybody."

Outings consisted mainly of trips into town to purchase groceries or pay bills, but only when necessary, and excursions for leisure or social activities were rare. Dwayne (UY1) mentioned going out cycling, and several others mentioned church attendance. As Rosemary (IM2) put it: "Sometimes I may want to go to the supermarket, but I don't go nowhere else like going out. Only place is church. I don't go anywhere else"; Gloria (WHH2) added: "I don't got nowhere else to go"; and Pauline (SW2) responded with: "I don't really go nowhere or nothing so. I does just stand home." Only the GM and the male UY, Dwayne, specifically mentioned leaving home to spend time with friends, and Sonia (UY2) said that she would sometimes call her girl-friend, and they would talk on the phone.

It appeared from many of the responses that spending time alone was a deliberate choice. A common sentiment expressed by the respondents was that they like to spend time alone, that they "keep to themselves" and "don't like company" because "people are not genuine". According to Pauline (SW2): "Anytime there have events or anything I don't go to none of them because a lot of foolishness does happen, and I ain't about that there. I does just stand home." She continued by saying: "I don't like so much company you understand, I does stand by myself."

For most respondents, families play a critical role in their general well-being – in providing all-round social and psychological, as well as financial and material support. Dwayne (UY1) lives with three adult family members – his father, stepmother and uncle. Though his father provides his main source of support in the form of money, food and clothes, it is his mother who lives elsewhere and whom he visits regularly. He also mentioned grandparents, aunts, uncles and cousins with whom he gets along, but they do not live nearby. Rosemary (IM2) receives support from her adult son and daughter who provide her with "everything" including money, food and "words of comfort". In the case of Gloria (WHH2), there is a close relationship with her mother who provides assistance with the daily care of children and, if she can afford it, financial assistance with lunch money or school tours. Sonia (UY2) has the most extensive and close family ties. She lives with her boyfriend and her two youngest children, both boys, aged two years and eight months, respectively. Four of her boyfriend's family members live in the home to which her dwelling is annexed. She comes from a large family. Her mother and nine siblings do not live nearby, but she gets along well with them. According to her: "We does get along good. You know every family would have their differences." She confidently confirmed that, if she needed help, she could call on her family, especially her older brother and her mother. She claimed that they would be there for her. In addition, she sometimes sends her two children to her family to spend time, and, on the occasions when she is "restless", she would spend a weekend with her family.

There was, however, considerable variation in the quality of family relationships and support. Co-residence does not appear to guarantee close ties. Dwayne (UY1), for example, though he lives with family members, said that he spends a lot of time at home alone. Karen (PLHIV1) resides in a large household consisting of thirteen other extended family members, ranging from an uncle aged seventy-six to a niece aged one, and has other family members, some of whom live in close proximity, but claims that relationships are not strong – she described them as "reasonable". Pauline (SW2) has two children, an eight-year-old son and three-year-old daughter who live with and are cared for by their respective grandparents but who visit her from time to time. At the time of the interview, her daughter was spending the weekend with her. When asked about any additional family members, she said that her mother passed away but that she has an aunt, brother and sister living in the parish of St Joseph. She described her relationships with them as "not bad", but said she does not see them regularly and has not "called for a little while", though she intends to. Both WHH revealed that, while they have other family close by, interaction with them is very limited. Pearl responded that although she has "loads" of family living nearby, "I only exist once a year" (Christmas). And Gloria, despite having uncles, cousins and aunts living in the same district, said she really associates only with her mother. As she put it: "I talk to everybody, but it's not much just a hi or hello. But majority of the time I does be here by my mother."

In the case of representatives of the vulnerable groups PLHIV and GM, they have found themselves disassociated from their families as a result of illness and sexuality, respectively. Both were forced to leave their family homes. Ryan, who is gay and HIV positive, explained that none of his family "agree" and that, when they found out he was ill, "scorned" and rejected him: "Them look at my point, that I sick, but everybody got things, there is God above to judge me, nobody else cannot judge me." He no longer lives at home, nor is he in contact with his family. Tony found his family's opposition to his sexuality intolerable and confided: "I was getting trouble at home as a gay person, so I decide to live on my own 'cause I ain't really about that. My mom and people in that environment weren't understanding." He feels that his standard of living has much deteriorated since leaving his family home but claimed that "things are worse, but better. I am still having trouble, but I'm living on my own." He concluded: "I do so much for them. But now them don't want nothing to do with me. Them don't want to see me. And that is not the way." He, however, maintains a relationship with an aunt and a few cousins who still talk to him and whom he visits once a week. Similarly, the interviewees in the vulnerable groups SW, WHH and IM all explained that they did not have strong ties with members of their families of origin.

Those respondents who are mothers, however, identify closest ties with their children. Joan (IM1), for example, lives with eight of her ten children, four sons aged twenty-six, twenty-five, seventeen and seven and four daughters aged fifteen, thirteen, thirteen and five. She also has two other children and a brother and sister who live at the other end of the island in St Philip. She described her relationship with her siblings as follows: "Me and my brother don't hit off but me and my sister, we get along." She expressed similar views in relation to her two non-resident children: "We get along."

Close friendships were rare, and the majority of respondents expressed caution over forming friendships. Even Pearl (WHH1), who revealed that she has about five friends whom she does not see as regularly as she would like but chats with on the phone and who visit her home occasionally, voiced the opinion that, "people don't know what friendship is today". The IM also expressed reluctance to engage in friendships. Joan stated that she did not have any friends to meet up with: "It's just me alone." And Rosemary said that she did not "keep any friends". She meets up "only with church people" and pointed out that none of them visit her home, so she sees them only at church. Even the UY expressed hesitation on the question of friendships. Sonia stated: "Well for me I don't like no lot of friends. That's the honest truth. I must have [only] two girlfriends." While her two friends do visit her home, this rarely occurs because they both work and have other responsibilities of their own. She explained: "His [her son's] god-mother, by she does work on a bank [bank holiday], I don't see her as often but my other girlfriend she does come sometime during the week if she is off." And though Dwayne mentioned friends, he qualified this by saying that "there are not really many people". He meets up with them "once in a while" if he has not seen them for some time and they "aren't doing anything", or he visits them at their homes. None of his friends ever visit him at home. When asked why, he said: "Because they studying and have exams or probably just busy during the week so they don't have time to come."

Monica (SW1) was the only respondent who mentioned close friendship and that with only one person. She lives with a woman, aged twenty-eight, who like her, is an unemployed non-national living in Barbados and engaged in the sex trade. She described her as "a friend", but when asked if she had any additional friends, family or a partner whom she associates with, she responded negatively – she does not meet up with anyone and no one visits her home.

The respondents also lack social engagement within their communities. When their knowledge of their neighbours was ascertained by asking whether they knew of anyone who had left the area, Joan (IM1), for example, replied "No". Rosemary (IM2) said, "Boy I don't know. I wouldn't even know" and went on to point out that she knew only of a young girl who lived with her grandmother right in front of her home who had moved away. They stated that their lack of social involvement stems from a lack of faith in the kindness of people and that, therefore, they prefer to keep to themselves. One might expect that, as immigrants, their knowledge of neighbours would be limited, but similar views expressed by other respondents suggested that they neither knew nor cared to know about their neighbours' lives. The PLHIV reported that they had no significant relationship with neighbours beyond polite conversation. The UY, although they are home during the day, do not often venture outside their homes to engage with neighbours and build social ties in the community. Sonia pointed out that she greets people respectfully but does not talk to anyone. Neither had any knowledge of neighbours moving away in the past five years.

Among respondents, there is also an absence of involvement in organizations, such as sports or leisure groups, and in political associations. Though several attend church, they are not involved in any religious groups. However, the two PLHIV are both members of Providing Relative Opportunities Through Togetherness (PROTT), a support organization formed of HIV positive individuals who attend the LMRU. This organization meets at least once or twice a week for group sessions.

Participation in social, community or political organizations was also minimal, and most respondents expressed no interest in any involvement. This was the case even among the UY. Dwayne has never thought about joining any groups and claims not to know what options are available to him. He was also unable to identify the political representative for his constituency and had no familiarity with the functioning of local constituency councils. Sonia, on the other hand, attributed her lack of social involvement to a scarcity of such organizations, stating that she was not involved because she did not think there were any in her neighbourhood. However, when asked if she was made aware, would she become a member, she answered negatively stating: "I can't say I would. To tell the truth I really don't know if I would be in it."

Respondents all expressed disdain with the political system and stressed the fact that political representatives "don't do nothing for you". Neither of the WHH, for example, is politically active; on the contrary, they expressed contempt for their political representative. Gloria spoke of experiencing an emergency situation during which she had asked for assistance from her political representative but received nothing despite continuous requests, personal visits to her home and several promises. When questioned about her political participation, she became visibly flustered and replied: "I don't deal with that. I just don't deal with that; I just don't deal with these people. . . . You see when my house get burn down, I learn so much. I see so much things that like turn me off of them kind of things." In general, there was also a lack of awareness of the functioning of local constituency councils and no direct engagement with them.

Experiences of stigma and discrimination were reported by members of all the vulnerable groups. They related incidents during which they faced hostility at many levels of social life – within their families and communities and in attempts to access social services. Fear of stigma and discrimination in some instances resulted in the unwillingness to join social and community organizations and therefore perpetuated social exclusion.

For the WHH, stigma and discrimination were realities of daily life. When asked if she felt she had experienced stigma as a result of her status as a poor single mother, Gloria replied: "When do I not?" She said that people see her and judge her, automatically assuming that her circumstances are by choice and that she could do better for herself instead of waiting for handouts. She described an experience at the welfare office where she was subjected to negative comments. She further revealed that she and her family were often on the receiving end of harsh comments and scornful laughter within her community as a result of their visible poverty, because they live in a "piece of house". Pearl has also confronted stigma but less as a result of her single parent status than of her son's autism, which manifests itself in physical and mental inability. In the past, people have made remarks such as: "Where he get way from, he should be in a zoo." Both women deal with the discrimination on their own and turn to no one for help. Gloria stated that she takes her problems to God. Even Dwayne (UY1) reported that children at his secondary school used to "pick on" him all the time and that, since leaving, his peace of mind has improved. Rosemary (IM2) disclosed that sometimes persons raise the question of her status as a non-national. This has never become a serious issue, and she herself sometimes jokes about it, telling others: "[W]unna can't tell me anything, I is a foreigner."

As might be expected, other vulnerable groups were more subject to stigma and discrimination on the grounds of lifestyles, illness and sexuality. The two SW, however, reported mixed experiences. While Monica did not feel she has ever experienced discriminatory treatment on the basis of her engagement in sex work, Pauline revealed that, whereas she has never faced stigma while trying to access a public service, there are those who sometimes come to the area and ridicule her for her life choice. One individual has even threatened her life. HIV and AIDS also attract strong stigma. Ann (PLHIV2) reported that a neighbour who saw her outside the LMRU "bring it out" that she was infected to other community members. As mentioned, she speculated that the reason she was suddenly laid off from her job six years ago with no explanation was the result of someone calling in to inform her employer of her HIV status. She also attributed her lack of involvement in social organizations to her fear of stigma from others once they become aware that she is HIV positive. Most significantly for her quality of life is her minimal interaction with her family, despite living in close proximity. She disclosed that this was the result of their negative reaction to her illness and that she therefore keeps as far away from them as possible. She has not taken these issues to any official authority but has found solace in talking to her social worker and her doctor.

The stigma and discrimination attached to homosexuality in Barbados are strong, and both GM acknowledged incidents in their daily lives. Ryan has been the recipient of negative remarks and comments from members of the public. He said: "They are some people that drop their little remarks . . . like you gay this . . . if you pass people will drop remarks to you." He further highlighted that previously when people "interfered with him", he would "curse and get on bad and block and do bad and fight" and report incidents to the police, but he is "getting older" and has changed. Now he turns to the police for assistance. When asked if the expectation of discrimination had prevented him from engaging with the community activities and organizations, he replied: "mussie" (must be), and when asked if he felt his sexuality and living conditions created a barrier to his receiving assistance from others, he replied that he was unsure. Tony also faces stigma and discrimination and revealed that he experiences feelings of hurt and sadness at the way he is treated. He reported that, when he goes out to eat, people would give him different cutlery and also approach him with attitude. In terms of access to government services, his response revealed stigmatization not on the part of social service providers but from fellow clientele: "Yes, people will give you the eye and look at you stink and make it harder for you to access the service." Most devastating for both GM is the hostility they have dealt with at the hands of their families, resulting in eviction from their homes.

As a result of their experiences with stigma, the GM tend to restrict their social lives to interactions with other gay men. They both currently live on Suttle Street, though in separate apartments, an area in the centre of Bridgetown that, according to them, is a favoured residential location for homosexuals – a small "gay community". They are also members of associations for gay men in Barbados and frequent the same social spots, sharing mutual gay friends and acquaintances.

In summary, there is significant evidence of social isolation across the vulnerable groups. Many respondents spend much time alone at home, with outings only when necessary and for specific functional purposes other than social or leisure activities. Only some of the female respondents mentioned close friendships and then only with one other woman. They were also wary of social engagement with neighbours, community members and social organizations, and there was minimal evidence of this. None mentioned political involvement; quite the reverse, as they expressed highly negative views on their political representatives and the political system in general.

Consequently, for many respondents, social interaction is confined mainly to family members. But beyond immediate family, in particular their mothers and their own children, contact was limited, and most relationships were described as somewhat distant. Alienation from family was reported by the PLHIV and also the GM, both of whom had been evicted from their homes.

Reasons given for this limited social engagement included their lack of finances and preoccupation with childcare, but also that they preferred to be alone and did not like company. Yet some admitted to feelings of loneliness, and many expressed a desire to improve their social lives. Their caution correlates with experiences of social stigma reported by all respondents. Their testimonies revealed that stigma was triggered by multiple factors including poverty, as evidenced by the condition of their homes, single parenting as a mother, and non-national status, but also and more intensely by lifestyle as a sex worker, illness in the form of HIV and homosexuality. The discrimination experienced by the GM has prompted them to confine their social lives mainly to interactions with other gay men.

Financial Assets

At the time of the interviews, none of the respondents, other than the sex workers, was engaged in steady, income-generating employment. All, however, conveyed that they were willing to work in any job and had made attempts to identify opportunities, however small. But they have met with no success and attributed this to their own lack of qualifications and certification. They also pointed out that employers are not hiring because finances are constrained, and they cannot afford to pay workers.

For those with responsibility to provide for their children's daily needs such as the WHH, the search to secure steady employment is especially urgent. Pearl, for example, has tried to find work in several places and has been interviewed by potential employers but without success. She explained that it appears that employers "don't have the funds to pay you", and this accounts for the lack of job opportunities. The UY have also been actively pursuing employment opportunities with no success. Dwayne has applied to several businesses and has received no response. He also visited the Ministry of Sports, Youth and Culture and completed an application for the job attachment opportunities it provides. He suggested that he has been unsuccessful due to his lack of certificates. Sonia looks in the newspaper every day for employment opportunities and contacts businesses but has failed to receive any response to her inquiries and applications. She has called spas, clothing stores, hotels and restaurants, prepared a curriculum vitae and filled out application forms to no avail. In her opinion, however, no barriers prevent her from securing employment. The two GM report similar experiences. Ryan has tried to secure employment at various businesses and has submitted job application forms, but there has been no response. As he put it: "I tried, I tried. And nothing. People say there ain't no work things slow, things this. I try cleaning firms, I try everything. I try all sorts of things and no help." Tony is sporadically employed, working only about once a week in a store in town. He has also been on the hunt for a job for some time and noted: "It's really hard. I don't know what is going on. They just call you for an interview and then don't call back after."

Others are less free for employment, especially on a full-time basis. Pearl (WHH1) is a single mother solely responsible for the care of her autistic son. Any employment she engages in would need to have flexible work hours for her to provide care on those days he is not at school. Her barrier to employment has been finding an accommodating employer or someone to care for her son. Karen (PLHIV1) has made no attempt to find a job. When asked why, she explained that she is fully occupied with housework and previously cared for her deceased mother and uncle. Therefore, she said: "[W]ork was never really on my list." For Sonia (UY2), the problem is compounded by her location in a distant rural parish. She reported that she sometimes makes money doing hair, but she does not do it often because people are unwilling to come to her in St Andrew, and she cannot meet them elsewhere because she has to care for her children.

The SW conduct their business in Nelson Street in Bridgetown, an area synonymous with the sex trade. Monica is a Guyanese immigrant. She lived in Barbados previously for a number of years, went home in 2012 for four years and has only recently returned and resumed earning a living as a sex worker. She stated that her general quality of life has declined somewhat and had been better previously. In contrast, Pauline feels that her life has only recently begun to improve, that is, since she began to engage in sex work. She worked previously at a local fast-food chain, and, when she lost that job, made the decision to become a sex worker. She explained that the birth of her second child, in 2012, initially imposed a significant financial burden on her as she was unemployed and unable to purchase the necessary basic items. In her words: "It was real bad before because, when she born, her father didn't give her nothing. . . . It's better now; It ain't too bad. I can't complain. I does get up on mornings and thank God for opening my eyes letting me see another day. I got food on the table and things there to eat."

Describing her experience as a sex worker, she expressed the opinion: "It isn't bad. You does get a little money on night." Nevertheless, she continues her efforts to find alternative employment, though these have been to no avail – she has applied for work and filled out forms at businesses. For reasons she cannot identify, no response has been forthcoming. In the case of Monica, she meets her needs with the money she makes as a sex worker independently of assistance from any individual or institution. She has not sought out alternative employment to enable her to leave the sex trade because she believes that her status as an immigrant with no work permit prevents her from securing employment.

Similarly, for Joan (IM1) her legal status acts as a barrier to steady employment. She has been employed off and on in the past and is willing to work, but her lack of National ID and a National Insurance Scheme card negatively impacts her job search. As she explained: "Well when they ask if I have any ID or NIS sometimes I does don't want to open my mouth. Just tell them I will come back. But it does affect me a lot. I used to work at a place in Warrens in One Accord Plaza, but I had to stop because I don't have an ID."

For others, for example Rosemary (IM2), illness has caused unemployment. At times, she is too sick to work for any duration, and, when employers become aware of her illness, they are unwilling to hire her. When asked if she has nonetheless sought employment, she replied:

> Yes. But getting jobs you have to tell them the truth and on two occasions I went for a job and after filling out the form and stating what my problem was, you know, I didn't even get a call from those people. Cause what they are saying is that when anything happen on the job it costs them. So you know it is better for me to wait until the doctor gives me that OK.

However, she also stated that she cannot afford the costs of the required medical examination. Ann (PLHIV2) expressed no desire to secure employment on account of her HIV status, which she predicted will expose her to discrimination and stigma.

There was considerable variation between respondents in terms of family support. At one extreme is Dwayne (UY1), a young man fully dependent on his parents and an aunt who, it seems, willingly provide daily support. His situation contrasts markedly with that of Tony (GM2) who has been stigmatized and rejected by his family and receives handouts from strangers. He disclosed that he would just ask people he meets for money, and, if they do not have their own business to deal with, they would help him. As he put it: "I would sometimes just talk to people and tell them about my situation and if they could help me they would help me if they could. If they can't help me, they can't help me." Of all the respondents, he is the most lacking in support.

Women, as mothers, spoke of child support received from the fathers of their children. Pearl (WHH1) said that she receives support from her daughter's father in the form of cash and basic essentials, along with her aunt and a few friends to the extent they can manage. This, she said, is minimal but enough to get by on. For Sonia (UY2), the main avenue of social support is her current partner and father of her last two children. He provides financially to meet their daily needs and to maintain the home. She also relies on her mother who, while not providing financial assistance, does help to care for the children and provide food if needed. However, like many other women in Barbados, she reports inconsistent child support contributions. She said that "the only thing" that causes her worry is the welfare of one of her four children because his father is not there for him financially, nor is he physically present in his life. It is for this reason, that is, to adequately provide for this son, that she is seeking employment. Her other children are sufficiently supported by their fathers.

Others, however, had a more limited social support system. The only sources of support for Joan (IM1), for example, are her social worker and landlord who provide food and clothes on occasion. In the case of the SW, their own earning capacity makes them relatively independent of others. Monica, for example, claimed to be self-sufficient with her earnings from sex work, supporting herself with no assistance from any individual or institution. Neither does she provide support to anyone other than her roommate whom she assists with chores such as washing or cooking. Pauline also supports herself but receives supplemental assistance from her current boyfriend infrequently and only when necessary. If things are really bad, she asks her aunt for money. Their desire for independence was echoed by Gloria (WHH2). She mentioned that a few people at church would give her food stuff if she asked but pointed out: "But I don't like to have to be asking people for help, I don't want to be doing that."

Given their unemployment status and inadequate sources of support otherwise, there was a high level of dependency on social institutions, specifically the Welfare Department. The negative reputation of the Welfare Department and the perceived lack of success in applying for assistance, however, act as deterrents. Rosemary (IM2) expressed surprise at her successful application: "I must be born lucky. . . . I went there and I got through and from there on I've never had a problem for sure. And everybody want to know how I get through so easy. But you know in God all things are well." But others have been put off. According to Sonia (UY2): "I never went. My mother always told me to go but I never went. I does just be scared they tell me I have too many children and to look for work." She subsequently changed her mind and, at the time of the interview, was receiving welfare assistance. Though Ryan (GM1) is currently the recipient of welfare assistance, he admitted being been denied on several occasions previously. It was his opinion that this and the way he was treated were due to his sexuality and HIV status. As he stated: "I went in there three times and the lady in there she scorn me three times. . . . So I went straight to the Nation [newspaper] and I put she in the papers." Tony (GM2) also reported stigma from the Welfare Department. He was denied assistance and met with "hostility and attitude" from the welfare officer. He believes that his poor reception was a direct result of his sexuality.

Limited and inconsistent sources of income have forced a reduction in spending and the concentration on items that are absolutely essential. Other than Tony (GM2), who stated that he is "very low maintenance" and that his spending has always been very minimal and he has therefore felt no need to cut back, all other respondents reported reductions in expenditure. They have cut back on entertainment, clothing and other non-essential items, and their priority is the purchase of food. Pauline (SW2), for example, noted that she "buys things that I need and things that I don't need, I leave. I buy the most important things like meat and stuff". She has also reduced expenditure on going out. She would like to go to a new club she has heard about or even to a movie but has been unable to do so. Rosemary (IM2) reported likewise: "I cut down on the clothes buying and all the little things I use to be fussy about. I don't do them anymore. All the hair buying and all of that. I cut back on those things." And Gloria (WHH2) noted that she has been forced to reduce her spending to such an extent that she is unable to buy toiletries such as sanitary napkins for herself and her daughters. Some, such as Joan (IM1), have even had to reduce spending on basic food essentials. According to her: "If I used to go supermarket and I would buy a big butter, now I buy a small one. Or I used to buy the big bag of English potato. . . . I have to buy the small bag."

The regular payment of utility bills is problematic for many. Ann (PLHIV2) stated that her bills go unpaid sometimes, and Gloria (WHH2) also reported overdue bills. Pearl (WHH1) has implemented a system for bill payment whereby she is always two months in arrears and pays only the minimum required to keep connected. Others are somewhat more fortunate. Karen (PLHIV1), for instance, lives in a household with a large number of persons who contribute to the payment of bills; Sonia's (UY2) boyfriend covers the household bills; and Joan's (IM1) utility bills are covered by the Bridge Programme.

Respondents acknowledged the importance of having savings and insurance in case of emergencies and for hard times, but the reality is that few have managed to do so. Only the two SW have set aside small amounts of money at home, but they have no savings in formal financial institutions, and neither has any insurance coverage. Monica has accumulated enough savings to last her for two weeks, and Pauline for "a week or so". Joan (IM1) has endeavoured to do the same: "So I does try to keep a little change in case anything with the children." Tony (GM2) claims that his "low maintenance" lifestyle has allowed him to accumulate a small sum, which he keeps in the bank. Dwayne (UY1) also has some savings in a bank account, which was opened and is financed by his mother, not by his own agency, and she has barred his access. But none of the other respondents has any savings set aside as a buffer in time of need and crisis. Ryan (GM1) lamented that the small amount of money he works for leaves nothing for savings. As he joked: "The only amount of money I got right now is ten cents inside." Neither have any of the respondents managed to acquire any formal insurance coverage.

In summary, none of the respondents, other than the SW, are employed or earn regular income. Illness, childcare responsibilities, non-national status and stigma were given as reasons for unemployment, but most expressed their willingness to work and have made the effort to find jobs. They also had ideas for self-employment, and some have been so engaged, but their lack of skills and finances limits capacity for entrepreneurial activity and the establishment of viable small businesses.

Unemployment and the absence of financial self-sufficiency meant dependence on others, mainly family members and occasionally friends. Respondents expressed their reluctance to ask for assistance and revealed levels of family support varying from total assistance to none, but for most, it was inadequate even for basic survival. They had no alternative but to turn to the Welfare Department, also reluctantly due to expectations or actual experiences of rejection and stigma.

Respondents had therefore to make fundamental decisions concerning their management of what little money they had, including spending reductions even on food and other basic essentials. They also avoid borrowing, even though they gave evidence of arrears on utility bills and hire purchases. All were aware of the importance of savings and insurance to provide a buffer in case of emergency, but their hand-to-mouth existence has made this impossible. Their helplessness and dependency were evident in cases of serious illness and the natural disasters that had wrought heavy damage on their homes.

ASSETS, POVERTY AND SOCIAL EXCLUSION

By any account, the respondents from each of the vulnerable groups would be described as asset poor. In terms of material possessions, none own land, home ownership is low, and, though there was some evidence of possession of household and personal items, these tended to be items for daily convenience rather than assets that might be invested for productive use and income generation. Homes, whether owned or rented, were often in poor condition, and, although several appreciated the peace and quiet of their neighbourhood environs, there were complaints about mosquitoes, garbage and noise. Human capital, in terms of education, was lacking as most respondents had left secondary school with no certificates. Those who had benefitted from vocational training were not putting these skills to use for income generation. Health-wise, although the physical and psychological profile of some respondents revealed serious problems, many seemed to be in denial especially as regards mental health issues, which are heavily stigmatized in Barbados. Respondents reported being "lonely", "downhearted" and "depressed", yet only the two PLHIV received professional support (at the LMRU). Others turned to their God or communicated with family or friends.

It was important for the research to move behind these realities and investigate the causes of asset deprivation and poverty. Critical in this respect was the impact, early in the respondents' lives, of the disruption of education, especially in view of the intersection between educational success and a good job. They cited their own poor intellectual incapacity and lack of confidence, as well as the absence of family encouragement and finances, as reasons for educational attrition. But for several of the female respondents, it was teenage pregnancy and motherhood that curtailed their education – this despite the advances made in Barbados by the official family planning and birth control programme. Teen pregnancy is well recognized as the trigger for an intergenerational cycle of early childbearing and poverty. The importance of education as a human capital asset was discussed in detail in chapter 2. In addition to developing basic intellectual capacity, education has also been seen as an important vehicle to rise out of poverty. Indeed, a number of poverty reduction strategies have cited education as being "one of the most powerful instruments societies have for reducing deprivation and vulnerability . . . and affords the disadvantaged a voice in society and the political system" (Aoki et al. 2001, 2). The participants generally, however, found themselves bereft of educational qualifications, forcing them to fall back on their own limited resources, effectively locked out of existing avenues for upward social mobility.

There was clear evidence from all respondents that their social exclusion is compounded by stigma and discrimination. Episodes of social rejection in all areas of life – by employers, by families and by the general public – were revealed in their narratives, particularly those of the SW, PLHIV and GM. For some, these reactions were intensified as a dual stigma as a result of their being gay and HIV positive, immigrant and living with HIV or engaging in sex work. In only one case was there any indication that recourse in response to discrimination had been sought in the form of a complaint to the press and an appeal to the police. For the rest, discrimination seemed to promote social withdrawal and the intensification of psychological problems, possibly also through self-stigma. While social exclusion is spatially related to place of residence and associated in the public's mind with undesirable communities, it is also socially constructed according to age and gender and correlated with a wide range of human qualities that attract stigma. That children, the elderly and women experience varying levels and forms of social exclusion that exacerbate their vulnerability to poverty is well recognized for the Caribbean and beyond. Significantly less well researched and reported, however, is the impact of disability, disease and sexuality on experiences of poverty, as described in these narratives. The combination of personal and communal resource deficiencies, stigmatization, isolation and marginalization relative to the rest of society produces feelings of non-belonging and alienation. The ruptures caused by these deficits in access to social assets have implications for the social cohesion and well-being of Caribbean communities and countries.

These narratives have revealed the complexity of factors and deficiencies in assets that have combined to generate social exclusion among participants. As discussed in chapter 2, social exclusion refers to the process by which individuals are unable to take part in critical societal activities. The preceding testimonies demonstrated that integral to this process were low levels of education and vocational skills. Participants also attributed their circumstances to ill health, including mental health evident in the loss of self-motivation and resilience, to the absence of financial and material resources that they might deploy to better their quality of life, and to stigma and discrimination. Although such material and financial resources are critical to the survival of those interviewed, their stories suggest that, as Townsend (1979) argued, poverty cannot be limited to issues of subsistence but must take into consideration the ability of individuals to participate in normal societal life.

The cyclical intersection between poverty and social exclusion is evident in the lifestyles of the participants – poverty caused social exclusion and was, in turn, the result of social exclusion.

All in all, the respondents have experienced little if any change in their lives over the past ten years or so. Though they have coped with emergencies, such as storms, serious illness and the deaths of close, supportive family members, any change for the better has tended to be short-lived, with brief periods of improvement followed by setbacks. Few have experienced improvements, and these have come at a cost. Joan (IM2) has had to move from her home into rental accommodation; Sonia (UY2) has become fully dependent on others – her boyfriend and "in-laws" – and on welfare; and Pauline (SW2) felt she had no choice but to become a sex worker. Even for them, though, and for the other respondents, there has been no escape from poverty, merely a day-by-day struggle for survival. The two PLHIV summed up the situation. Ann stated: "[S]ometimes it's good and sometimes not", and Karen feels as if she is "at the same crossroad financially . . . back in the rut".

CHAPTER 5

RESILIENCE

THE CARIBBEAN HUMAN DEVELOPMENT REPORT (2016) ADOPTED A multidimensional approach to addressing vulnerability and resilience in which the concept of resilience was expanded beyond state capacity to include human resilience at the household and community levels. If people are vulnerable as a result of a lack of agency due to a restriction of access to resources critical to human development, then resilience must involve the empowerment necessary to improve human agency. This involves both the state and individuals themselves. Indeed, as discussed in chapter 2, Narayan, Pritchett and Kapoor (2009) found that resilience is most heavily influenced by two factors: (1) the creation of a local social, political and economic environment that provides the necessary opportunities to adapt and innovate and (2) the characteristics of the poverty-stricken individual or household members and the nature of initiatives they undertake to improve their situation. With this in mind, therefore, this chapter explores avenues for the provision of the critical assets needed to alleviate conditions of deprivation and to facilitate individual and collective resilience. The local social, political and economic environment is discussed by way of the institutional, economic and social support infrastructure in Barbados. These data were collected as part of the macro social and economic assessment (MSEA) portion of the CALC. The MSEA used an "analytical historic" approach and relied on historical data collected mainly from secondary sources (Barbados Statistical Service, Central Bank of Barbados, Ministries of Government and regional and international agencies such as the Caribbean Development Bank [CDB], World Bank, Inter-American Development Bank [IDB] and the International Monetary Fund [IMF]). Individual-level characteristics were obtained as part of the qualitative interviews described in chapter 4.

THE INSTITUTIONAL, ECONOMIC AND SOCIAL SUPPORT INFRASTRUCTURE IN BARBADOS

As noted in chapter 1, the so-called Barbados Model is one traditionally based on socio-economic development through consistent social investments and the development of its human resources, a strategy deemed necessary due to the limited prevalence of natural resources available for economic exploitation. The following analysis of the institutional environment in the country highlights the main factors at this level that facilitate the link between individuals and asset-building mechanisms, the "intervening factors" of the conceptual model.

Governance and Development Strategy

The Constitution of Barbados proclaims equal treatment of all regardless of race, place of origin, political opinions, colour, creed or sex. The fundamental rights relate to

a. life, liberty and security of the person;
b. protection for the privacy of his home and other property and from deprivation of property without compensation;
c. the protection of the law; and
d. freedom of conscience, of expression and of assembly and association.

Barbados operates a Westminster-style parliamentary democracy, comprised of a lower house of thirty elected constituency representatives and an upper house of twenty-one unelected senators, with twelve nominated by the government, two by the opposition and the remaining seven nominated to represent the second (private sector) and third (social sector) sectors. For a population of 280,000, there is an elected representative for approximately every 9,000 persons. The administration of government is directed by the Cabinet, comprised of the prime minister and ministers of the various government ministries. There are currently twenty members of Cabinet, comprised of thirteen of the sixteen elected members of the lower house, and seven nominated members of the upper house.

In addition to the Office of the Prime Minister and the Office of the Attorney General as the legal counsel of the government, the fifteen ministries of government seek to serve a number of individual groups, services and sectors. (See table 5.2.) While youth issues are highlighted at the ministerial level in the Ministry of Culture, Youth and Sports, gender and elderly issues are subsumed within the Ministry of Social Care (Bureau of Gender Affairs and the National Assistance Board). Social safety net support is overseen both by the National Insurance Scheme (NIS), overseen by the Ministry of Labour, and by the Welfare Department under the Ministry of Social Care.

Of the fifteen specific government ministries, nine seek to address material deprivation as a core element of social exclusion, while eight seek to provide for social rights such as education, health, housing, social security and safety. Only two ministries directly seek to address insufficient social participation (the Ministry of Culture, Youth and Sports; the Ministry of Social Care). In addition to these ministries addressing social participation, only one other seeks to address cultural and normative integration, the Ministry of Home Affairs, which oversees the police force and the prisons.

Current and past governance frameworks in Barbados have been guided by a number of development strategies over time. In the early 1990s, the strategic direction and vision for the development of the country were provided by the Development Plan 1993–2000, followed by the National Strategic Plan 2006–2025, and the Medium-term Development Strategy 2010–2014. Barbados has adopted a largely indicative approach to planning, with the private sector propelling economic growth through the key sectors of agriculture, manufacturing and services (especially tourism and international business). The government has facilitated the development process by creating an "enabling environment" through a series of incentives, infrastructural development and rules and regulations. The government, through its planning process, has focused on improving productivity and promoting the export of goods and services via several trading agreements. A deliberate effort has been made to reposition and diversify the economy, namely, from an agricultural to a services orientation. Over the years, the government has been able to build its human and social capital and introduce several measures to reduce the incidence of poverty in the country. The vision in the National Strategic Plan 2006–2025 is to be fully developed and people centred by the end of the planning period.

In the area of the environmental policy, the government has been promoting the need for sustainable development in a small, vulnerable developing economy. In recent times, there has been a push to achieve a "green economy" that would see an integration of environmental and economic policy measures (Government of Barbados 2013).

With respect to human development, by international standards, Barbados has been able to achieve a "high human development" status according to the UNDP's Human Development Index (HDI), which combines indicators of health and education status and livelihood; in 2015 the country ranked fifty-fourth on the HDI. By 2007, the country had made good progress with the achievement of four of the eight Millennium Development Goals (MDGs) and was expected to achieve the other unmet goals by 2015. The four MDGs that were achieved include Goal 2 (Universal Primary-level Education), Goal 3 (Gender Equality and Empowerment of Women), Goal 4 (Reduction in Child Mortality) and Goal 5 (Improvement in Maternal Health).

Directly addressing social exclusion, policy measures have involved a range of legislative,[1] institutional and programme initiatives. In addition to the supply of education and health services and long-standing social institutions such as the Welfare Department, the National Assistance Board and the National Housing Corporation, more recent institutions and programmes include Rural and Urban Development Commissions, a Social Investment Fund, a specific poverty alleviation programme, the Youth Entrepreneurship Scheme (YES), and general skills training programmes under various ministries and departments. Through a social partnership between the government, employers' representatives and workers' representatives, a series of protocols have been developed to guide wage/salary increases and other related conditions of work. During the period since 1995, five protocols agreed among the three parties have been enforced.

While the ideology of socio-economic development has been based on human resource development as a pathway to growth and development and as a means to escape poverty in the contemporary period, since 2008, one of the most symbolic actions representing a change in focus was the name change of the Ministry of Social Transformation to the Ministry of Social Care, suggesting a philosophical reversion to the remedial focus of the welfare state over the developmental objective of positive social change. More detrimental, however, was the change in conception of education as investment to education as cost, where in 2013, in an effort to address fiscal deficits, the government instituted significant cuts in funding for tertiary education.

Structural Change

The strategic direction of government has led to notable changes in the economy since independence. As previously noted, there has been a steady decline in the contribution of the agricultural and industrial sectors to GDP over the years. While the share of the agricultural sector declined from 3.4 per cent in 1990 to 1.4 per cent in 2014, the share for industry fell from 18.7 per cent in 1990 to 9.5 per cent in 2014. Over this period, the contribution of services increased from 67.2 per cent to 73.3 per cent, and the government's share in GDP rose from 10.7 per cent to 15.8 per cent.[2]

There have been changes in the international market for sugar and other agricultural products with the push to dismantle a preferential system as part of the trade liberalization process. There has also been a fall-off in the regional and extra-regional markets for manufacturing products. While the tourism sector is a major contributor to GDP and foreign exchange earnings, there is still a high level of market concentration in the sector with the United States, the United Kingdom, Canada and selected CARICOM countries being the main sources of tourist arrivals. As part of the diversification effort, the government has actively promoted the international business and financial sector. However, the sector has been subject to threats from international organizations such as the OECD with regard to the tax concessions provided by the government. The domestic financial services sector, especially the credit union sub-sector, has grown significantly over the years. Credit unions have become a major source of funds for personal loans for their members. In recent years, there has been a discussion on promoting the cultural sector as part of the productive diversification process.

The Macroeconomic Environment

The focal areas of macroeconomic policy management over the period were maintaining balance in the balance of payments (BOP) and containing the deficit in the fiscal accounts – the so-called twin deficits. Barbados has generally experienced a chronic balance of visible trade deficit over the years as the exports of goods have usually been significantly less than the imports of goods, though services exports, namely tourism, have allowed the current account of the BOP to realize a surplus in some years. In 2013, the BOP was in deficit by 3.5 per cent of GDP;[3] this fell to 1.0 per cent of GDP in 2014 and was expected to be only marginally in surplus in 2016 at 0.1 per cent of GDP. With respect to the fiscal deficit, this was estimated as 7.0 per cent of GDP in 2015 and was expected to remain in deficit over the near term, while government debt was estimated at 141.6 per cent of GDP in the same year and was 143.6 per cent in 2017.

In seeking to address these macroeconomic issues, initially due to the Global Crisis, the government undertook a number of contractionary policies to increase revenue through the removal of a number of tax concessions, mainly from the middle class, as well as reducing expenditures in the form of the removal of tax credits to those on the lowest incomes and, as the situation became more severe, the retrenchment of public sector workers. These actions have to some degree contracted economic activity; the IMF notes that increasing recurrent expenditures and debt interest have crowded out capital spending and led to "excessive central government deficits" (International Monetary Fund 2016, 20).

Given this poor macroeconomic performance, Barbados is ranked 132nd out of 144 countries with respect to the macroeconomic environment in the 2014–2015 Global Competitiveness Report.[4] Overall, the country ranks well but is underperforming with respect to goods market efficiency, business sophistication and innovation. In addition, the World Bank Doing Business survey for Barbados[5] for 2017 ranks the country as 117th out of 190 economies with respect to the ease of doing business in the country, with a distance to frontier score (DTF) of 57 per cent. DTF is a measure of how well the country is performing in relation to an ideal, ranging from zero to the frontier (the ideal) of 100 per cent. However, the country outperforms its overall score in relation to starting a business (85 per cent), getting electricity (69 per cent), paying taxes (73 per cent), trading across borders (62 per cent) and resolving insolvency (70 per cent). Despite these relatively good scores, the country performs worse in relation to dealing with construction permits (55 per cent), registering property (52 per cent), getting credit (35 per cent), protecting minority investors (35 per cent) and enforcing contracts (38 per cent).

The Natural Environment

Over the years, Barbados has witnessed a reduction in the amount of land used for agricultural purpose (especially sugar cane) and an increase in the allocation of land for residential purposes. This has been associated with the growth of the construction sector as persons have had ready access to mortgage finance and land. There has also been a shift of residents from the urban areas to the rural/suburban areas such as St Thomas and St Phillip.

There is an increasing prevalence of squatting in the country, especially on government lands (Office of the Auditor General 2014), and the housing conditions of the poor are largely substandard. There has been an increase in vehicular traffic on the main roads in urban areas, and this has resulted in pollution and congestion challenges. The ground water is protected through a zoning system that is closely monitored. A solid waste management system is also in place, but there is growth in the volume of waste occasioned by increased domestic consumption and tourism activity. The recent attempts to move the country to a Green Economy are intended to reduce the environmental burden on such a small, vulnerable island state.

As a small island in the Caribbean, Barbados is subject to such environmental and natural hazards as storms, hurricanes and associated flooding, as well as sea level rise and marine environment damage due to climate change. However, the country has not experienced a hurricane since 1955, with the most prevalent disasters relating to flooding as a consequence of heavy rainfall. To address potential environmental hazards, the government has established the institutional framework to address any disasters arising from such natural/ environmental events, including a catastrophe fund, the Department of Emergency Management and a National Disaster Management Plan. To accommodate those in vulnerable housing, there are also twenty-seven public emergency shelters available across the island. To address the detrimental effects of climate change, the government is undertaking a number of activities related to monitoring, infrastructure development and institutional strengthening. An inventory of the activities being undertaken are detailed in Cashman (2014).

The Social Sector

Developmental Interventions

Education constitutes an important element of human development with the government contributing approximately 20 per cent of its expenditure to all levels of education. As indicated earlier, Barbados enjoys universal secondary-level education. Enrolment data indicate that there was a slight upward trend in primary-level education. Secondary-level educational enrolment was relatively constant, while there was a significant rise in enrolment at the tertiary level. Such increased enrolment is reflected in the improved educational attainment of the labour force.

The public health sector accounts for 16 per cent of government expenditure. There has been a steady growth in the number of health professionals (for example, doctors, nurses, laboratory technicians) with the development of several specialty areas. Barbados has witnessed a decline in its birth rate and the degree of child mortality and a slight fall in the death rate. Most of the public facilities cater for curative care, although there has been a push to strengthen the preventative aspects of medicine in recent times. The health facilities have improved over the years with the strengthening of the polyclinic system. There is very high (almost 100 per cent) access to drinking water and improved sanitation. The public drug service provides a selection of free medication.

There has also been a significant growth in the housing sector, which has in turn boosted the construction sector. The government has been very active in the housing sector by constructing low- and middle-income housing through the National Housing Corporation and providing assistance to individuals through the Urban and Rural Development Commissions (UDC and RDC).

Government and NGO Poverty and Social Welfare Remedial Programmes

A range of poverty and related social welfare programmes were introduced by the government during the 1995–2010 period. Several new institutional arrangements were established to complement the traditional institutions. For example, the UDC and the RDC, along with special poverty alleviation programmes, were established to complement the traditional Welfare Department, National Assistance Board and the Child Care Board. The focus of several of the requests for social assistance has been on the areas of house repair and the payment of water arrears. The government introduced a reverse tax credit for low-income earners, thus assisting the working poor; however, this has been reduced in recent times. Assistance is also provided to the disabled and to the elderly through home help, meals on wheels, transportation and financial assistance. The unemployed are able to claim unemployment insurance once they qualify, and children at the primary level receive free school meals and, in some cases, free uniforms. School children also have access to free textbooks and public bus transportation. A number of non-governmental organizations (NGOs) have also organized support programmes to help alleviate the plight of the poor and needy.

In order to assess the level and nature of social services provided by government and non-governmental organizations, an institutional assessment was undertaken in 2010.[6] Following the completion of the data collection process, the information obtained was organized in a manner that would enable a comprehensive investigation into the main issues to emerge. The assessment concentrated mainly on the types of living conditions addressed, the type of support provided, as well as the vulnerable groups targeted by each institution. From this information, a grid was constructed that matched the indicators of living conditions with the types of methodologies used by each institution to improve them. An aggregated grid was then constructed to identify overlaps and gaps in total support provision.

The analysis revealed that a variety of methodologies were employed in order to achieve the individual mandates of improving living conditions. Table 5.1 outlines the number of institutions that adopt the various approaches to improving specific living conditions.

There are areas of overlap in institutional focus as well as areas of neglect or gaps in support provision. These are illustrated in the table. The majority of the programmes address level of income, access to education and social discrimination. The majority of the methodologies used focus on advocacy, finance/resource provision to individuals, care and counselling and technical assistance to individuals. More importantly, however, the analysis also revealed a number of gaps or areas of relative neglect in terms of service provision. Relatively few programmes addressed access to productive

Table 5.1. Composite Matrix of Institutional Methodologies

Indicators of Living Condition	Methodologies Used										
	Vocational training	Other skills training	Advocacy	Technical assistance to individuals	Technical assistance to organizations	Infrastructure provision	Finance/resource provision (individuals)	Finance/resource provision (organizations)	Research	Care and counselling	Total
Level of income	9	7	3	5	1	3	5	3	1	4	41
Access to productive resources	0	0	2	6	3	1	3	3	0	0	18
Access to education	5	5	3	2	3	2	2	2	3	2	29
Morbidity/ mortality from illness			0		0	1	4	0	0	0	5
Homelessness			5		0	2	1	0	0	3	11
Housing facilities			2	1	1	6	3	2	0	1	16
Physical and social environments		1	3	1	2	3	1	1	2	3	17
Social discrimination and exclusion		0	5	2	4	1	2	3	2	6	25
Total	14	13	23	17	14	19	23	14	8	19	162

resources, physical and social environments, housing facilities, homelessness and, in particular, morbidity/mortality from illness.

Analysis and Summary

At an institutional level, through a social exclusion lens and from the perspective of the most socially excluded, the government provides support for the unemployed, the retired and the working poor through a number of direct provisions. Direct monetary support is provided through the National Insurance Scheme and, for those not qualifying, through the Welfare Department. Low-income housing and support for the elderly are also provided. Gender is a cross-cutting issue, and the country is signatory to the Convention on the Elimination of All Forms of Discrimination Against Women (CEDAW).

The government is active across all forms of asset-building mechanisms, from the facilitation of self-employment through microfinance, to community development interventions and facilities, and to free transportation for schoolchildren. In the absence of personal asset stocks and to provide greater access to asset-building mechanisms, the government provides access to health care and education, infrastructural construction and maintenance, welfare transfers and employment enhancement services. (See table 5.2.) However, as noted previously, the focus is predominantly on addressing the material deprivation and social rights elements of social exclusion, with less attention paid to increasing social participation and greater cultural/normative appreciation and integration.

INDIVIDUAL AND HOUSEHOLD INITIATIVES

Human Assets

Although respondents were clearly aware of the potential contribution of further education and skills training to the improvement of their life chances and socio-economic situation, enrolment was low. The primary reasons were the cost and, for women, the responsibilities of childcare. Although both WHH expressed a desire to pursue further education and training, one of them, Gloria, referred to the lack of family finances: "Cause it was just my mother. I was raised by a single parent and she wasn't working on a regular basis so there

Table 5.2. Governance, Groups Served and Relevant Components of Social Exclusion

Offices and Ministries of Government	Groups	Intervening Factors	Mechanisms	Element of Social Exclusion Addressing
Finance and economic affairs		Macroeconomic conditions		Material deprivation
Civil service	Public servants		Labour markets	Material deprivation
Labour, social security and human resource development			Labour markets Welfare systems Educational systems	Material deprivation Social rights
Home affairs		Institutions, legislation and regulations		Social rights Cultural/normative integration
Health	Population		Health systems	Social rights
Education, science, technology and innovation	Population		Educational systems	Social rights
Housing and lands and rural development	Poor		Infrastructure	Social rights
Tourism and international transport	Population	Macroeconomic conditions	Labour markets Infrastructure	Material deprivation Material deprivation

Transport and works Culture, youth and sports	Population Youth	Macroeconomic conditions Social and cultural conditions	Infrastructure Social networks	Social rights Social participation Cultural/normative integration
Environment and drainage	Population	Environmental conditions	Natural ecosystems	Social rights
Social care, constituency empowerment and community development	Poor women Elderly	Social and cultural conditions	Welfare systems Social networks Educational systems	Social rights Material deprivation Social participation Cultural/normative integration
Foreign affairs and foreign trade	Population	Politics Macroeconomic conditions	Trade in goods and services	Material deprivation
Industry, international business, commerce and small business development	Population	Macroeconomic conditions	Trade in goods and services Labour markets	Material deprivation
Agriculture, food, fisheries and water resource management	Population	Macroeconomic conditions Environmental conditions	Trade in goods and services Labour markets Natural ecosystems	Material deprivation

was no money available for tuition." Pearl, who would like to become a Care Giver for Children with Special Needs as her son is autistic, mentioned her own lack of financial capacity for further education: "That is something that I think about, but the money. These classes does be real expensive. It is something that I does be thinking about. But then, financially I cannot afford it."

Joan, who took responsibility for her sister's children, stated her willingness to resume training in a vocational skill but was somewhat vague in intention. She had no specific plans or area of training in mind other than a liking for the care of the elderly and children and for cleaning, and she strongly believed that she is unable to obtain any educational certification at this stage in her life (she is fifty-five years old with ten children). Most significant, however, is her immigrant status. which places her in a precarious situation. As she stated: "I don't have an ID Card, if not I could have gone places. That's what keeping me back, but them trying. Everything in process but we only waiting on papers."

Although formal vocational training was generally lacking, there was evidence of self-taught skills in areas such as cosmetology, sewing, hair dressing and cookery from their life experiences that could be used for employment generation. As adults, the SW took no steps to further their education and acquire even basic educational certification. Rosemary (IM2), who is from Jamaica, has learned to use a sewing machine and has cookery skills gained while working in the kitchens of Jamaican guest houses and restaurants and "can do a little hair if necessary". And Monica (SW1) highlighted that she has self-taught skills in cosmetology and her interest in pursuing a certified course in that area in the near future, though she has not started to explore her options.

While several of the respondents expressed interest in acquiring vocational skills, this was not the case with the PLHIV, one of whom stated: "Maybe, but right now unless it's something I can do without a cost or someone sponsor it. . . . I'm not even sure, I would like to do like designing and fashion." It would appear that continued education and training to improve her life chances is not something to which she has given much consideration.

With regard to health, despite complaints of various physical and mental issues, when asked about plans to improve their physical and mental health, responses echoed those in relation to education in that respondents had plans but that, for the most part, these had not been acted on. Additionally, these plans related more to the improvement of physical than mental health. The

UY, for example, indicated that they would like to increase their physical activity through exercise; the SW highlighted plans to exercise more and to work on eating habits, respectively. Pearl (WHH1) noted that she would like to resume evening walks, as did one of the SW, but she has not started as yet because she does not feel like moving. However, Sonia (UY2) pointed out that she is currently on a diet in an effort to lose the weight gained during her last pregnancy, though she did not indicate how successful this was. Tony (GM2) specifically indicated his reluctance to deal with mental health issues. He said he plans to make more regular trips to the doctor, but, despite noting that his psychological well-being was poor, he does not intend to visit a counsellor or talk to anyone about his problems, claiming that he does not really like to talk.

Social Assets

Chapter 2 highlighted the importance of social networks, particularly at the level of the community, in fostering resilience as this can lead to future employment and skills development. Among the respondents, against the background of a lack of community engagement and organizational involvement, several indicated a desire to improve their social lives and go out more by engaging in leisure and entertainment activities. They expressed interest in going to the cinema, socializing at bars and attending cultural events, picnics and other entertainment activities. Both SW, for example, said they'd like to see changes to their social life, and Monica pointed out that "when you get out, sometimes you meet good people", but neither has made any attempt to implement this. For some, the lack of funds for entertainment and their involvement in childcare or the absence of babysitting services were deterrents. Ann (PLHIV2), who lives with her son who spends much time visiting his girlfriend elsewhere, reported experiencing great feelings of loneliness and wished for her social life to improve with opportunities to attend picnics and socials, visit bars and other places to "chill out" but lamented that she is unable to afford this. Similarly, Ryan (UY1) expressed discontent with the quality of his social life and said that he would like to "go out a little bit more and do fun things" but that "the problem is with money . . . and if my father say he doesn't have any money, well I can't go". Sonia (UY2) said she would have welcomed more social activity, "one time not now . . . because really and truly, my main concern is my children. That [social activity] will always be there, but I don't really worry about that right now." Likewise, Pearl (WHH1) stated that she would like to go out more to places like the cinema, as she had not done so in over fourteen years. She, however, noted that she would need a reliable childcare facility or babysitter for her son first.

Conversely, an equal number of persons stated that they were content with their social lives and did not wish to see any changes. Gloria (WHH2) stated that she is not an "outtey person" and has no real interest in going out. Instead, she associated an improvement in her social life with an increase in her children's happiness, comfort and improved living conditions. On the other hand, Ryan (GM1) described himself as very active – always out and about outside the home. He discussed how the following day he and some friends were going out together and that the previous weekend, he had been to a bar with friends. In relation to the quality of his social life, he declared: "I'm fine, I don't got no problems." Karen (PLHIV1) expressed complete satis-faction with her current social life, though this is centred on her family (she lives with thirteen family members), weekly interaction with members of a support group for persons living with HIV and her one female friend. When asked if she would like to see any changes, she answered: "No, no, no, I am comfortable as it is right now."

Among the most socially isolated is Tony (GM2). When asked if he desired an improvement to his social life, his initial response was, "so-so". Later, he disclosed that he would like to see "a lot" of change to his social life, but this would depend on changing his personality: "I don't talk a lot. But I want to be more open and talk to people, I want to go more places and meet people I can talk to." He went on to say that he has recently taken some positive action and has struck up friendships with a few people. Yet he attributed his failure to engage socially to his preference for isolation and his belief that involvement would make no positive contribution to his well-being: "I don't like the crowds and I think some of these groups don't really even do anythin."

Financial Assets

Given the absence of employment opportunities and their lack of success in securing jobs, several respondents have turned to self-employment and have used their skills, mostly self-taught, in cosmetology, cooking and handicraft.

The two PLHIV are so engaged. Karen utilizes her self-taught skills in sewing to make and alter clothing, while Ann also earns a little money on the rare occasions that the bags and jewellery that the members of PROTT create are sold. But she believes that her lack of skills prohibits her from making money: "I don't have the skills to make money. I would just like a little small business selling snacks and things." Their efforts have been on a small-scale, irregular basis by offering the service to persons they know, and none of the respondents have, as yet, conceptualized a viable and consistent entrepreneurial strategy. Their lack of access to finances also curtails their capability to develop ideas into viable businesses. Pauline (SW2) has plans to start a small catering business with her boyfriend, but they have got no further than adding a wooden structure to their dwelling for this purpose.

Several respondents do "odd jobs" for community members or friends for which they receive some compensation, though minimal. Pearl (WHH1), for example, does chores for two older persons in the community. However, they indicated that such casual labour often exposes them to exploitation. Ryan (GM1) occasionally does small household chores such as cleaning and laundry – "[S]ome people does call me to press and wash for them" – but he pointed out that persons attempt to take advantage of him and either not pay him or "short" his pay.

For others, entrepreneurial ideas are evident, but translation into action has not occurred. For the two WHH, Pearl has skills in creating canvas mats and would like to start a small business making and selling them, but she cannot afford to purchase the necessary raw materials. Gloria wishes to start making and selling food, but she believes that the public will not be willing to purchase meals from her once they see the dilapidated condition of her home. According to her: "My surroundings would have to be different. . . . [P]eople would look and say well anything coming from in there cannot be clean. So, if I had to have a different housing arrangement, I would pursue that." In line with her love for cosmetology, Monica (SW1) has an interest in completing training in cosmetology and opening her own salon, while Pauline (SW2) was planning to set up a small catering outlet. Joan (IM1) suggested knitting clothing, and Rosemary (IM2) would like to open a cook shop or make pillows to sell. When asked if he has any plans or ideas, Ryan (UY1) answered positively: "My plans to make money right now is doing photography, starting my own photography or art business."

In the absence of employment or sources of regular, adequate income, respondents were all heavily dependent on others, and most acknowledged receipt of money, food and clothing. For most, their families are the first resort, and some receive support from friends, but much of this assistance is in kind and inadequate even to cover basic needs. The majority has therefore sought institutional support, primarily from the government Welfare Department. Nine of the respondents have received welfare assistance at some time in the past, four currently receive assistance and two respondents were scheduled to attend intake interviews with the department. For instance, Joan's monthly rental payments are covered by the Welfare Department; Sonia (UY2) receives money and food vouchers; and Ryan (GM1) was homeless until welfare provided accommodation and some financial assistance. He commented: "A few things change but not really. . . . Right now, I get a roof over my head. Welfare does give me little money."

Dependence on welfare, though, is generally viewed as neither reliable nor satisfactory. Respondents expressed reluctance to access social assistance, mainly as a result of their experiences or expectations of poor treatment meted out by welfare officials, of being "talked down to" as several put it. In addition, the WHH, PLHIV and GM have all been denied social assistance in the past, and this has served to deter them from further application. Pearl (WHH1) previously received assistance from the Welfare Department, but this has been discontinued and she has experienced challenges in reinstating it. She recounted that on her last visit to the office, due to the "ignorance" of the welfare officer, her request for assistance was denied, and it was suggested that she "finds a job" – this despite her explanation that her son is autistic and she lacks a support system to care for him to free her for work. Pauline (SW2) received financial assistance from the Welfare Department in the past, but she has made the decision not to reapply as she believes she will be refused. She explained:

> I ain't went back since that time. Cause I tell myself I may not get through again cause they does start giving you and then give you for a good little while and then they does stop it. They send you a review letter *telling* you to come in to them and when you come in to them that's when they stop it.

Karen (PLHIV1) also spoke negatively of the procedure required for the receipt of welfare assistance, viewing it as a deterrent. She disclosed that, when she applied, she found the line of questioning to be overly intrusive, the process time-consuming and the monetary assistance provided insufficient.

Despite their poor living conditions and inability on occasions to make ends meet, respondents are not in favour of borrowing money. Most expressed disdain at this coping strategy. As Pauline (SW2) put it: "I just don't like borrowing, I like my own", and Joan (IM1) noted that she has not borrowed money because "people aren't good". She also stated that she knows no one from whom she can borrow. The difficulty of repayments was also cited. Rosemary (IM2) has found herself in debt. She is unable to pay her bills including a hire purchase bill at a local furniture store. She also owes money to the bank but cannot make the payments. She has not borrowed money from a financial institution because she has a bad credit record, which reduces her likelihood of her success. Neither has she borrowed from other individuals – she believes no one will lend her money because they already know she cannot afford to repay.

Forward planning for emergency situations has proved impossible for most respondents. The majority have no idea what they would do in an emergency situation, though these are not unknown. The homes of three of the respondents have been badly affected by environmental hazards. When Joan's (IM1) home was destroyed by a storm, she says she coped by "the grace of Jesus". At the time, she presented herself and her children to the Welfare Department requesting assistance and was successful. The roof of Pearl's (WHH1) home was damaged in 2010 as a result of a tropical storm. She said that she had no savings or support system and "could not function" as a result. Six years later, the roof remains unfixed. A house fire destroyed Gloria's (WHH2) home. At the time, she had no measures in place to deal with such an emergency and said, "Up to this day, I don't even know how I'm coping."

Unexpected unemployment also generates emergency situations. Rosemary (IM2) lost her job suddenly two years ago, and this left her in a predicament. However, with careful planning and budgeting of the income provided by her children, they were able to cope. Additionally, in the past when she was sick and had to be hospitalized, a sister who lives in the United States sent money to support the children, and she was able to deal with her situation. In other cases when serious illness has caused emergencies, the support of families and occasionally others has seen the respondents through. When Sonia (UY2) was unwell and had to be hospitalized, she dealt with the

situation with the assistance of her daughter's father. Both GM respondents
have experienced health emergencies. Ryan took sick as a result of his chronic
HIV illness. He said that at first he was bad, but then he coped with assistance
from the woman who was his landlady at the time. Tony also faced a health
emergency that he found "really stressful". However, he coped with the social
support provided by his aunt.

Environmental and Physical Assets

Housing conditions among the respondents ranged from good, to adequate,
to poor with roughly equal numbers falling into each category. There was
very little indication of any effort to improve their homes and safeguard them
against the possibility of natural disasters. This was either because they could
not afford to make the necessary repairs or because they were living in a
rented home and believe repairs to be the responsibility of the owner. In most
cases, however, the respondents did make efforts to ensure that their homes
and immediate surroundings were kept clean and tidy.

Both WHH expressed clear discontent with the condition of their homes.
Gloria lamented: "Well 2010, since my house get burn down everything has
been downhill." Her home was completely destroyed by fire in 2010, and she
lost all of her personal possessions. Since then, she "sponges off" her mother
and is not satisfied with this state of affairs. She has made efforts to rebuild
her home but to date has managed only to place concrete slabs – her home has
no electricity or running water, no back door, and the roofing is incomplete
and open in some areas. Pearl's home was damaged by Tropical Storm Tomas
in 2010. It was previously in poor condition, but the storm resulted in further
degradation and the loss of the roof, which she has been unable to replace.
The physical structure of her home is poor with holes in the boarding, termite
infestation and small, cramped and dark spaces. Even her security of tenure
has become precarious as the owner of the land on which her house is situated has requested that she move it. When asked what steps they have taken
to make improvements to their homes, their responses reflected helplessness.
Gloria stated: "Well what can you do? I does try. Honest to God, I got material there, but then to pay a carpenter. All I can do is keep it clean. . . . I just
living here." She concluded with: "There is nothing you can do. . . . You see
the house?" And Pearl said: "There isn't really much you can do with it. I try

to keep it as tidy and comfortable as possible." They both felt that their homes were beyond repair.

The two GM also live in poor housing. Both are in rented communal apartments in which each has a personal bedroom, but the shower, toilet and kitchen are shared by all residents. Utilities including electricity and water are provided, but there is no telephone service. Both homes, however, are dirty and dilapidated, with inadequate lighting and an oppressive atmosphere.

On the other hand, Joan (IM1) shifted location to improve her living conditions. Though noting that her surroundings are still not ideal, she mentioned significant changes as a result of moving. When asked about her previous environment, she said: "It is a book to write, very, very, very hard, there ain't had no water, there ain't had no light and I didn't have any toilet. Anybody could have walk in the house and pull me out."

Although the SW have only recently assumed residence at their present location, they were both able to identify improvements to the physical structure of their homes. Monica lives in a rented home that she described as being in good condition – the owners have constructed an additional room and also changed the furniture. Pauline has lived at the home of her boyfriend for approximately a month. He has added a wooden structure onto the house with the intention of opening a food kitchen. Additionally, they have patched the roof to minimize leaking through holes in the galvanized roofing.

Dwayne (UY1) lives with his family in a government-owned house. It is constructed of concrete, but time has contributed to the degradation of the physical structure, and there are cracks along some of the walls. Though not owning the property, they have taken steps to improve the home by tiling the inside, adding a patio to the back and ensuring that the interior and exterior are cleaned. On the other hand, the PLHIV showed no efforts to improve their living surroundings and to safeguard against disasters. Karen stated that while her home actually is in need of repairs, nothing has been done, while Ann declared that, since she rents her home, she has done nothing to improve it as she believes this is the landlord's responsibility; she simply tries to maintain the cleanliness of the surroundings.

As property renters, also, neither of the IM has enhanced her home. Joan stated that the landlady takes care of those things – she had promised to fix up the home and recently attended to leaks in the roof. Though Joan does not contribute to the repairs and maintenance, she attempts to improve the external surroundings: "I does try out there in the yard to plant a little thing and see if I can fork it up and plant a little greens." No repairs have been done to the home that Rosemary rents since its construction ten years ago. But she, too, makes an effort: "Well all we is like just keep it clean, try to keep the walls tidy the best I can. You know doing a little painting."

SUMMARY

We have argued that the fostering of resilience among the socially excluded requires efforts both at the local government level as well as on the part of the excluded themselves. Individuals living in poverty are likely to develop a variety of strategies to acquire the basic necessities that they need for survival. The more effective the strategy, the greater the likelihood that individual resilience will increase and upward social mobility will occur over time. There are, however, certain socio-economic preconditions, controlled by and large by the state, that must exist in order to create an empowering environment and provide those living in poverty with the requisite skills, finances and tools.

At the governmental level, the country has historically sought to build asset stocks at the individual level through the state provision of universal primary and secondary education and currently some support for tertiary education. Provision of free health care, as well as welfare and social security support, complements these efforts to enhance social inclusion. Through the development of public institutions and legislation, the government has also provided the means through which individuals access asset-building mechanisms such as employment and self-employment to reduce economic and structural exclusion. However, while these mechanisms have allowed for the accumulation of physical, financial and human capital assets, less attention has been paid to sociocultural exclusion. While institutions exist to build social assets, such as efforts at community development, there appears to be less of a focus on building social networks and reducing stigma and discrimination than on human capital development. The process of increasing social participation and reducing stigma and discrimination are inextricably linked, and while there are some efforts at promoting community activities, apart from constitutional statements that require equal treatment, there is no

comprehensive legislation preventing discrimination in employment, education or health care.

There is a clear delineation between social and economic issues at the
governance level in the country, with limited interventions to address the
interactions between the two. While there is an understanding of these
interactions, there is also a level of institutional inefficiency in addressing the
interplay between sociocultural mechanisms and economic/structural
exclusion. An example of this is the manner in which youth issues are
addressed. While high levels of youth unemployment are a major concern
and a development constraint, both nationally and regionally, with several
social consequences, the issue is viewed more through a social lens while the
underlying causes are also economic. However, within the public sector,
youth issues are subsumed within a ministry also concerned with culture
and sports, as opposed to a more effective association with ministries related
to education and labour. This is not to suggest that an issue such as youth
unemployment is solely an economic issue but merely to highlight that the
current approach is overly addressed from a social point of view rather than
appreciating that disconnects between the education system and the needs of
the labour market have a significant role to play.

At the individual level, responses to poverty were affected by a lack of both
human and social capital. Responses revealed small social support networks,
limited to family – and then to more immediate relations, mainly mothers
and their own adult children – and one or two friends. Without employment,
other than occasional "odd jobs", the financial resources of respondents were
minimal, sufficient only for basic survival, not to cope with emergencies or to
escape poverty.

Barbados's record of investment in public education and health is evident
in social services that are comprehensive, accessible, free to nationals and of
good quality. The paradox in relation to the experiences of respondents is
why they continue to not access these opportunities and services to enhance
their quality of life, to achieve social mobility and to gain relief from poverty.
Responses suggest that they do take advantage of health services offered in
the polyclinics and that, on the whole, they appreciate their treatment and
have not experienced stigma from health providers but that they do not seek
assistance for psychological health issues. Some testimonies, however, suggest
that these problems have a marked impact on their daily lives and well-being.

Though respondents were fully aware of the potential for education and vocational training to lift them from poverty and knew of available opportunities, none were actually enrolled. Yet they specifically attributed their own inability to find work to their lack of education and skills. This apparent apathy was a theme also identified by Safa (1999). Participants in her study described their poverty almost as an inevitable manifestation of their own personal inadequacies. Also, given as reasons for unemployment in the present study were the burden of childcare, the expectation of stigma in the selection process and, in one case, non-national status and the lack of a Barbados ID card. The intersection between health and employment was also evident in that some respondents cited their own poor health as a deterrent to work.

Many respondents, nevertheless, have made considerable efforts to find employment. Without success in the formal job market, they have developed ideas for self-employment and setting up small businesses using whatever skills they have – mainly self-taught in areas such as cookery and hairdressing. But none of these ideas has been formulated into a valid plan and operationalized. And, although the lack of investment capital was mentioned, none of the respondents said that they had investigated small business training and soft loan opportunities on offer in Barbados. Instead, their testimonies suggest that they were risk averse and reluctant to borrow money. Similarly, although many expressed the desire to improve their social lives by going out more, there was also great reluctance to enhance social assets and expand their social networks by engaging with neighbours or becoming involved in community, political or other organizations. Indeed, there have been similar findings relating to social exclusion elsewhere, in that structural unemployment and declines in welfare provisions are accompanied by the retreat from mainstream society, increasing individualism and the disintegration of community (Bailey 2004).

This chapter has demonstrated that at the individual/household level, as well as at the level of the local social, political and economic environment, there have been numerous efforts at improving the living conditions of the poor in Barbados. We have, however, identified existing gaps and deficiencies at both levels that may be hindering resilience. The following chapter will discuss the manner in which these gaps can be addressed.

CHAPTER 6

CONCLUSION

AS A SMALL ISLAND DEVELOPING STATE, BARBADOS HAS survived many challenges during its history both before and after independence in 1966. When compared with most neighbouring Caribbean countries, the Barbados record of development has been positive. The country has made much progress in overcoming the vulnerabilities related to small size and a lack of natural resources, as well as a legacy of slavery and colonialism. Economic growth with diversification, sound financial management and the creation of occupational opportunities, coupled with political democracy and stability, and sustainable environmental policy and programming have enabled Barbados to emerge as a modern nation state. Playing perhaps the most significant role in this achievement are continuous investments in education, health and social welfare that have promoted a transformation towards social and gender equality, maintained low crime rates and ensured relatively low levels of poverty. Since 2008, however, with the onset of the global financial crisis, Barbados has been confronted with what history may record as the most potentially devastating challenge, one that threatens to undermine political, economic, social and environmental achievements. Evidence of the erosion of development has already become especially apparent in economic indicators of weak growth, escalating public debt burdens and deficits, rapidly shrinking foreign exchange reserves, continued dependence on a narrow economic base of tourism and financial services, growing unemployment and austerity. Signs of recovery have been described as "weak and uncertain", and the outlook for the future is bleak. The present situation demands a fundamental rethink of the Barbados model of development.

Our task in this research has been less ambitious and holistic, though directly related to Barbados's present-day crisis and a reframing of the way forward. We have focused specifically on the intersectionality between asset-poverty, social exclusion, resilience and human rights and, in the process, sought to rethink and remodel approaches to tackling these social and economic problems.

Thus far, we have used the Barbados experience in order to broaden the dialogue on poverty beyond merely the use of absolute measures towards a more comprehensive understanding of the realities of those living in deprivation within the Caribbean. A number of concepts were advanced towards this aim. Our framework is located against the background of an *asset-based approach* to understanding poverty, in which the traditionally common income-based definitions have been replaced by a more complex conceptualization that acknowledges a set of four assets that are necessary to maintain an acceptable standard of living. (1) Physical assets are those that have a direct monetary value, whatever their level of liquidity. Here, unemployment acts as a significant barrier to the accumulation of physical or financial assets. Added to this are the feelings of inadequacy, isolation and alienation that develop as a result of chronic unemployment whereby individuals feel victimized by an exclusionary system. (2) Human assets are those skills and benefits that afford individuals the ability to generate goods and services. The role of education assumes particular relevance here as it remains an integral part of upward social mobility. Within the Caribbean, however, socio-economic status has emerged as a significant predictor of educational attainment, as among the poor, there is a general absence of skills and academic qualifications. Similarly, access to an acceptable level of health care – also an important aspect of human asset accumulation – is negatively affected by factors that include socio-economic status, as well as, in some cases, gender and sexual orientation. (3) Social assets relate to the social relations between and among individuals such as family and community networks. The benefits of social capital to physical and psychological well-being are well established. Social capital, however, also has significant effects on economic status since social mobility is positively affected by integration into groups and organizations. Such social relations are important within disadvantaged communities in the Caribbean, particularly as they intersect with stigma and discrimination. Finally, (4) environmental assets are the naturally produced raw materials that are critical to human existence. At the micro level, there is the ability to protect oneself from natural disasters such as hurricanes and earthquakes. This is complicated by the fact that the poor tend to depend on occupations that are vulnerable to climatic shifts. At the macro level, there is the ability to harness and exploit valuable natural resources. Access to these assets is critical to the well-being of individuals and societies. Low-income residents are, however, typically relegated to undesirable neighbourhoods beset by decay. Linked to this is the fact that these locations tend to be vulnerable to the effects of natural disasters and climate change.

We have argued that the absence of these critical assets or, indeed, an ability to access them renders individuals *socially excluded*. This concept transitions the focus away from a model of deprivation that sees material needs as paramount towards one in which a broader array of issues are considered. In doing so, we stress the multidimensional nature of deprivation that includes the simultaneous absence of these assets, resulting in a lack of access to social services, political representation and productive employment. In order to mitigate the effects of this exclusion, the poor are compelled to employ strategies aimed at effectively managing their situation with the aim of acquiring the goods and services necessary for their survival. The factors that cause some but not all of the excluded to successfully manage their situation in such a way that they are able to make changes to improve their living conditions are the essence of *resilience*. Research shows that strategies may include a re-budgeting of income or indeed "going without"; where kinship and community networks are strong, some may also engage in informal arrangements designed to share financial burdens; others may also engage in illegitimate activities as a means of improving their situation. Oscar Lewis portrayed the poor as unresourceful, disorganized and alienated. Our findings lend support to early criticisms of his work and the myth of his *culture of poverty*. Indeed, Safa (1974), in what signalled a paradigm shift in poverty scholarship, depicted her sample as self-reliant, cooperative and ingenious. This manuscript reinforces this characterization. The ability of those living in deprivation, to be resilient in the face of their exclusion, is directly related to the likelihood that they will or will not emerge from poverty. In keeping with Narayan, Pritchett and Kapoor (2009), however, we have suggested that resilience is not determined purely by the characteristics or actions of those living in poverty but that the creation of a local social, political and economic environment that provides the necessary opportunities for advancement is integral to this process.

Within the existing framework, therefore, fostering resilience among the excluded is essential to their emergence from poverty. We have advanced the concept of *social inclusion* to this end. This is a dynamic and multilayered term that, when confronting social policy, is faced with the critical dilemma of whether to seek to address deficiencies in social and economic structures or to seek to provide pathways for marginalized groups into fair and adequate versions of these structures. One school of thought (social integrationist discourse, SID) sees exclusion from paid work as paramount and, as such, places emphasis on addressing unemployment through the development of skills. Similarly, another (redistributionist, RED) views unemployment as the main cause of exclusion but sees the responsibility of creating inclusion resting with the wider society. As others have noted, however, such interpretations suggest that full participation in economic, social and political life will be the result of involvement in paid work. In reality, the positive effects of paid work can be undermined by other factors such as stigma, lack of access to health, poor social contacts and other inequalities. Social inclusion efforts, therefore, must move beyond the mere provision of paid employment towards intervention at the national (economic, social, political, environmental) level, as well as at the individual and household levels.

Finally, our framework is in keeping with a conceptualization of *human rights* that, while not ignoring the importance of employment and social protection, advocates for a more holistic interpretation of well-being in which the range of assets essential for an acceptable standard of living includes physical, human, social and environmental assets. These encompass a number of entitlements such as property rights, rights to education and adequate health care, as well as citizenship rights. Essential to this conceptualization is the notion that these rights are non-discretionary. They are due to all persons irrespective of factors such as age, sex, sexual orientation, gender, nationality or economic status. In the current Caribbean reality, however, several countries are characterized by scarce resources and the exclusion of large sectors of society, leaving them bereft of the aforementioned assets. This reality falls short of the UN agenda for human rights that has mandated the provision of these assets to all persons. Social inclusion is dependent not only on access to assets but also on the realization of human rights, in particular the right to a life free of stigma, discrimination and violence. Foremost in this regard are rights guaranteed under the law and, by extension, protected by social policy and programming. Modern Barbadian law and policy reform have, as mentioned, promoted the rights of citizens, women and children in particular, though the process remains incomplete. But, if anything, these legal reforms have further entrenched the heteronormative moral imperative of sex for procreation and reinforced the criminalization of gay sex and sex work (Robinson 2009). Even though legal sanctions are rarely enforced, anal sex in Barbados carries a penalty of life imprisonment. As the voices of our informants from vulnerable groups revealed, stigma and discrimination persist, against gay men and sex workers in particular, and are exacerbated by association with HIV infection, immigrant status and poverty.

Human rights in Barbados stand poised between increasingly vociferous conservative religious forces and the quiet, gradual growth of public tolerance. Evidence of the latter was revealed in surveys showing that, since 2004, public "acceptance" of homosexuals rose from 17 to 28 per cent, and, by 2013–2014, 67 per cent of Barbadians were either "tolerant" or "accepting" of homosexuals (Caribbean Development Research Services Incorporated 2013). Tolerance rhetoric often drives stigma (Barrow and Aggleton 2013) but may also become a first step towards social acceptance. Realizing this trajectory requires the strengthening of social agency to build resilience and advocate for the human rights of all persons. Such activism supported by public campaigns tends to activate political will and leadership to drive social transformation and law reform.

Our research findings point to the prevalence of asset poverty and social exclusion especially evident among the working-poor, the unemployed, and retirees. The analysis revealed several correlates of social exclusion common across these three groups. First, there were general macroeconomic issues, in particular the lack of employment opportunities, that combined to render asset-building mechanisms deficient. Among the unemployed, there was a lack of awareness of employment opportunities as well as an indication of self-exclusion due to disillusionment with the conditions of work available to them. Second, levels of human capital were low as these related to education and skills and, in turn, the ability to secure decent work. As retirees, those who were poor and vulnerable had limited means through which to access asset-building or asset-preserving mechanisms since they were without physical and financial assets such as rent from buildings, interest on savings and dividends from investments. Though several received incomes from pensions, these were generally too low to ensure an adequate standard of living. A third explanatory factor was the high level of household dependency. Even when individuals secured employment, household obligations reduced earned income to the extent that poverty often ensued. Among the unemployed, women in particular, the burden of care for children, the elderly and other dependents also constrained entry into the labour market. Retirees generally found themselves without supplementary household support and may even have had to share their pensions with other family members. Across these groups, the inability to build assets also correlated with age and gender in that social exclusion was most evident among the youth, females in particular, and the elderly.

The explanation of social exclusion relates to both the demand and the supply sides. On the one hand, there was an absence of employment opportunities due to the present condition of the economy and the structure of industry; on the other, a lack of education, skills and experience reduced individuals' employability. In addition, high levels of intra-household dependency with income pooling and expenditure sharing put constraints on individual progress, and family care duties were a deterrent to labour market participation. What this added up to is the incapacity on the part of individuals and households to utilize asset-building mechanisms to preserve and further build physical and financial assets to alleviate poverty and social exclusion.

The narratives of our respondents added further in-depth perspectives to these findings on social exclusion in Barbados. On all measurements, whether material or intangible, respondents were asset poor. Few owned their homes, none owned land, and several expressed great concerns about the dilapidated condition of homes, in some cases rendered virtually beyond repair as a result of destruction by storm or fire. However, there was little evidence of structural repairs or renovations either because they were unable to afford this or because they felt the onus to be on their landlords. The material items in their possession were mainly small, convenience household and personal goods. Other than the occasional laptop or sewing machine, there was little evidence of items that could be put to productive use. However, despite their residence mainly in poor urban neighbourhoods, most respondents expressed satisfaction with their lived environments in terms of peace and security, access to amenities and services and the supply of utilities, though there were complaints about mosquitoes, rats and garbage.

Human assets were also lacking. As regards education, although most respondents had accessed secondary schooling, there was little evidence of certification or of vocational training. In many cases, educational attrition was attributed to family poverty and a lack of parental encouragement, their own low confidence and incapacity for academic work and, for female respondents, teenage pregnancy and motherhood. All were aware of the importance of education and training in enhancing employment opportunities, and all knew of opportunities provided in Barbados, but none was enrolled in further education or skills training. By way of explanation, respondents pointed to costs and, for women in particular, the burden of childcare. Even their self-taught vocational skills were not being put to use for income generation. Poor physical and mental health also contributed to unemployment and social exclusion. Mentioned were chronic health issues, hunger and poor diets and, though rare and not abusive, the use of alcohol and marijuana. Though there was little evidence of self-help in terms of dietary change and exercise, respondents have taken full advantage of public health services, and there were few complaints of poor treatment or discrimination from health service providers. More problematic than physical health were psychological issues of sadness, loneliness, worry, stress and depression. Beckford (1972) argued that one of the most important characteristics of poverty in the Caribbean was a pervasive psychological or social ill-being, leading to low self-esteem and feelings of inferiority. However, the notion of psychological poverty is empirically difficult to operationalize. Perhaps as a result of the strong stigma against mental illness in Barbados, respondents rarely sought help from either family or other social and professional sources. Instead, they tended to be in denial about poor mental health and also to rely on prayer.

Social assets were also in short supply, and there was significant evidence of social isolation. The general pattern was to spend much time alone and at home, and, though some mentioned social interaction with family members, this was generally confined to immediate family and was often limited and somewhat distant. The PLHIV and the GM were alienated from their families, having been evicted from their homes. Friends are also few; only female respondents mentioned close friendships and then only with one other woman, and there was minimal evidence of social engagement with neighbours, community members or social and political organizations. Reasons given included a lack of finances and involvement in chores and childcare, but respondents also stated a preference for being alone. This correlates with experiences of social stigma reported by all of the respondents in relation to a range of social characteristics, including their visible poverty, single parenting, non-national status, lifestyle as a sex worker, illness in the form of HIV and homosexuality. The stigmatization of the GM, in particular, confined their social lives mainly to interactions with other gay men.

None of the respondents, other than the SW, was employed or earning regular income. This they attributed to illness, childcare responsibilities, non-national status and stigma and discrimination. Most, though not all, however, expressed their willingness to work and had searched for jobs and opportunities for self-employment, but their lack of skills and finances limited the capacity for entrepreneurial activity. The result has been dependence on others, mainly family members. This, however, has generally been inadequate even for basic survival, and most have sought welfare support, albeit reluctantly. Respondents have also made fundamental decisions on financial management that included spending reductions even on food and other basic essentials. They also avoided borrowing. Though aware of the importance of savings and insurance, their hand-to-mouth existence has made this impossible. Asset poverty and dependency became most evident during periods of serious illness and natural disasters that severely damaged their homes.

A number of general issues emerged from the respondents' narratives. There was some reluctance on their part to access the opportunities available in Barbados in relation to asset provision for poverty relief, for example, in skills training and small business development. Respondents expressed a desire for more education and, in particular for vocational training, but none was so engaged. Similarly, although several had made efforts to use their skills, largely self-taught, for employment, none had taken advantage of opportunities for small business development. Their comments also indicated that they were risk averse and especially reluctant to borrow funds for investment since, in their view, this would inevitably lead to repayment problems and a downward spiral into indebtedness. Their efforts, therefore, tended to be small-scale, irregular, informal and personal in that they undertook "odd job" services by word of mouth to family and friends. As regards their health, respondents took advantage of public health clinics and other services, but more for physical than for mental health and well-being.

Only the PLHIV were receiving both counselling and treatment and that at their specialist clinic. The teen pregnancies and early childbearing among female respondents also suggest non-access to established reproductive health and family planning services. Most respondents had received support from the Welfare Department, though that was seen as a last resort. Although these general services for education, training and health are available in Barbados, specialist NGOs and other agencies for specific vulnerable social groups are either lacking or embryonic. In relation to our respondents, gay men and sex workers were particularly without group support.

Although unaffordable costs and the absence of babysitting services were mentioned as deterrents to the access of assets for social inclusion, respondent experiences also revealed low self-motivation for action, specifically in relation to the translation of intention into implementation. Many expressed a desire to avail themselves of education and vocational training but had taken no action. Business ideas were vaguely formulated and not converted into viable plans. A disconnect between intention and action was also evident in other areas of life. Plans to improve health by diet and exercise were postponed, and the wish to renovate their homes and surroundings was minimally realized. Virtually all also expressed their desire to improve their social lives, but there was little evidence of action in this regard.

Underlying much of this inaction was the dearth of social assets, which, in turn, generated social isolation. For many, social interaction was limited to family and friends. Even then, contacts were confined to a few family members and one or two friends. Community and organizational engagement was almost completely lacking, and none mentioned political involvement – indeed they expressed highly negative views of their political representatives and of politics in general. Much of this social isolation was attributed to their experiences of stigma and discrimination to which all, in particular the sex workers, persons living with HIV and gay men, had been exposed in a variety of social contexts – at school and work, in government agencies (the Welfare Department in particular), in public spaces and at home. The fear and expectation of further negative treatment also generated self-isolation and, to some degree, self-stigma and mental health problems. Assessments of their own psychological health revealed problems of loneliness, downheartedness and depression. This and their negative social experiences had resulted in the mistrust of and avoidance of dependence on others.

Several indicated that they were not social beings and preferred to be alone. In other words, stigma and discrimination have reinforced social withdrawal, rather than stimulating social organization and activism on their own behalf to advocate for and ensure human rights. There was evidence in only one case, that of a gay man, of formal complaint as a result of discrimination and that to a local newspaper, not to the police or legal authorities.

Within the context of asset poverty and a day-to-day struggle for survival, our informants have generally managed to cope with crises in the form of serious illness, the death of a family breadwinner and natural disasters wreaking destruction on their homes. This has, however, entailed dependence on agencies and other persons and generally exposed them to stigma and discrimination with mental health consequences. Furthermore, any change for the better has been short-lived. They remain trapped in an intergenerational cycle of chronic poverty and social exclusion triggered by a variety of personal experiences. The evidence points to the need for multi-level and multi-pronged policies and strategies to facilitate social agency and build resilience for social inclusion, poverty alleviation and human rights. Respondents' testimonies suggest that entry points for such interventions should include family poverty, chronic illness and hunger, educational disruption, early childbearing and experiences of stigma and discrimination.

At the most basic level, age, gender and other human qualities that drive stigma and discrimination appear as the main characteristics associated with social exclusion. The household survey revealed that social exclusion was mostly related to youth, mostly young females, and the retired. The phenomenon of the working poor was also observed, with many of the same correlated factors, including lack of human capital and residence in households with high levels of dependency. The lack of human capital was mostly due to a lack of utilization of education and skills as development opportunities, with the consequential outcome of unemployment.

Examining the situation of the most socially excluded through targeted interviews confirms some of the findings from the national survey and also gives voice to individual experiences. Central to the experiences of those most vulnerable were the current and historical lack of access to asset-building mechanisms, particularly decent employment and education. These factors also have cumulative effects, with the most vulnerable lacking the ability, as individuals, to access asset-building mechanisms such as through self-employment and also suffering stigma and discrimination due to their age, sexuality, health, nationality or poverty. Exclusion from institutional support was also seen in relation to immigrant status.

Narayan, Pritchett and Kapoor (2009) suggest that the pathway to resilience is built on both the provision of opportunities at the societal, political and economic levels, as well as at the level of the individual in the manner in which they seek to build their own resilience. This observation is particularly relevant to the situation in Barbados where issues at both the structural and the individual levels have contributed to the social exclusion observed; in this sense, the provision of access to asset-building mechanisms will need improvement, but there is also notable reluctance to utilize these mechanisms as well as a lack of knowledge among the socially excluded as to their existence and how to access them.

In addressing these issues, there are two broad approaches: first, proactive developmental measures to prevent social exclusion and, second, remedial measures to enhance the inclusion of those currently excluded. With reference to the conceptual framework and the identification of the main factors causing social exclusion, interventions would be most critically required at the level of institutions, legislation and regulations, as well as in relation to social and cultural conditions and values. While it is appreciated that politics and macro social, economic and environmental conditions all have roles to play as facilitators or inhibitors of access to asset-building mechanisms, the focus here is on direct, feasible and short- to medium-term interventions that can address the most pressing causes of social exclusion at the individual level. While all of these factors have covariate effects, it is considered that interventions at the level of institutions and sociocultural conditions and values will be most effective in dealing with the idiosyncratic risks faced by socially excluded individuals. The interventions in this case are intended to provide greater access to asset-building mechanisms.

In the preceding discussion, we focused on identifying the causes, consequences and processes that lead to sociocultural, economic and structural exclusion, the main elements of social exclusion proposed by Jehoel-Gijsbers and Vrooman (2004). The following discussion seeks to offer recommendations for Barbados and provide lessons for other small Caribbean states and small island developing states in general, to promote greater social inclusion and, through this mechanism, build resilience. In addressing social inclusion, and for matters of parsimony, we take the converse of social exclusion by seeking to achieve:

1. Active social participation in both formal and informal networks and activities, the provision of social support to reduce social isolation; and
2. Cultural and normative integration, not only in the sense of achieving "compliance with core norms and values" (Jehoel-Gijsbers and Vrooman 2004, 4) but addressing the promotion of core norms and values that are in keeping with individuals' human rights, as well as promoting compliance with respect to the development of strong work ethics, desires for educational achievement, reduced deviant behaviour, and respect for gender-based and children's rights;
3. Material asset building with access to asset-building mechanisms to meet basic short-term needs and to build longer-term resilience through access to employment and self-employment opportunities, and financial services (savings, insurance, credit, investment) to facilitate asset building with respect to physical, financial, social, and human capital. The issue of longer-term resilience is particularly important with respect to the lack of access to mechanisms to provide for the most basic of needs among retirees, one of the three most socially excluded groups along with those not in employment, education or training (NEET) and the working poor;
4. Access to "social rights" providers of health care, childcare, education, decent housing, social safety nets, utilities, advocacy, mobility and protection from crime and violence.

The development of interventions to address these issues cannot, however, take place in isolation, as many of the issues raised overlap with the various dimensions of sociocultural, economic and structural exclusion. As shown in table 6.1, several of the specific constraints are related to more than one of the core elements of social inclusion. For example, the lack of familial encouragement to education undermines the achievement of all four of the elements of social inclusion just noted. However, some constraints that relate to only a single element, specifically lack of knowledge of sources of social support, negative views of the political system and a preference for not asking for assistance, would only relate to Activating Social Participation. Similarly,

Table 6.1. Social Inclusion Components and Constraints

	SOCIAL INCLUSION		
Activating Social Participation	Cultural/Normative Appre-ciation and Integration	Building Material Assets	Meeting "Social Rights" Obligations
	GENERAL CONSTRAINTS TO SOCIAL INCLUSION		
Lack of encouragement	Lack of encouragement	Lack of encouragement	Lack of encouragement
Stigma and discrimination	Stigma and discrimination	Stigma and discrimination	Stigma and discrimination
Lack of knowledge of sources of support	Personal: Poor work ethic, education, health	Lack of knowledge of sources of support	Lack of knowledge of sources of support
Insularity and fear	Lack of employment opportunities	Personal: Poor work ethic, education, health	Personal: Poor work ethic, education, health
Lack of networks		Insularity and fear	Insularity and fear
		Lack of employment opportunities	Lack of social security support
		Lack of social security support	
		Lack of networks	

Table 6.1 continues

Table 6.1. Social Inclusion Components and Constraints (*cont'd*)

SOCIAL INCLUSION			
Activating Social Participation	**Cultural/Normative Appreciation and Integration**	**Building Material Assets**	**Meeting "Social Rights" Obligations**
SPECIFIC CONSTRAINTS TO SOCIAL INCLUSION			
• Lack of familial encouragement to education • Lack of social networks: curtails finding employment, and assistance with burden of care • Lack of social networks due in part to stigma and discrimination • Self-exclusion due to mistrust and fear of stigma and discrimination • Social exclusion due to stigma and discrimination because of health status or sexuality	• Lack of familial encouragement to education • Discouragement with the labour market • Weak work ethic • Stigma and discrimination from social service providers and their clientele	• Lack of familial encouragement to education • Lack of social networks: curtails finding employment and assistance with burden of care • Lack of social networks due in part to stigma and discrimination • Discouragement with the labour market • Weak work ethic • Lack of education, certification and skills	• Lack of familial encouragement to education • Self-exclusion due to mistrust and fear of stigma and discrimination • Social exclusion due to stigma and discrimination because of health status or sexuality • Stigma and discrimination from social service providers and their clientele • Lack of knowledge of how and where to find employment

- Lack of knowledge of sources of support
- Negative view of political system
- Prefer not to ask for help

- Psychological issues caused by stigma and discrimination
- Poor state of the economy
- Lack of knowledge of how and where to find employment
- Poor health for individual as well as effect on carers
- Limited savings and insurance
- Lack of pension-building activity
- Reluctance to borrow
- Exclusion from opportunity to gain qualifications within education system
- Migration legislation and regulations

- Poor health for individual as well as effect on carers
- Limited savings and insurance
- Lack of pension-building activity
- Reluctance to borrow
- Exclusion from opportunity to gain qualifications within education system
- Migration legislation and regulations

Table 6.2. Interrelationship Between General Constraints and Elements of Social Inclusion

General Constraints	Activating Social Participation	Cultural/ Normative Appreciation and Integration	Building Material Assets	Meeting "Social Rights" Obligations
Lack of knowledge of support sources	x		x	x
Lack of support networks	x		x	
Insularity and fear	x		x	x
Stigma and discrimination	x	x	xx	x
Personal: Poor work ethic, education and health		x	xxxxxx	xxx
Lack of encouragement	x	x	xx	x
Lack of social security support			x	x
Lack of employment opportunities		x	x	

education levels, psychological issues and the general state of the economy relate only to Building Material Assets. This abstraction is not to deny the existence of feedback effects with other elements of social exclusion but merely to indicate where the direct relationships exist.

The interrelated effect of general constraints on multiple elements of social inclusion is demonstrated in table 6.2.

The interrelationships shown may mask the complexity of the actual relationships to some degree but do show the main areas where interventions are required. This is particularly in relation to addressing personal qualities as they relate to enhancing participation in the labour market through human capital development in order to assist in building material assets, while also meeting social rights obligations. However, although development in this area is critical, the most pervasive constraints relate to stigma and discrimination and a lack of encouragement, two constraints that affect all of the core elements of social inclusion.

Relating these findings to the conceptual framework, the specific areas in which action is required (although overlaps in effects are noted) are

- **Intervening factors:**
  - Institutions, legislation and regulations to address
    - the lack of knowledge of sources of support, specifically as it relates to social support and identifying employment opportunities; and
    - the lack of social security support.
  - Macroeconomic conditions to enhance employment opportunities.
  - Social and cultural conditions and values to address:
    - the lack of encouragement to undertake education; and
    - insularity and fear, specifically in relation to addressing stigma and discrimination.

- **Asset-building mechanisms:**
  - Trade in goods and services and labour markets to address the lack of employment opportunities, as well as to promote the option of self-employment.
  - Health systems to address poor health as a source of stigma and discrimination and as a constraint to undertaking employment.
  - Educational systems to address a lack of qualifications and relevance of education to industry as a barrier to obtaining employment.
  - Social networks to strengthen both bridging and bonding social capital to address issues related to stigma and discrimination, the burden of care and the securing of employment opportunities.

In the following discussion, we seek to establish interventions to address these constraints as observed in the Barbadian case.

ADDRESSING CONSTRAINTS TO SOCIAL INCLUSION IN BARBADOS

> Social inclusion . . . is a concept with universal appeal. . . . However, the challenge lies at the core: how to apply the concept in real life situations, and how to operationalize it through mobilizing all actors in society. (DESA 2009, 29)

For Barbados and other small island developing states, the challenge is not solely related to practical implementation but also funding of interventions, given tight fiscal constraints. The implementation of interventions will need to be either expenditure neutral, funded from sources outside the public purse, or funded under a new fiscal regime. If the idea of social transformation is one grounded in social inclusion, one to be funded by governments due to the public good nature of interventions, then this will require a sea change in the manner in which wealth is distributed in society. This is unlike the "see-saw" change that is characteristic of political decision making in the region.

Political will and funding are integral to the implementation of any institutional, legislative or regulatory change. Political will aside and seeking to draw lessons from countries with high levels of social inclusion, the discussion inevitably turns to the Nordic region and the key features of the so-called Nordic model. The Nordic countries are prominent as the top performers in the Inclusive Development Index (IDI), accounting for four of the top ten (Norway first, Iceland fourth, Denmark fifth and Sweden sixth), with countries adopting similar approaches also in the top ten (Netherlands seventh and Austria tenth).[1] Andersen et al. (2007, 13–14) outline the principal features of the Nordic model as:

> a comprehensive welfare state with an emphasis on transfers to households and publicly provided social services financed by taxes, which are high notably for wage income and consumption;

> a lot of public and/or private spending on investment in human capital, including childcare and education as well as research and development (R&D); and

> a set of labour market institutions that include strong labour unions and employer associations, significant elements of wage coordination, relatively generous unemployment benefits and a prominent role for active labour market policies.[2]

The level of social support (security), with the Nordics noted for having large public sectors, makes adaptation to changes (flexibility) enforced by globalization acceptable. Underlying these features are trust and a sense of fairness: "Underpinning this virtuous interaction of security and flexibility is the widespread feeling of trust – among citizens and in public administration – and a sense of fairness related to the egalitarian ambitions of the welfare state (education, social policy)" (Anderson et al. 2007, 14).

This observation suggests that trust in government is central to the effectiveness of the Nordic model, which is noted as grounded historically in "ethnic and religious homogeneity" (ibid., 39).

While the Nordic model is put forward as an exemplar of promoting social inclusion, the system is by no means perfect in implementation. Despite high levels of taxation, the Nordics still suffer fiscal constraints. Andersen et al. (2007) propose a number of recommendations to reform the Nordic model under conditions of increased competition due to globalization and an ageing population, which is placing pressure on public finances. Some of the relevant specific recommendations made to facilitate the sustainability of the Nordic model include the following:

- A continuation of the utilization of collective agreements in the labour market but restricting the scope to non-wage issues such as working times and setting the rules for wage-setting. Wage-setting should be decentralized to the local level to give greater flexibility in the setting of remuneration and incentives based on economic conditions.
- Privatization or outsourcing of non-core public services.
- Greater efficiency in education with respect to students making the transition to work earlier in life.

The removal of government subsidization of "consumption education", that is, education undertaken "because one likes it and has chosen . . . as one would choose sports, going to the movies, or buying a bigger house" (Census Bureau 1975, 165).

- The enhancing of labour force participation to increase tax revenue and reduce unemployment in order to reduce government expenditure by removing schemes that discourage employment and matching the demands of industry with the supply of education and skills.

- Reframing of the requirements to access unemployment benefits and greater monitoring of job search efforts.
- An increase of the retirement age and reduced incentives for early retirement. Encouragement to pensioners to continue work could be facilitated by provision of tax allowances for pensioners that continue in employment.
- The rationalization (including privatization where feasible), clearer delineation and potential of capping/rationing of welfare services. Clearer outlines of entitlements for citizens (greater knowledge dissemination) are expected to allow for greater ability to plan and save for future needs.

All of these recommendations are underpinned by a "social contract" between the government and the citizenry. Previous to the commencement of employment (particularly for children and youth) and when employment ceases, either through unemployment or retirement, the government commits to a net expenditure on the citizen. During employment, the citizen is then expected to contribute, through taxation, to the support of others not in employment.

While Barbados does not follow a Nordic model in the strictest sense, the underlying philosophy has guided development in the country with a focus on social security and welfare support, education as means to escape material poverty and a high level of representation of labour. With these underlying ideals and the lack of fiscal space to fund a welfare state and high levels of debt, many of the recommendations made by Andersen et al. (2007), as previously noted, would apply in the case of Barbados.

Turning to interventions aimed at addressing the issues arising in Barbados, and as noted in the earlier discussion, there are two main categories of intervention: proactive developmental interventions to prevent social exclusion and remedial interventions to reduce current experiences of social exclusion. The following discussion highlights some of the options available to address these constraints in relation to the area of the intervention and the specific constraints to be addressed. While we note that this is not an exhaustive list and that the options will not be applicable to all countries, these options provide a starting point for addressing the main issues seen in the case of Barbados.

Institutional, Legal and Regulatory Measures to Enhance Social Inclusion

Several broad institutional[3] measures can be undertaken to enhance the level of social inclusion in Barbados. The main issues to emerge from the analysis that require attention relate to a lack of knowledge of sources of support and a lack of social safety nets. In this vein, despite a wide prevalence of support sources, as noted in Caribbean Development Bank (2012b), ranging from public support for the elderly (National Assistance Board) to third-sector support for parental education (PAREDOS), interviewees still indicated that they did not know where to go for support in time of need. The national survey also revealed a lack of utilization of the public employment bureau and greater utilization of word of mouth to secure employment. Given the lack of social networks seen among the socially excluded, this word-of-mouth methodology in securing employment would be inefficient.

In essence we see a clear demonstration of the trend noted earlier, the existence of institutional support but a lack of utilization.[4] The clear requirements here are greater dissemination of information on sources of support for all sectors, public safety net support, advocacy channels to address the idiosyncrasies of specific socially excluded groups and opportunities for employment in both the public and the private sectors. The government has a key role to play here in relation to ensuring that all sources of support are clearly catalogued and utilizing various mediums to disseminate this information. At a developmental level, such dissemination would take place in educational institutions, informing children from an early age as about the institutional structure of the country, while third sector organizations could ensure that their various constituents are knowledgeable about the availability of specific types of support in the event of crisis.

While it is understood that many of the most socially excluded do not interact with these organizations, remedial measures would be required through proactive community involvement to identify and inform them of the support available. Linkages between organizations in the various sectors and within the various sectors will also need to be strengthened to allow them to act as access points to wider support available. In this sense, individuals with particular idiosyncratic needs that enter the system through the

Welfare Department could be informed of specific support in other organizations to meet their needs.

The issue of lack of access to employment opportunities, when they exist, is one based in a lack of dissemination of opportunities, as well as in relation to the of knowledge of sources of information. This suggests the need for greater visibility of public employment services (PES), especially their electronic presence (e-presence), among both potential employers and employees. The current lack of utilization of PES across the region, due to low levels of visibility (Lashley et al. 2015), can be enhanced through the adoption of proactive strategies to engage both with the private sector[5] and with organizations that come into direct contact with the socially excluded, as well as drawing on the high utilization of mobile technology in the country. The National Employment Bureau has a web presence and provides a number of related job-seeking services through its One Stop Resource Centre; however, the household survey indicated that only 6 per cent of the unemployed utilized the Bureau to find information on vacancies.

The issue of revisions to social security support is complex, especially as any revisions would seek to address the National Insurance Scheme's (NIS) pensions for retirees, non-contributory pensions for those who have not made sufficient contributions,[6] as well as benefits for the unemployed. To address the financial constraints in providing this support, the NIS is systematically raised the retirement age from 65 to 67 by 2018. There is also the introduction of a flexible retirement age, up to age 70, introduced in 2003.

While contributory pensions provide for 60 per cent of average insurable earnings, non-contributory pension are approximately Bds$7,200 per annum. Of note is that the poverty line for Barbados in 2010 was Bds$7,861 and for the elderly, due to greater nutritional and non-food requirements than young children, was approximately Bds$8,770 (Caribbean Development Bank 2012a). For an individual receiving only a non-contributory pension, this means consistently living in material poverty or, if residing with others, contributing to the burden of care that has been shown to be a characteristic of the lives of the working poor. There is a need to address the quantum of support for those who have not contributed sufficiently to the NIS; however, this is an actuarial issue beyond the scope of the current exercise.

In addition to an actuarial analysis to enhance the provision of monetary support for the retired, other measures can be employed to address the situation of the retired over the longer term. However, first, there is a need to identify why contributions are not made to the NIS, as this is not solely related to not wanting to work over a lifetime. Illness, disability or informal employment are all issues that contribute to non-participation in the labour force. While remedial support for illness and disability relates directly to the provision of health care, the issue of informal employment is also a significant factor contributing to a lack of sufficient social security support in later life. The Caribbean Development Bank (2012a) indicates that approximately 49.6 per cent of self-employed persons were operating informally, that is, the business was not registered, and operated outside of any formal institutional structure. This suggests that efforts would need to be made to increase formality among the self-employed, not only to the benefit of the self-employed persons themselves but also their employees. Again, the dissemination of information in relation to the benefits of formality will be required.

Also of concern is the issue of social security support to the unemployed and casually employed, particularly the youth. The current system of unemployment support is based on being insured for at least a year before becoming unemployed, having made at least twenty contributions in the three quarters preceding unemployment and at least seven contributions in the quarter preceding unemployment.[7] The notable gap here is that persons with no formal employment history or experience have no access to social security support. This is a critical situation for youth attempting to make the school-to-work transition, as they lack "employability" in a competitive labour market. From the household survey, 24 per cent of unemployed youth, that is, those actually seeking work, have never worked, and, overall, 69 per cent of the unemployed had less than one year of work experience. This does not account for the unemployed who are not seeking work. This finding can assist in understanding the extremely strong links seen in the data between unemployment and poverty; while there are unemployment benefits available, a large proportion of the unemployed cannot access them.

While there are also actuarial issues to be investigated in relation to the provision of adequate quanta for non-contributory pensions and the provision of unemployment benefits with greater breadth of access, other policy interventions can be undertaken such as minimum income support, if a more Nordic model approach is adopted.

Income support schemes for people of working age (*whether in or out of work*) which provide a *means-tested* safety net for those not eligible for social insurance payments or those whose entitlement to these payments has expired. They are in effect *last resort schemes*, which are intended to *prevent destitution* and to ensure a decent minimum standard of living for individuals and their dependants when they have no other or insufficient means of financial support. (Frazer and Marlier 2016, 5–6) (emphasis added)

Minimum income support in this sense addresses both the unemployed and the working and pension poor, the most vulnerable groups identified previously. However, while the direct provision of a financial asset may be appealing in addressing the material element of social exclusion, it may have the added complication of extenuating stigma and discrimination by the attachment of poverty labels to individuals, exclusion due to judgements made on the work ethic of individuals and classification as a drain on the state.

In addition to social security as a safety net, a number of other issues emerging from the research need to be addressed at the institutional level in relation to enhancing social inclusion. The prevalence of stigma and discrimination in relation to health status, discussed in more detail later, has led to withdrawal and is cited as a reason for the inability to secure employment. While improvements in preventative and curative health care have a role to play by removing the source of stigma, there is also the need to reduce misconceptions by both service providers and society in general. The provision of sensitization training and campaigns, as utilized with respect to HIV and AIDS, would need to be undertaken. This would require, again, the greater development of linkages between service providers and advocacy groups.

While lack of employment has been a recurring theme in the preceding discussion, the key causal links between unemployment and social exclusion are qualifications, skills and their relevance to the needs of employers. The household survey revealed that 24 per cent of NEET had no qualifications, and 19 per cent had only a school leaving certificate; that is, 43 per cent of those currently excluded from education or employment are not attractive to employers. What is also surprising is that 81 per cent of household survey respondents who had left education had at least competed secondary education, while only 56 per cent had at least obtained the equivalent of an

O-level qualification. This suggests a need to address some of the noted issues in the formal educational system as a developmental exercise, as well as enhancing the effectiveness and outreach of less formal technical and vocational education and training (TVET) programmes for those who have exited formal education without any certification.

The main goals for transformative change in the educational system in general, formal and programmatic, relate to first understanding the needs and abilities of students and, through this, providing appropriate channels through which they can obtain qualifications. There is also the need to ensure the relevance of education to the labour force needs of the country. These approaches would apply to both developmental and remedial interventions.

Understanding the needs and abilities of students is also a priority. While, as indicated, the Barbados educational system provides tuition-free education at the primary, secondary and, until recently, tertiary levels, and enrolment rates are high and gender balanced, problems of low achievement and attrition are evident, especially among boys. Our informants' views made it clear that their early dropout from the educational system and their lack of educational and vocational qualifications marked a turning point in their lives, one that drove them into asset deprivation and social exclusion. The reasons they gave for their lack of educational success were varied and point to critical entry points for social policy. Included among them were family poverty and the absence of family encouragement, as well as their own incapacity for academic studies and lack of confidence. Several female informants revealed early pregnancy and childbirth as their reason for leaving school, and the gay men mentioned stigma and discrimination at school as deterrents to educational achievement.

The interviews with the socially excluded revealed a reluctance to associate with others, while a lack of confidence can result in anxiety in new social situations (Hazenberg 2012) and hence lead to avoiding such situations as job interviews or social gatherings. If mechanisms can be implemented to provide measures of students' needs, such as self-efficacy tests to reveal levels of introversion, then a curriculum can be developed to address any issues arising. A similar assessment of practical abilities would allow students to be streamed into areas of greatest interest and ability, within a system structured to allow lateral movements between wholly academic and wholly technical instruction. Such systems exist in Europe and are detailed in Lashley et al. (2015).

An educational system established around the needs and abilities of students would assist in not excluding students from opportunities to obtain qualifications as is currently the case with students in secondary schools placed in non-CXC classes who bide their time until they reach the compulsory age for remaining in education, currently sixteen years.

Integrated within an approach that is appreciative of the needs and abilities of students would need to be strategies to assist students in entering the "real world", not just the world of work. UNICEF (2010) presents a number of teaching and learning strategies that relate to active, participatory and experiential learning. This Active Learning Process is student centred, utilizing "the experience, opinions, and knowledge of the students" and promoting "the development of action competence for use in the real world" (ibid., 18).

Other areas in which the educational system could be adapted to address some of the other factors constraining social inclusion include the promotion of volunteerism, either in the local community or with specific groups, to address the development of social networks and social responsibility. The implementation of a youth guarantee scheme would also assist. Youth guarantee schemes in Europe provide a guarantee to school leavers of a place in a training course or subsidized/alternative employment (apprenticeships, public works) if they are unable to find employment in the regular labour force within a certain time frame after leaving school. A discussion of this and other issues related to addressing the youth unemployment issue in the Caribbean, such as support for micro enterprise development (finance, entrepreneurship education within the curriculum and technical assistance) can be found in Lashley et al. (2015).

Macroeconomic Measures to Enhance Employment Opportunities

The health of the macroeconomy has many implications for social inclusion. Low levels of aggregate demand during times of recession result in fewer opportunities to participate in the labour market, with attendant consequences. As noted in the discussions throughout, unemployment is one of the main drivers of social exclusion, not only in relation to an individual's inability to build material assets and meet basic needs but also in relation to withdrawal and feelings of isolation or low self-worth. While our discussions suggest measures to address the consequences or prospects of unemployment by improving the ability to access channels of support and improving the quality and effectiveness of education, without adequate demand for labour, there will be limited prospects of achieving social inclusion.

In capitalist societies, economic growth is driven by the activities of the private sector. Government's role is facilitative, providing the institutional, legislative and regulatory framework for efficient business operations. In this respect, for the public good, governments also seek to address market failures through the provision of systems or the correction of systems with respect to finance, training and education, along with technical assistance. All of these activities have the objective of increasing competitiveness to promote economic growth and development, with the private sector as the main driver.

Narayan and Smyth's (2004) observation that resilience is built on the provision of institutional support, as well as on individual action, can be easily applied to the situation of marginalized businesses. This is highly relevant to Barbadian enterprises given that, while imperfect, institutional support is provided, but enterprises themselves fail to take advantage of this support (Lashley 2010). This in essence mirrors the situation seen with socially excluded individuals, as previously discussed.

Further lessons can be drawn from our discussion of social exclusion. Drawing on Jehoel-Gijsbers and Vrooman (2004), the exclusion of businesses can be conceptualized within the framework of social exclusion to relate to:

- Insufficient participation in business networks and lack of collaborative behaviour;
- Insufficient professionalism (integration of core business norms and goals);
- Exclusion from access to the factors of production (land, capital, labour, technology), whether supplied by the government or capitalists; and
- Inadequate provision of and access to governmental support in the areas of finance, training and technical assistance.

As with social inclusion having "universal appeal" (DESA 2009, 29), so does the business goal of integration in global value chains. This is, however, not characteristic of Barbadian businesses, a situation seen across the Caribbean, with businesses focused on the domestic economy in sectors characterized by high levels of competition, low skills and low value added (Nicholson and Lashley 2016). If the marginalization of the private sector can be reduced, this would assist in enhancing the private sector's contribution to economic growth.

Drawing on extant information on Barbadian enterprises,[8] some stylized tendencies can be seen that relate to a framework of exclusion:

- **Network participation:** Between 2012 and 2014, only 20 per cent of businesses attempted to form alliances. Of these only attempts, 16 per cent were successful. For manufacturing firms, only 36 per cent were members of the local manufacturing association, 18 per cent were members of the local chamber of commerce and 16 per cent members of the local small business association (Lashley 2010).

- **Professionalism:** As with the discussion of cultural/normative integration in relation to social exclusion, the setting of "acceptable practice" is determined by those in power. When we switched our discussion from social exclusion to inclusion, we noted there was not only a need to achieve "compliance with core norms and values" (Jehoel-Gijsbers and Vrooman 2004, 4) but also the promotion of core norms and values that are in keeping with individuals' human rights. A similar approach can be taken with businesses. Power in dictating acceptable business practice lies with government and the providers of capital. A lack of understanding of the reality at the level of the enterprise has led to the rigorous application of economic, rational, "professional" assessments of enterprises in the region seeking finance, leading to exclusion, both self- and externally imposed, of family-owned and women-owned businesses (Nicholson and Lashley 2016). These businesses are considered less professional. Nicholson and Lashley (2016) note that family-owned businesses account for approximately 70 per cent of businesses in the region, and survey data reveal that 41 per cent of businesses in Barbados had either majority or equal ownership by women, suggesting that a high proportion of enterprises in the region are "excluded". The high level of informality of enterprises, as noted previously, is also a demonstration of a lack of compliance.

- **Access to factors of production:** The three largest barriers to operating in Barbados are noted by businesses as an inadequately educated workforce (43 per cent), lack of access to finance (37 per cent) and the cost of finance (33 per cent).[9] These factors relate to lack of access to suitable labour and capital as factors of production and also constrain access to the acquisition of technology. The issue of access to land was less of a constraint, mentioned by only 11 per cent of respondents. The constraints noted demonstrate some gender differences in relation to ownership. Whereas the labour issue was more prevalent as a constraint to fully male-owned enterprises (52 per cent as opposed to 38 per cent for enterprises with female ownership). In addition, enterprises with some female ownership had a greater proportion considering cost of finance as a main constraint, 40 per cent versus 21 per cent for fully male-owned enterprises. In examining the issue of access and cost of finance in some detail, Nicholson and Lashley (2016) highlight a level of self-exclusion among enterprise owners due to fear of having loan applications rejected or due to a high level of bureaucracy in the process of obtaining finance.

- **Access to government support in finance, training and technical assistance:**
  - *Finance:* The government provides a number of financing sources for the private sector including debt, equity, grants and guarantees.[10] However, only 11 per cent of enterprises in the sample utilized funding from a government agency in the last year for working capital, and 2 per cent for purchase of fixed assets.
  - *Training:* The government provides TVET services through a number of institutions.[11] However, while 50 per cent of enterprises ran training programmes, only 9 per cent of enterprises utilized public support for training. The main reason for not running a training programme was the lack of available funds. This is despite the existence of government programmes to assist. Some of the shortcomings of the education and training system in the country, which were rated as very important or critical factors causing the skill shortages for enterprises, were overall lack of quality of education and training (57 per cent), lack of soft skills provided by local institutions (36 per cent), lack of personal qualities such as

honesty and integrity (63 per cent noted this was a barrier for recruitment), general lack of educational background (80 per cent noted this as a barrier for recruitment) and 53 per cent noted the motivation of job applicants as a barrier for recruitment.

o   *Technical assistance:* As with finance and training, technical assistance services are also provided by the government,[12] and as with utilization, while 50 per cent of enterprises are aware of sources of technical assistance, only 20 per cent of enterprises actually utilize it.

This brief analysis of the private sector in Barbados suggests that many of the issues raised in our discussion of the socially excluded are relevant here, namely a level of separation from networks and advocacy agencies designed to support their interests; a lack of adherence to externally imposed accepted business norms and practices related to perceived lower levels of professionalism in family- and women-owned businesses; difficulty in accessing suitable levels of the factors of production, mainly labour and capital; and a disconnect between support services provided by government and the level of utilization by enterprises.

While government provides the framework for the functioning of the private sector, a number of shortcomings of the system can be addressed to enhance the productivity of enterprises and contribute to economic growth and development. As identified by the World Bank Doing Business survey for Barbados[13] for 2017, the main areas that need addressing are in relation to dealing with construction permits, registering property, getting credit, protecting minority investors and enforcing contracts – all issues affecting the efficient operation of the economy. Government will need to address these areas as a matter of priority in order to enhance the quality of private sector activity in the country.

In addition to the institutional, legislative and regulatory actions required, other areas in which action can be taken to enhance the state of the macroeconomy would relate to the undertaking of greater research, development and innovation (RD&I), as well as greater sectoral diversification and exploitation of opportunities in new and emerging sectors (Moore 2013). Moore (2013) identifies potential new and emerging sectors in Barbados as international business and financial services, alcoholic beverages and green energy.

In addition to promoting the growth, development and competitiveness of the private sector, government can also take measures in relation to increasing revenue and reducing expenditure, measures critical to reducing the high debt levels currently experienced that have contracted the fiscal space within which the government has to operate. This contracted fiscal space constrains the ability to meet current social obligations, as well as the ability to implement transformative change in the social sector, as previously discussed. Some of the areas in which government can reduce fiscal deficits can emanate from restructuring its debt, privatization, retrenchment, consolidation of institutions and the implementation of user fees in health and education. While the spectre of higher unemployment may cause many of these approaches to be considered unviable by politicians and representatives of labour, taken in consort with other measures to promote private sector growth and development, social security provision and actions in the education and training sector can result in more sustainable economic growth and development.

Measures to Address Social and Cultural Conditions to Enhance Social Inclusion

> It is important to recognize, that when tackling poverty, it involves not only economic measures and improvement in infrastructure and services, but also requires building social capital: the networks, norms and trust that facilitate co-ordination and co-operation for mutual benefit. (DESA 2009, 56)

Perhaps the most pervasive issue to arise throughout the discussion is the issue of social capital assets and the role this plays in experiences of stigma and discrimination, the burden of care and the inability to access sources of support and employment. While many of the broad measures discussed here can assist in enhancing social inclusion, there is a need to also improve social networks.

Participation in social networks assists in building bonding and bridging social capital among different social groups. Portes (1998) believed that poor inner-city neighbourhoods could not exist effectively without networks and relationships and that when assumptions are made about their absence, they are usually based on value judgements (see also Portney and Berry [1997]).

An individual's social network ranges from immediate to extended family, to participation in various community and national groupings. Community groupings here are related not strictly to spatial proximity but also to communities with common interests, where physical association is no longer required with the prevalence of social media. Common interests may relate to sports, the arts or other areas of recreational activity, while also applying to groups with common vulnerabilities.

Interviews with the socially excluded revealed a lack of participation in social networks, neither for recreational activity nor for much needed support. Alienation from family, as well as lack of encouragement to build their own asset base, has contributed significantly to individuals' social exclusion. A lack of understanding by other community groupings has led to stigma and discrimination, further exacerbating social exclusion. These results emphasize the need for the development of greater levels of bonding and bridging social capital. However, while institutional measures can be implemented directly to address an issue, the development of social capital is a more organic procedure, built on the gradual development of trust and understanding, concepts that cannot be "legislated".

The main aims of building social capital are to ease the means of access to asset-building mechanisms, through the reduction of stigma and discrimination and the burden of care, as well as motivating socially excluded individuals to take advantage of these mechanisms through reducing fear of social participation.

Greater bonding social capital will increase an individual's direct support network, which not only acts to increase social participation but also reduces the ill effects of stigma and discrimination from the immediate and extended network of family and friends and lightens the burden of care that can prevent participation in education or employment. The development of bridging social capital, at a broader societal level, can contribute to reduced stigma and discrimination and can permit greater access to other asset-building mechanisms. Having made the case for the importance of social capital in addressing exclusion, text box 6.1 provides an example of an intervention that both utilizes and fosters social capital towards the ultimate goal of reducing exclusion.

Text Box 6.1. Community Land Trusts (CLTs)

The CLT model was developed as membership corporations in the 1960s in the United States by community activists who felt that a democratically controlled institution could hold land for the common good and make it available to individuals through long-term land leases (Peterson 1996). Some of them are directed towards solving problems faced by those who already own their homes. These individuals are equity rich but income poor. The CLT offers them an opportunity to sell their land in exchange for cash to do their repairs. Others focus on increasing home ownership by eliminating the cost of land in the housing equation. There are those who act as developers of special needs housing, and some provide space for low-income entrepreneurs. The CLTs are community based, and they acquire land within a community and hold it permanently for the benefit of that community. They usually decide on a geographical area from which most members would be drawn, and this could comprise a region or a neighbourhood. The definition of the boundaries is usually determined by whether the people see their area as distinct from others, whether there is a "critical mass" for organizing a CLT on the one hand, but at the same time whether it is small enough to encourage grass roots participation.

The CLTs acquire land and financing for their projects in a variety of ways. They sometimes obtain donated property or cash donations to buy property. They obtain money from state housing finance agencies and acquire city-owned property from local governments. The CLTs own the land and arrange long-term leases (99 years) that are assignable to heirs of the leaseholders. Residents therefore have the security of tenure that encourages them to build their own housing units gradually and so obtain the equity they build up in their units through their investments and improvements (DeFilippis 2001).

Recently, there has been increased recognition of the role the CLTs can play in asset-based community development or poverty alleviation. CLTs have the potential to facilitate the transfer of assets such as land, buildings and other property and, in so doing, increase levels of social capital towards the ultimate goal of empowering communities and individuals. The ownership of community assets presents a range of benefits that impact directly on levels of social capital. These include the creation of jobs, community pride and confidence, community cohesion, and psychological boosts in the form of hope for the future (Cabinet Office 2007). Community empowerment is an integral part of

Text Box 6.1 continues

Text Box 6.1. Community Land Trusts (CLTs) (*cont'd*)

addressing social exclusion. Achieving this requires active citizens, strengthened communities, as well as partnership with public bodies. CLTs, through their asset-based approach, have the ability to positively affect each of these by transforming individuals and groups from consumers to producers (Mathie and Cunningham 2003). CLTs strengthen existing levels of social capital by shifting ownership into the hands of the local community.

For communities to be self-sustaining, however, one has to look beyond the realm of property ownership to employment, and one of the advantages of the CLT approach to poverty alleviation is that they can be the vehicle for launching a wide range of small-scale income-generating community projects. Micro enterprise lending programmes, in which loan decisions are made by the group and evaluations of creditworthiness are character based, can stimulate the development of small-scale enterprises and expand self-employment, allowing community members to make a decent living (DeFilippis 2001). These schemes recommend themselves because, unlike others, they, at one and the same time, provide benefits to individuals and strengthen social networks and communities.

Addressing Integration at the Institutional Level

Overriding many of the issues emerging is the issue of stigma and discrimination. The UN Department of Economic and Social Affairs (DESA) (2009) identified two institutional approaches to enhance social integration of migrants: one in Germany, the Frankfurt Municipal Department of Multicultural Affairs (AMKA), and the other in Madrid, Madrid Plan for Social and Intercultural Coexistence. Although these institutional approaches attempted to deal with social tensions arising from a high prevalence of inward migration from different cultures, the actions can inform addressing the issues facing other vulnerable groups suffering from stigma and discrimination. Friedman and Lehrer (1997) speak to the formation of AMKA in 1989, noting the importance of political will on the city council (the election of the Green Party) and the importance of a prominent champion, Daniel Cohn-Bendit, a green activist with a global reputation. The primary aim of the AMKA was to assist in the formation of a "multicultural society", with a number of related conditions, including: "participation, equal rights, and the acceptance of cultural diversity with a framework of [universal] human rights" (Friedmann and Lehrer 1997, para. 38). One relevant area of work of the AMKA included the formation of a Foreign Residents' Advisory Board, with members having access to City Council meetings and the opportunity to comment on budget proposals for the City. In addition, compilation of registers of migrant organizations and financial and technical support for multicultural events were also undertaken.

The Madrid Plan took a similar course, including forums for discussion, the promotion of associations to address immigrant issues and intercultural programmes. The main objectives were "fostering the institutional progress of immigrant reception at the municipal level, to provide better access to civil rights and resources for immigrants, as well as to improve coexistence between Spaniards and foreigners in order to create dynamic and harmonious neighbourhoods" (Borkert et al. 2007, 47).

While the details of broad strategies at this "partnership" level may vary, as outlined across Europe by Borkert et al. (2007), the general point is that there is the recognition of an issue, that of social exclusion, along with an institutional structure in place to address it. While these policies described for Europe apply to addressing integration of immigrants, the general premise can apply to all vulnerable and excluded groups. In Barbados, there is an institutional structure for dialogue between some elements of society, the government, employers' representatives and trade unions. This social partnership, which is representative only of the main economic actors, not the wider civil society, could be augmented to include organizations that represent the voice of the excluded.

APPENDIX: DESCRIPTION OF
THE INTERVIEW PROCESS

Respondents were selected mainly through contact with government agencies and other individuals who offer social services to poor and vulnerable persons. Given the intimate and sensitive nature of the questions, researchers approached potential respondents with caution, generally through the snowball method of sampling. There was some difficulty in accessing representatives from specific vulnerable groups, namely the PLHIV, SW and GM. Given the nature of their lifestyles and conditions, as well as their exposure to stigma and discrimination, these groups are among the most socially excluded and hard to reach. It was necessary first to make contact with other individuals well associated with and trusted by representatives of vulnerable groups in order to arrange the interviews. This proved to be worthwhile in that the participation of persons willing to share intimate details of their lives was secured.

There were no concerns over confidentiality. Respondents were informed at the start of the interviews that the information they shared would be confidential and that their names would not be published in any documentation.[1] Names and contact details were, however, collected should it be necessary for the interviewer to get in touch in order to acquire additional information or clarify details of the interview. These details were willingly given with no concerns raised over this requirement. In the event, it proved to be unnecessary. All respondents also signed the Consent Form without hesitation.

On average, interviews lasted fifty minutes with the longest extending over a period of one hour and ten minutes and the shortest for thirty-five minutes. It was important, as far as possible, to ensure privacy and to avoid interruptions during the interview process. Nine of the twelve interviews were conducted in the homes of the respondents, which proved to be private spaces. There were no major interruptions other than, in some instances, incoming telephone calls, which were taken. Interviews with the two PLHIV were conducted at the Lady Meade Reference Unit (LMRU), a specialist centre where persons living with HIV receive treatment and counselling and where they indicated they felt most comfortable. Arrangements were made by a staff member who made the necessary contacts and facilitated the interviews. All interviews were conducted in private rooms, out of earshot of others, with minimal distraction and no interruptions. The exception was the interview with one SW which took place on the street where she was conducting business. Though she lives in the area, the interview process did not take place in her home due to the lack of privacy there. She was asked if she would prefer to go to a more private area but insisted not. There were interruptions as she occasionally engaged in conversation with some passers-by as well as answered incoming calls to her mobile phone, but these were minor.

Before the commencement of each interview, respondents were made comfortable with light conversation and thanked for their contribution. The purpose of the interview and of their participation in the process was explicitly explained. All respondents understood this, and no one questioned their role. The interview sought mostly qualitative information. Questions were open-ended and accompanied by probes asked in an easy conversational rather than interrogative style. Respondents were further put at ease by the avoidance of any approving or disapproving comments or gestures by the interviewer. Patience and empathy were required on occasions when questions evoked painful memories. Questions were easily understood by the respondents, apart from one concerning their "diet", which posed a challenge. This question was interpreted by them as inquiring about dietary restrictions, not regular nutritional intake.

The respondents responded willingly, though some were more conversational and others somewhat more reserved indicating that they were not "talkative" by nature. All, however, were open and shared information with little hesitation. Prior to the commencement of the interviewing process, researchers were warned that, as a result of a recent spate of research projects dealing with issues around poverty and social exclusion, interview fatigue and a reluctance to engage in the process once more might be encountered. As it turned out, this was not the case. In addition, in order to express gratitude on the part of the researchers, a token non-monetary gift was presented to the respondents after the interview had been completed. This was unexpected, and many respondents expressed surprise and appreciation on receipt.

Although the interviews ran smoothly, the question of interviewer security, particularly the requirement that the interviews preferably be conducted in the homes of the informants, became a point of concern. Many of the respondents lived in what can be considered unsafe neighbourhoods, and some of their homes were in poor condition. This placed the interviewer in a situation where she had to be "constantly aware" of her safety. The gender of the interviewer and whether interviewers should operate in pairs should be a consideration in future research projects of this nature.

NOTES

CHAPTER 1

1. Also commonly known as the Moyne Report after the chairman of the Commission Lord Moyne.
2. Also see Teekens (1990).
3. This study was conducted with the assistance of the Inter-American Development Bank (IDB) and completed by the Barbados Statistical Service as a Poverty and Living Conditions module attached to the Continuous Labour Force Household Sample Survey conducted quarterly.
4. (1) The Participatory Poverty Assessment is a compilation of data gathered from in-depth interviews and focus group sessions conducted with individuals in low-income communities about their daily living conditions and coping strategies. (2) The Institutional Assessment examines the contribution of public, private and civil society organizations to the state of living conditions of citizens. (3) The Survey of Living Conditions provides primary data that is utilized to construct poverty estimates and to determine the distribution of poverty.
5. Similar definitions of poverty have been offered in CPA/CALC documents throughout the region. For example, the *Anguilla Country Poverty Assessment 2007/2009* defines the poor (those who suffer from poverty) as "those in society who suffer disadvantage with regard to their lack of possession of those goods, or facilities deemed to be necessary according to some generally accepted social standard or some fundamental physical need. There are two facets to this definition, one relative, the other absolute; both are utilized in the study" (3). The poverty rate was estimated at 5.8 per cent of individuals in the population based on a poverty line of EC$16,348.

    The *Grenada, Carriacou and Petit Martinique Country Poverty Assessment 2008* notes, "There is hardly any disagreement now that poverty is about the failure of an individual, a group, or community to achieve some acceptable standard of living that has a material base. The poverty line is the consumption (or income) level that separates the poor from the rest of the population on the basis of this material base: it is comprised of an absolute and a relative component" (2).

CHAPTER 2

1. Nam, Huang and Sherraden (2008) have defined "assets" as anything that can provide positive financial return. Assets can be tangible or intangible. Tangible assets include (1) money savings, (2) stocks, bonds and other financial security, (3) real property/estate, (4) hard assets other than real property such as automobiles, jewellery, art and collectibles, (5) machines, equipment, tools and other tangible components of production, (6) durable household goods, (7) natural resources, and (8) copyrights, patents and other intellectual property. Intangible assets include (1) access to credit, (2) human capital, (3) cultural capital, (4) informal social capital, (5) formal social capital or organizational capital and (6) political capital.

2. See   http://www.nationnews.com/nationnews/news/94732/rock-hall-bursting -squatters (accessed 20 May 2017).

3. Amartya Sen (1999, 63), in his renowned work *Development as Freedom*, discusses the adaptation of persons to their conditions of poverty and inequality to make their lives more bearable. He states, "The deprived tend to come to terms with their deprivation because of the sheer necessity of survival and they may, as a result even adjust their desires and expectations to what they unambitiously see as feasible." Therefore, despite conditions of poverty not being ideal, poor individuals often train themselves to be contented with their circumstances and adjust their expectations and aspirations to align with their reality and avoid feelings of disappointment and hopelessness.

4. Christophe, Newsham, Davies, Ulrichs and Godfrey-Wood (2014, 607) note that coping strategies that involve a reduction in consumption and access to resources can have detrimental effects on the overall well-being of the family and can also negatively impact their ability to climb out of poverty. There are a variety of "unacceptable trade-offs", such as reduced meals, poor diets, dropping out of school and not seeking medical attention for health issues.

5. The fifteen countries from which data were gathered are Malawi, Morocco, Senegal, Tanzania, Uganda, Afghanistan, Bangladesh, India, Sri Lanka, Cambodia, Indonesia, Philippines, Thailand, Columbia, Mexico.

CHAPTER 3

1. Other data sources are utilized where relevant.
2. Youth are defined as those in the age group 15 to 24; middle-aged as between 25 and 54; and elderly as 55 and over.
3. Chi-squared significance tests indicate an Asymp. Sig. value of 0.004, Chi-square value of 8.239.
4. t-statistic = 7.35.

CHAPTER 4

1. A full description of the interview process is available in the appendix.
2. The Barbados ISEE (Identification, Stabilization, Enablement, Empowerment) Bridge Programme is an intervention at household-level modelled on the Chilean Puente Programme of conditional cash transfers, and it is intended to reduce poverty and promote social inclusion.

CHAPTER 5

1. Appendix 2 of the Barbados Habitat III report provides a list of relevant legislation directed at social protection of vulnerable groups. See https://www2. habitat3.org/bitcache/2a5a50290a7d7ba1f5999f7fecce92db9d60b912?vid=5722 47&disposition=inline&op=view (accessed 27 March 2017).
2. Source: http://databank.worldbank.org/data/reports.aspx?source=2&country =BRB (accessed 27 March 2017).
3. Data from: https://www.imf.org/external/pubs/ft/scr/2016/cr16279.pdf (accessed 27 March 2017).
4. See https://reports.weforum.org/global-competitiveness-report-2014-2015/economies /#economy=BRB (accessed 27 March 2017).
5. See http://www.doingbusiness.org/data/exploreeconomies/barbados (accessed 25 March 2017).
6. Face-to-face interviews were held with the head of each organization or with someone nominated by him or her. An interview schedule was designed specifically for this assessment and solicited information on a variety of issues. These included the organization of the institution, financial information, long- and short-term goals, target population, living conditions addressed, type of support provided (methodologies), networking and challenges faced.

CHAPTER 6

1. The Inclusive Development Index is based on twelve indicators at the country level: GDP per capita; employment; labour productivity; healthy life expectancy; median household income; poverty rate; income Gini coefficient; wealth Gini coefficient; adjusted net savings; public debt (as percentage of GDP); dependency ratio; and carbon intensity of GDP (Samans et al. 2017).

2. Active labour market (ALM) policies are direct interventions by a government to provide employment. Interventions include the provision of public employment bureaux, training schemes, wage subsidies and direct provision of employment in public works projects. Lashley et al. (2015) provide a review of such ALM policies in practice as well as recommendations for enhancing their effectiveness in the Caribbean to address the issue of youth unemployment.

3. We use the term broad institutions to relate to institutions, legislation and regulations in all the three sectors of the economy: the public sector, the private sector and the third sector which includes non-state/non-market institutions such as charities, advocacy groups and other groups with a focus on addressing societal issues.

4. In addition to perceived stigma and discrimination reducing the lack of utilization, other factors such as high levels of bureaucracy, the need to supply very private information, the inadequacy of benefits viewed as not being worth the effort and a desire to remain independent all contribute to a lack of utilization.

5. Drawing on a survey of establishments in Barbados in 2014, only 18 per cent of enterprises utilized the National Employment Bureau to locate new employees. Data available from http://competecaribbean.org/proteqin (accessed 25 March 2017).

6. Currently, in order to access a contributory pension, at least 150 contributions have to made during a person's working life.

7. See http://www.nis.gov.bb/Benefits/?page=GenPage&subsection=Unemployment %20Benefit (accessed 24 March 2017).

8. Unless otherwise stated, all data are drawn from a 2014 survey on productivity, technology and innovation (PROTEqIN) undertaken in thirteen countries in the region. Data is presented only for Barbados. Data available from http://competecaribbean.org/proteqin (accessed 25 March 2017).

9. Multiple responses were allowed so figures would total to more than 100 per cent. Also note that electricity was also cited by 33 per cent of respondents.

10. The main multi-sectoral government agencies providing finance include Enterprise Growth Fund Limited, Barbados Investment Development Corporation and

FundAccess. The government also provides a small business loan guarantee through the Central Bank of Barbados.

11. In addition to the provision of compulsory education up to the secondary level and partial funding of tertiary education, the government also provides TVET services through the Barbados Institute of Management and Productivity, the Barbados Vocational Training Board, the Barbados TVET Council, Barbados Investment Development Corporation, the Samuel Jackman Prescott Polytechnic and the Barbados Community College.

12. Several institutions provide technical assistance as a component of normal operations; the most prominent is the Barbados Investment Development Corporation.

13. See http://www.doingbusiness.org/data/exploreeconomies/barbados (accessed 25 March 2017).

APPENDIX: DESCRIPTION OF THE INTERVIEW PROCESS

1. This report uses pseudonyms to conceal interviewees' identities.

REFERENCES

Alcock, Pete. 1997. *Understanding Poverty*. London: Macmillan.

Amendah, D. D., S. Buigut and S. Mohamed. 2014. "Coping Strategies Among Urban Poor: Evidence from Nairobi Kenya". Accessed 27 August 2016. http://dx.doi.org /10.1371/journal.pone.0083428.

Anderson, Torben, Bengt Holmstrom, Seppo Honkapohja, Sixten Korkman, Hans Soderstrom and Juhana Vartianen. 2007. *The Nordic Model. Embracing Globalization and Sharing Risks*. Helsinki: ETLA B.

Aoki, Aya, Barbara Bruns, Michael Drabble, Mmantsetsa Marope, Alain Mingat, Peter Moock, Patrick Murphy et al. 2001. *Education: Poverty Reduction Strategy Sourcebook*. Washington, DC: World Bank.

Araujo, Ariana, Andrea Quesada, Lorena Aguilar and Rebecca Pearl. 2007. *Gender Equality and Adaptation*. New York and Gland: Women's Environment and Development Organization and International Union for Conservation of Nature.

Atkinson, A. 2003. "Multidimensional Deprivation: Contrasting Social Welfare and Counting Approaches". *Journal of Economic Inequality* 1: 51–65.

Attanasio, Orazio P., and Miguel Székely. 1999. "An Asset-Based Approach to the Analysis of Poverty in Latin America". Working Paper R-376, Inter-American Development Bank, Washington, DC.

Azmat, Ghazala, Guell, Maia and Alan Manning. 2006. "Gender Gaps in Unemployment Rates in OECD Countries". *Journal of Labour Economics* 24 (1): 1–37.

Bailey, Barbara, and Suzanne Charles. 2010. *Gender Differentials in Caribbean Education Systems*. Georgetown: CARICOM.

Bailey, Corin. 2004. "Crime and Social Exclusion in the Kingston Metropolitan Area". Thesis, University of the West Indies, Mona, Jamaica.

———. 2013. "Exploring Female Motivations for Drug Smuggling on the Island of Barbados". *Feminist Criminology* 8 (2): 117–41.

———. 2016. *Crime and Violence in Barbados*. Washington, DC: Inter-American Development Bank.

Bailey, Wilma. 1981. "Clinical Undernutrition in the Kingston/St Andrew Metropolitan Area: 1967–1976". *Social Science and Medicine* 15 (4): 471–77.

Barbados Office of the Auditor General. 2014. *Report of the Auditor General*. Bridgetown: Barbados Audit Office.

Barbados Statistical Service. 2013. *Population and Housing Census*. Volume 1. Bridgetown: Barbados Statistical Service.

Barker, Judy L. 1997. *Poverty Reduction and Human Development in the Caribbean*. Washington, DC: World Bank.

Barrow, Christine. 2001. "Contesting the Rhetoric of 'Black Family Breakdown' from Barbados". *Journal of Comparative Family Studies* 32 (3): 419–41.

———. 2009. "Contradictory Sexualities: From Vulnerability to Empowerment for Adolescent Girls in Barbados". In *Sexuality, Social Exclusion and Human Rights: Vulnerability in the Caribbean Context of HIV*, edited by Christine Barrow, Marjan de Bruin and Robert Carr, 215–38. Kingston: Ian Randle.

Barrow, Christine, and Peter Aggleton. 2013. "Good Face, Bad Mind? HIV Stigma and Tolerance Rhetoric in Barbados". *Social and Economic Studies* 62 (1–2): 28–52.

Bass, Steven, Tom Bigg, Joshua Bishop and Dan Tunstall. 2006. "Sustaining the Environment to Fight Poverty and Achieve the Millennium Development Goals". *Review of European Community and International Environmental Law* 15 (1): 39–55.

Beckford, George. 1972. *Persistent Poverty: Underdevelopment in Plantation Economies of the Third World*. New York: Oxford University Press.

Begum, Sharifa, and Binayak Sen. 2003. "Unsustainable Livelihoods, Health Shocks and Urban Chronic Poverty: Rickshaw Pullers as a Case Study". CPRC Working Paper (46). Bangladesh Institute of Development Studies, Bangladesh.

Bene, Christophe, Andrew Newsham, Andrew Davies, Martina Ulrichs and Rachel Godfrey-Wood. 2014. "Review Article: Resilience, Poverty and Development". *Journal of International Development* 98 (6): 598–623.

Bennett, Fran, and Mary Daly. 2014. *Poverty Through a Gender Lens: Evidence and Policy Review on Gender and Poverty*. Oxford: Joseph Rowntree Foundation.

Berkham, Heather. 2007. *Social Exclusion and Violence in Latin America and the Caribbean*. Washington, DC: Inter-American Development Bank.

Bolin, Robert, and Lois Standford. 1998. *The Northridge Earthquake: Vulnerability and Disaster*. London: Routledge.

Borkert, Maren, Wolfgang Bosswick, Friedrich Heckman and Doris Luken-Klaben. 2007. *Local Integration Policies for Migrants in Europe*. Dublin: European Foundation for the Improvement of Living and Working Conditions.

Bourguignon, F., and S. Chakravarty. 2003. "The Measurement of Multidimensional Poverty". *Journal of Economic Inequality* 1 (1): 15–49.

Bourne, Paul. 2009. "Socio-demographic Determinants of Healthcare-seeking Behaviour, Self Reported Illness and Self-evaluated Health Status in Jamaica". *International Journal of Collaborative Research on Internal Medicine and Public Health* 1 (4): 101–30.

Bowles, Samuel, and Herbert Gintis. 1976. *Schooling in Capitalist America*. London: Routledge and Kegan Paul.

Boyce, James, and Manuel Pastor. 2001. *Building Natural Assets: New Strategies for Poverty Reduction and Environmental Protection*. Amherst, MA: Political Economy Research Institute.

Bryant, Toba, Chad Leaver and James Dunn. 2009. "Unmet Healthcare Need, Gender, and Health Inequities in Canada". *Health Policy* 91 (1): 24–32.

Bynner, John, and Will Paxton. 2001. *The Asset Effect*. London: Institute for Public Policy Research.

Cabinet Office. 2007. *Making Assets Work: The Quirk Review of Community Management and Ownership of Public Assets*. Norwich: Office of Public Sector Information.

Cagatay, Nilufer. 1998. "Engendering Macroeconomics and Macroeconomic Policies". Social Development and Poverty Elimination Division, Working Paper (6). UNDP, New York.

Campbell, Donovan, and Clinton Beckford. 2009. "Negotiating Uncertainty: Jamaican Small Farmers' Adaptation and Coping Strategies, Before and After Hurricanes – A Case Study of Hurricane Dean". *Sustainability* 1: 1366–87.

Caner, Asena, and Edward Wolff. 2004. "Asset Poverty in the United States, 1984–99: Evidence from the Panel Study of Income Dynamics". *Review of Income and Wealth* 50 (4): 493–518.

Caribbean Development Bank. 2012a. *Barbados Country Assessment of Living Conditions 2010*. Volume 3: *Survey of Living Conditions*. Bridgetown: Caribbean Development Bank/Government of Barbados.

———. 2012b. *Barbados Country Assessment of Living Conditions 2010*. Volume 6: *The Institutional Assessment (IA)*. Bridgetown: Caribbean Development Bank.

———. 2016. *The Changing Nature of Poverty and Inequality in the Caribbean: New Issues, New Solutions*. Barbados: Caribbean Development Bank.

Caribbean Development Research Services Incorporated. 2013. *Attitudes Towards Homosexuals in Barbados*. Bridgetown: Caribbean Development Research Services.

Case, Anne, and Christina Paxson. 2005. "Sex Differences in Morbidity and Mortality". *Demography* 42: 189–214.

Cashman, A. 2014. "Water Security and Services in the Caribbean". *Water* 6: 1187–203.

Census Bureau. 1975. *A Numerator and Denominator for Measuring Change.* Washington, DC: US Bureau of the Census.

Chambers, Robert. 1995. "Poverty and Livelihoods: Whose Really Counts?" *Environment and Urbanization* 7 (1): 173–204.

Chen, Jiajian, and Feng Hou. 2002. "Unmet Needs for Health Care". *Health Reports* 13 (2): 23–34.

Clark, David. 2007. *Adaptation, Poverty and Well-being: Some Issues and Observations with Special Reference to the Capability Approach and Development Studies.* Manchester: Institute for Development Policy and Management, University of Manchester, Global Poverty Research Group.

Clark, Kim, and Lawrence Summers. 1979. "Labour Market Dynamics and Unemployment: A Reconsideration". *Brookings Papers on Economic Activity* 1: 13–60.

Clark, Sherrill. 2007. "Social Work Students' Perceptions of Poverty". *Journal of Human Behaviour in the Social Environment* 16 (1–2): 149–66.

Clemente, Frank, and Michael Kleiman. 1977. "Fear of Crime in the United States: A Multivariate Analysis". *Social Forces* 56: 519–31.

Cohen, Barney. 2006. "Urbanization in Developing Countries: Current Trends, Future Projections, and Key Challenges for Sustainability". *Technology in Society* 28 (1–2): 63–80.

Cox, Eva. 1995. *A Truly Civic Society.* Sydney: ABC Books.

Craine, Steve. 1997. "The Black Magic Roundabout: Cyclical Social Exclusion and Alternative Careers". In *Youth, the "Underclass" and Social Exclusion*, edited by Robert McDonald, 130–52. London: Routledge.

Cresswell, Tim. 2000. *The Tramp in America: An Explanation of Knowledge, Mobility and Marginality.* New York: Reaktion Books.

Cutter, Susan. 2005. "Are We Asking the Right Question?" In *What Is a Disaster? New Answers to Old Questions*, edited by Ronald Perry and Enrico Quarantelli, 39–48. Philadelphia: Xlibris.

Dankelman, Irene. 2010. *Gender and Climate Change: An Introduction.* London: Earthscan.

Davy, Ulrike. 2014. "How Human Rights Shape Social Citizenship: On Citizenship and the Understanding of Economic and Social Rights". *Washington University Global Studies Law Review* 13 (2): 201–63.

DeFilippis, Joseph. 2001. "The Myth of Social Capital in Community Development". *Housing Policy Debate* 12 (4): 781–803.

De la Fuente, Alejandro. 2007. "Climate Shocks and Their Impact on Assets". Paper no. 23. Human Development Report 2007/2008. United Nations Development Programme. Oxford University Press, New York.

Denton, Margaret, Steven Prus and Vivienne Walters. 2004. "Gender Differences in Health: A Canadian Study of the Psychological, Structural and Behavioural Determinants of Health". *Social Science and Medicine* 58 (12): 2585–600.

Dercon, Stefan. 2000. *Income Risk, Coping Strategies and Safety Nets.* Oxford: Oxford University, Department of Economics.

DESA. 2009. *Creating an Inclusive Society: Practical Strategies to Promote Social Integration.* New York: United Nations, Department of Economic and Social Affairs.

Deutsch, J., and J. Silber. 2005. "Measuring Multidimensional Poverty: An Empirical Comparison of Various Approaches". *Review of Income and Wealth* 51: 145–74.

Devicienti, Francesco, and Ambra Poggi. 2011. "Poverty and Social Exclusion: Two Sides of the Same Coin or Dynamically Interrelated Processes". *Applied Economics* 43 (25): 3549–71.

Dewey, John. 1953. *Democracy and Education: An Introduction to the Philosophy of Education.* New York: Macmillan.

Department for International Development (DFID). 1999. *Sustainable Livelihoods and Poverty Elimination.* London: Department for International Development.

Dhongde, S., and R. Haveman. 2017. "Multi-dimensional Deprivation in the US". *Social Indicators Research* 133: 477–500.

Diez de Medina, Rafael. 1998. *Poverty and Income Distribution in Barbados 1996–1997.* Washington, DC: Inter-American Development Bank.

Donald, Alice, and Elizabeth Mothershaw. 2009. *Poverty, Inequality and Human Rights.* New York: Joseph Rowntree Foundation.

Dugarova, Esuna. 2015. "Social Inclusion, Poverty Eradication and the 2030 Agenda for Sustainable Development". Working Paper, United Nations Research Institute for Social Development, Geneva.

Durkheim, Emile. 1961. *Moral Education: A Study in the Theory and Application of the Sociology of Education.* New York: Free Press.

Duryea, Suzanne, Sebastian Galiani, Hugo Nopo and Claudia Piras. 2007. *The Education Gender Gap in Latin America and the Caribbean.* Washington, DC: Inter-American Development Bank.

Elliott, Dawn. 2006. "The Jamaican Female Skills Surplus and Earnings Deficit". *Journal of International Women's Studies* 8 (1): 65–82.

Ellis, Frank, and Edward Allison. 2004. "Livelihood Diversification and Natural Resource Access". Livelihood Support Programme Working Paper. UN Food and Agriculture Organization, Rome.

EU Social Protection Committee. 2014. "The Working Poor in Europe". SPMM Thematic Reviews on the 2012 Social Trends to Watch. Accessed 15 May 2015. https://ec.europa.eu/social/BlobServlet?docId=14887&langId=en.

Fagin, Leonard, and Martin Little. 1984. *The Forsaken Families*. Harmondsworth: Penguin.

Farchamps, Marcel. 2003. *Rural Poverty, Risk and Development*. Cheltenham: Edward Elgar.

Ferguson, C., C. Moser and A. Norton. 2006. "Claiming Rights: Citizenship and the Politics of Asset Distribution". In *Reducing Global Poverty: The Case for Asset Accumulation*, edited by C. Moser, 273–88. Washington, DC: Brookings Institution Press.

Fernandez-Kelly, Maria. 1995. "Social and Cultural Capital in the Urban Ghetto: Implications for the Economic Sociology of Immigration". In *The Economic Sociology of Immigration*, edited by Alejandro Portes, 213–47. New York: Russell Sage Foundation.

Field, Christopher, Vicente Barros, Thomas Stocker, Qin Dahe, David Jon Dokken, Kristie Ebi, Michael Mastrandrea et al. 2012. *Managing the Risks of Extreme Events and Disasters to Advance Climate Change Adaptation: Special Report of the Intergovernmental Panel on Climate Change*. New York: Cambridge University Press.

Figueroa, John. 2008. "The HIV Epidemic in the Caribbean: Meeting the Challenges of Achieving Universal Access to Prevention, Treatment and Care". *West Indian Medical Journal* 57 (3): 195–203.

Flint, John. 2010. *Coping Strategies? Agencies, Budgeting and Self-esteem Amongst Low-income Households*. Sheffield: Centre for Regional Economic and Social Research, Sheffield Hallam University.

Food and Agriculture Organization (FAO). 2015. *State of Food Insecurity and the CARICOM Caribbean. Meeting Hunger Targets: Taking Stock of Uneven Progress*. Barbados: Subregional Office for the Caribbean, FAO.

Ford Foundation. 2004. *Building Assets to Reduce Poverty and Injustice*. New York: Ford Foundation.

Foster, J., J. Greer and E. Thorbecke. 1984. "A Class of Decomposable Poverty Measures". *Econometrica* 52 (3): 761–66.

Frank, Robert. 2007. *Falling Behind: How Rising Inequality Harms the Middle Class*. Berkeley: University of California Press.

Frazer, Hugh and Marlier Eric. 2010. "In-work Poverty and Labour Market Segmentation in the EU: Key Lessons". Synthesis Report (based on National Reports by EU Network of National Independent Experts on Social Inclusion). Brussels: European Commission.

———. 2016. *Minimum Income Schemes in Europe: A Study of National Policies, 2015*. Brussels: European Commission.

————. 2013. *Assessment of Progress Towards the Europe 2020 Social Inclusion Objectives.* EU Network of Independent Experts on Social Inclusion. Brussels: European Commission.

Frey, Bruno, and Alois Stutzer. 2002. *Happiness and Economics.* Princeton, NJ: Princeton University Press.

Friedman, John, and Ute Lehrer. 1997. "Urban Policy Responses to Foreign-migration: The Case of Frankfurt-am-Main". *Journal of the American Planning Association* 63 (1): 61–78.

Fukuyama, Francis. 1995. *Trust, the Social Virtues and Creation of Prosperity.* New York: Free Press.

Gallie, Duncan, and Carolyn Vogler. 1994. "Unemployment and Attitudes to Work". In *Social Change and the Experience of Unemployment,* edited by Duncan Gallie, Catherine Marsh and Carolyn Vogler, 115–53. Oxford and New York: Oxford University Press.

Garba, Tukur. 2011. "Shocks, Coping Strategies and Subjective Poverty: Evidence from Nigeria's National Core Welfare Indicators Questionnaire Survey". *Journal of Sustainable Development in Africa* 13 (6): 129–64.

Garfinkel, I., and R. Haveman. 1977. *Earnings Capacity, Poverty and Inequality.* New York: Academic Press.

Girvan, Norman. 1997. *Poverty, Empowerment and Social Development in the Caribbean.* Kingston: Canoe Press.

Gordon-Rouse, Kimberly. 1998. "Resilience from Poverty and Stress". *Human Development and Family Life Bulletin* 4 (1): 1–10.

Government of Barbados. 2013. *Barbados National Assessment Report for the Third International Conferences on Small Island Developing States.* Bridgetown: Government of Barbados.

————. 2015. *National Report for the Third United Nations Conference on Housing and Sustainable Development, Habitat III.* Sir Arthur Lewis Institute of Social and Economic Studies (SALISES) and the Centre for Resource Management and Environmental Studies (CERMES) of the University of the West Indies, Cave Hill, Barbados: Ministry of Housing, Lands and Rural Development of the Government of Barbados.

Halpern, David. 1999. *Social Capital, Exclusion and the Quality of Life.* London: Institute for Public Research.

Halsey, Albert, Jean Floud and Charles Anderson. 1961. *Education, Society and Economy.* New York: Free Press.

Harriott, A. 2003. "Social Identities and the Escalation of Homicidal Violence in Jamaica". In *Understanding Crime in Jamaica: New Challenges for Public Policy,* edited by A. Harriott, 89–112. Kingston: University of the West Indies Press.

Haveman, R., and L. Buron. 1993. "Escaping Poverty Through Work: The Problem of Low Earnings Capacity in the United States. 1973–88". *Review of Income and Wealth* 39 (2): 141–57.

Haveman, Robert, and Melissa Mullikin. 1999. "Alternatives to the Official Poverty Measure: Perspectives and Assessment". Paper presented at Poverty: Improving the Definition after Thirty Years. Institute for Research on Poverty, University of Wisconsin–Madison.

Haveman, Robert, and Edward Wolff. 2001. *Who Are the Asset Poor? Levels, Trends and Composition, 1983–1998*. Institute for Research on Poverty Discussion Paper 1227-01. Madison: IRP Publications.

———. 2004. "The Concept and Measurement of Asset Poverty: Levels, Trends and Composition for the US, 1983–2001". *Journal of Economic Inequality* 2 (2): 145–69.

Hazenberg, Richard. 2012. "Work-integration in Social Enterprise: A NEET Idea?" Doctor of Philosophy. University of Northampton.

Healy, Karen, Michele Haynes and Anne Hampshire. 2007. "Gender, Social Capital and Location: Understanding the Interactions". *International Journal of Social Welfare* 16: 110–18.

Henry, Ralph, and Juliet Melville. 2001. "Poverty Revisited: Trinidad and Tobago in the Late 1980's". In *Caribbean Sociology: Introductory Readings*, edited by Rhoda Reddock and Christine Barrow, 223–33. Kingston: Ian Randle.

Henry-Lee, Aldrie, and Elsie Le Franc. 2002. "Private Property and Gender in Guyana and Barbados". *Social and Economic Studies* 51 (4): 1–30.

Hospes, Otto, and Joy Clancy. 2011. "Unpacking the Discourse of Social Inclusion in Value Chains". In *Value Chains, Inclusion and Endogenous Development: Contrasting Theories and Realities*, edited by Bert Helmsing and Sietze Vellema, 23–41. London: Routledge.

International Fund for Agricultural Development (IFAD). 2011. *Annual Report 2010*. Rome: IFAD.

International Labour Organization (ILO). 2014. *Global Employment Trends: Risk of a Jobless Recovery*. Geneva: International Labour Organization.

International Monetary Fund (IMF). 2016. "National Insurance Scheme Reforms in the Caribbean". IMF Working Paper. Washington, DC: (IMF).

James, Christopher, Kara Hanson, Barbara McPake, Dina Balbanova, David Gwatkin, Ian Hopwood, Christina KIrunga et al. 2006. "To Retain or Remove User Fees? Reflections on the Current Debate in Low and Middle-income Countries." *Applied Health Economics and Health Policy* 5: 147–53.

Jehoel-Gijsbers, Gerda. 2004. *Social Exclusion in the Netherlands*. The Hague: Netherlands Institute for Social Research.

Jehoel-Gijsbers, Gerda, and Cok Vrooman. 2004. "Social Exclusion in the Netherlands: Construction of a Model of Key Risks on Poverty and Social Exclusion". Third Round Table on Poverty and Social Exclusion. Rotterdam, 18–19 October. Accessed 23 January 2016. https://www.researchgate.net/publication /236981323_Social_exclusion_in_the_Netherlands_Construction_of_a_model _of_key_risks_on_poverty_and_social_exclusion.

Kairi Consultants Limited. 2008. *Final Report Country Poverty Assessment: Grenada, Carriacou and Petit Martinique.* Grenada: Government of Grenada and Caribbean Development Bank.

Kawachi, Ichiro, Bruce Kennedy and Roberta Glass. 1999. "Social Capital and Self-rated Health: A Contextual Analysis". *American Journal of Public Health* 87 (9): 11491–98.

Kempson, Elaine, Alex Bryson and Karen Rowlingson. 1994. *Strategies Used by Low Income Families with Children to Make Ends Meet.* London: Joseph Rowntree Foundation.

Kenney, Catherine. 2004. "Cohabiting Couple, Filing Jointly? Resource Pooling and US Poverty Policies". *Family Relations* 53 (2): 237–47.

Knack, Stephen, and Philip Keefer. 1997. "Does Social Capital Have an Economic Payoff? A Cross Country Investigation". *Quarterly Journal of Economics* 112 (4): 1251–88.

Krishna, Anirudh. 2006. "Pathways out of and into Poverty in 36 Villages of Andhra Pradesh, India". *World Development* 34 (2): 324–404.

Laguerre, Michel. 1990. *Urban Poverty in the Caribbean: French Martinique as a Social Laboratory.* Basingstoke: Palgrave Macmillan.

Lashley, Jonathan. 2010. "External Enticements and Internal Inertia: Constraints to Enterprise Growth in Barbadian Manufacturing Enterprises". Paper presented at the SALISES Annual Conference: Turbulence in Small Developing States: Going Beyond Survival. Port of Spain, Trinidad and Tobago.

———. 2012. *Weather Related Insurance and Risk Management: A Demand Study in the Caribbean.* Bonn: German Association for International Cooperation.

Lashley, Jonathan, Don Marshall, Corin Bailey and Karen Lord. 2015. *Youth Are the Future: The Imperative of Youth Employment for Sustainable Development.* Bridgetown: Caribbean Development Bank.

Lavesque, Jean, Mark Harris and Grant Russell. 2013. "Patient-centered Access to Health Care: Conceptualising Access at the Interface of Health Systems and Populations". *International Journal for Equity in Health* 12: 12–18.

Levitas, Ruth. 1996. "The Legacy of Rayner". In *Interpreting Official Statistics*, edited by Ruth Levitas and Will Guy, 7–25. London: Routledge.

————. 1998. *The Inclusive Society? Social Exclusion and New Labour*. Basingstoke: Macmillan.

Lewis, Oscar. 1965. *La Vida*. New York: Random House.

Light, Ivan, and Stavros Karageorgis. 1994. "The Ethnic Economy". In *Handbook of Economic Sociology*, edited by Neil Smelser and Richard Swedberg, 650–77. Princeton, NJ: Princeton University Press.

Lister, Ruth. 2004. *Poverty*. Cambridge: Polity Press.

Marston, Stephen. 1975. "The Impact of Unemployment Insurance on Job Search". *Brookings Papers on Economic Activity* 1: 169–203.

Mathie, A., and Gord Cunningham, G. 2003. "From Clients to Citizens: Asset-Based Community Development as a Strategy for Community-Driven Development". *Development in Practice* 13: 474–86.

McNeil, Patrick, and Charles Townley. 1986. *Fundamentals of Sociology*. London: Hutchinson.

Mechler, Reinhard, Joanne Linnerooth-Bayer and David Peppiatt. 2006. *Disaster Insurance for the Poor: A Review of Microinsurance for Natural Disaster Risks in Developing Countries*. Geneva: Prevention Consortium.

Mitchell, Andrew, and Richard Shillington. 2002. *Poverty, Inequality, and Social Exclusion*. Toronto: Laidlaw Foundation.

Mitchell, Tom, and Katie Harris. 2012. *Resilience: A Risk Management Approach*. London: Overseas Development Institute.

Monroe, Pamela, Vicky Tiller, Carol O'Neil and Lydia Blalock. 2007. "We Make Our Ends Meet Good: Coping Strategies of Former Welfare-reliant Women". *Journal of Loss and Trauma* 12: 199–221.

Moore, Winston. 2013. *Private Sector Assessment of Barbados*. Washington, DC: Inter-American Development Bank.

Moser, Caroline. 1998. "The Asset Vulnerability Framework: Reassessing Urban Poverty Reduction Strategies". *World Development* 26: 1–19.

Moser, Caroline, and Jeremy Holland. 1997. *Urban Poverty and Violence in Jamaica*. Washington, DC: World Bank.

Nam, Valerie. 2016. *Trends in Adolescent Motherhood and Fertility, and Related Inequalities in the Caribbean 1990–2010*. ECLAC: Population and Development Series no. 115. Santiago: United Nations.

Nam, Yunju, Jin Huang and Michael Sherraden. 2008. *Assets, Poverty and Public Policy: Challenges in Definition and Measurement*. St Louis, MO: Center for Social Development, Washington University.

Narayan, Deepa, Raj Patel, Kai Schafft, Anne Rademacher and Sarah Koch-Schulte. 2000. *Voices of the Poor: Can Anyone Hear Us?* Washington, DC: Oxford University Press for the World Bank.

Narayan, Deepa, and Patti Petesch. 2007. "Agency, Opportunity and Poverty Escapes". In vol. 1, *Moving Out of Poverty: Cross Disciplinary Perspectives on Mobility*, edited by Deepa Narayan and Patti Petesch, 1–44. Washington, DC: Palgrave Macmillan and World Bank.

Narayan, Deepa, Lant Pritchett and Soumya Kapoor. 2009. *Moving Out of Poverty: Success from the Bottom Up*. Washington, DC: Palgrave Macmillan/World Bank.

Narayan, P., and R. Smyth. 2004. The Relationship Between the Real Exchange Rate and Balance of Payments: Empirical Evidence for China from Cointegration and Causality Testing. *Applied Economics Letters* 11: 287–91.

Nicholson, Lawrence, and Jonathan Lashley. 2016. *Understanding the Caribbean Enterprise: Insights from MSMEs and Family Owned Businesses*. London: Palgrave Macmillan.

Nilsen, Øivind Anti, and Katrine Holm Reiso. 2011. *Scarring Effects of Unemployment*. Bonn: Institute for the Study of Labour.

Nishikiori, Nobuyuki, Tomoko Abe, Dehiwala Costa, Samath Dharmaratne, Osamu Kunil and Kazuhiko Moji. 2006. "Who Died as a Result of the Tsunami? Risk Factors of Mortality Among Internally Displaced Persons in Sri Lanka: A Retrospective Cohort Analysis". *BMC Public Health* 6: 73–74.

Novick, Marvyn. 2001. "Social Inclusion: The Foundation of a National Policy Agenda". In *The Laidlaw and Canadian Council on Social Development Conference: A New Way of Thinking? Towards a Vision of Social Inclusion*. Ottawa: Laidlaw Institute.

Office of the Auditor General. 2014. *Report of the Auditor General for the Year 2013*. Bridgetown: Barbados Audit Office.

Oliver, Melvin, and Thomas Shapiro. 1997. *Black Wealth/White Wealth*. New York: Routledge Press.

OPHI. 2017. *Oxford Poverty and Human Development Initiative*. Accessed 14 August 2018. https://www.ophi.org.uk/wp-content/uploads/B47_Global_MPI_2017.pdf.

Organization of American States. 2005. "The Economics of Disaster Mitigation in the Caribbean: Quantifying the Benefits and Costs of Mitigating Natural Hazards Losses. Lessons Learned from the 2004 Hurricane Season". *Working Paper*. Accessed 11 May 2016. http://www.oas.org/dsd/MinisterialMeeting/Documents/economics_disaster_mitigation_caribb_full_report.pdf.

Osei, Phillip. 2001. "Has Poor Relief Declined in Jamaica? A Preliminary Investigation". *Social and Economic Studies* 50 (1): 229–62.

Parry, Martin, Osvaldo Canziani, Jean Palutikof, Paul van der Linden and Clair Hanson. 2007. *Climate Change 2007: Impacts, Adaptation and Vulnerability*. New York: Cambridge University Press.

Parsons, Talcott. 1961. "The School Class as a Social System". In *Education, Economy, and Society*, edited by Albert Halsey and Charles Anderson, 434–55. New York: Free Press.

Pemberton, Simon, Eileen Sutton and Eldin Fahmy. 2013. "A Review of the Qualitative Evidence Relating to the Experience of Poverty and Social Exclusion". Poverty and Social Exclusion in the UK, Working Paper Series. Economic and Social Research Council, Bristol/Birmingham.

Perlman, Janice. 2007. "Elusive Pathways out of Poverty: Intra- and Inter-generational Mobility in the Favelas of Rio de Janeiro". In vol. 1, *Moving out of Poverty: Cross-disciplinary Perspectives on Mobility*, edited by Deepa Narayan and Patti Petesch, 227–73. Washington, DC: Palgrave Macmillan and World Bank.

Peters, David, Anu Garg, Gerry Bloom, Damian Walker, William Brieger and Hafizur Rahman. 2008. "Poverty and Access to Health Care in Developing Countries". *Annals of New York Academy of Sciences* 1136: 161–71.

Peterson, Tom. 1996. "Community Land Trusts: An Introduction". *Planning Commissioners Journal* 23: 10–15.

Planning Institute of Jamaica. 2013. *Economic and Social Survey of Jamaica*. Kingston: Planning Institute of Jamaica.

———. 1999. *Economic and Social Survey of Jamaica*. Kingston: Planning Institute of Jamaica.

Portes, Alejandro. 1995. "Economic Sociology and the Sociology of Immigration: A Conceptual Overview". In *The Economic Sociology of Immigration: Essays on the Networks, Ethnicity and Entrepreneurship*, edited by Alejandro Portes, 1–41. New York: Russell Sage Foundation.

———. 1998. "Social Capital: Its Origins and Applications in Modern Sociology". *Annual Review of Sociology* 24: 1–24.

Portney, Kent, and Jeffrey Berry. 1997. "Mobilizing Minority Communities: Social Capital and Participation in Neighbourhoods". *American Behavioural Scientist* 40 (5): 632–44.

Potter, Robert B., David Barker, Dennis Conway and Thomas Klak. 2014. *The Contemporary Caribbean*. London: Routledge Taylor & Francis Group.

Putnam, Robert. 1993. *Making Democracy Work: Civic Traditions in Modern Italy*. Princeton, NJ: Princeton University Press.

———. 2000. *Bowling Alone: The Collapse and Revival of American Community*. New York: Simon & Schuster.

Renard, Yves, and Eleanor Wint. 2007. *Participatory Approaches, Social, Policy and Poverty Reduction*. Kingston: Ian Randle.

Robinson, Tracy. 2009. "Authorized Sex: Same-sex Sexuality and Law in the Caribbean". In *Sexuality, Social Exclusion and Human Rights: Vulnerabilities in the Caribbean Context of HIV*, edited by Christine Barrow, Marjan de Bruin and Robert Carr, 3–22. Kingston: Ian Randle.

Ruthven, Orlanda, and Sushil Kumar. 2003. "Making and Breaking Poverty in Koraon, Utter Pradesh" Paper presented at the conference Chronic Poverty and Development Policy, University of Manchester, 7–9 April.

Safa, Helen. 1974. *The Urban Poor of Puerto Rico: A Study in Development and Inequality*. New York: Holt, Rinehart & Winston.

———. 1999. "Female-headed Households in the Caribbean: Deviant of Alternative Form of Family Organization". *Latino(a) Research Review* 4 (2): 16–26.

Sahin, Aysegul, Jeseph Song and Bart Hobijn. 2010. *The Unemployment Gender Gap during the 2007 Recession*. New York: Federal Reserve Bank of New York.

Samans, Richard, Jennifer Blanke, Gemma Corrigan and Margareta Drzeniek Hanouz. 2017. "Rising to the Challenge of Inclusive Growth and Development". In *Inclusive Growth and Development Report*, edited by Richard Samans, Jennifer Blanke and Margareta Drzeniek Hanouz, 1–46. Geneva: World Economic Forum.

Sanders, Anne, Lim Sungwoo and Sohn Woosung. 2008. "Resilience to Urban Poverty: Theoretical and Empirical Considerations for Population Health". *American Journal of Public Health* 98 (6): 1101–6.

Secombe, Karen. 2002. "Beating the Odds Versus Changing the Odds: Poverty, Resilience and Family Policy". *Journal of Marriage and Family* 64: 384–94.

Seers, Dudley. 1969. "The Meaning of Development". *IDS Communications 44*. Accessed 20 May 2019. https://www.ids.ac.uk/files/dmfile/themeaningofdevelopment.pdf.

Seguino, Stephanie. 2003. "Why Are Women in the Caribbean so Much More Likely to Be Unemployed?" MPRA Paper No. 6507. University of the West Indies, St Augustine, Trinidad and Tobago.

Sen, Amartya. 1999. *Development as Freedom*. New York: Alfred Knopf.

Shaffer, Paul. 2002. "Participatory Analyses of Poverty Dynamics: Reflections on the Myanmar PPA". In *Knowing Poverty. Critical Reflections on Participatory Research and Policy*, edited by Karen McGee and Rosemary Brock, 44–68. Oxford: Earthscan Publications.

Shapiro, Thomas. 2001. "The Importance of Assets". In *Assets for the Poor: The Benefits of Spreading Asset Ownership*, edited by Thomas M. Shapiro and Edward N. Wolff, 11–33. New York: Russell Sage Foundation.

Shapiro, Thomas, Melvin Oliver and Tatjana Meschede. 2009. "The Asset Security and Opportunity Index". Research and Policy Brief. Institute on Assets and Social Policy, Boston.

Sherman, Jennifer. 2006. "Coping with Rural Poverty: Economic Survival and Moral Capital in Rural America". *Social Forces* 85 (2): 891–913.

Sherraden, Michael. 2001. *Assets and the Poor: Implications for Individual Accounts and Social Security: Invited Testimony to the President's Commission on Social Security* (CSD Perspective No. 01-17). St Louis, MO: Washington University, Center for Social Development.

Socias, Maria, Mieke Koehoorn and Jean Shoveller. 2016. "Gender Inequalities in Access to Health Care Among Adults Living in British Columbia, Canada". *Women's Health Issues* 26 (1): 74–79. doi: 10.1016/j.whi.2015.08.001.

Tchombe, Shalo, Almon Shumba, Joseph Lo-oh, Theogene-Octave Gakuba, Martina Zinkeng and Tanyi Teku. 2012. "South African Psychological Undertones of Family Poverty in Rural Communities in Cameroon". *South African Journal of Psychology* 42 (2): 234–39.

Teekens, Rudolph. 1990. "Poverty Data from Two Family Budget Surveys in Trinidad and Tobago, 1989". World Bank.

Theodossiou, Loannis, and Alexandros Zangelidis. 2009. "Should I Stay or Should I Go? The Effect of Gender, Education and Unemployment on Labour Market Transitions". *Labour Economics* 16 (5): 566–77.

Thomas, Clive. 1993. "The State of Poverty and Poverty Studies in Guyana". Paper presented at the seminar Poverty in Guyana: Finding Solutions. Institute of Development Studies, Georgetown, Guyana.

Townsend, Peter. 1979. *Poverty in the United Kingdom*. London: Penguin.

UNAIDS. 2015. "UNAIDS 2016–2021 Strategy: On the Fast Track to End AIDS". Accessed 16 May 2017. aidsdatahub.org/sites/default/files/publication/UNAIDS_Strategy_2016-2021.pdf.

UNICEF. 2010. *Health and Family Life Education Regional Curriculum Framework*. Bridgetown: UNICEF.

United Nations Development Programme (UNDP). 2013. *Overview of Linkages Between Gender and Climate Change*. Gender and Climate Change Asia and Pacific Policy Brief 1. New York: UNDP.

———. 2016. *Caribbean Human Development Report. Multidimensional Progress: Human Resilience Beyond Income*. New York: UNDP.

United States Department of State. 2016. "Country Reports on Human Rights Practices for 2016". *Barbados 2016 Human Rights Report*. Accessed 15 May 2017. www.refworld.org/docid/58ec8a7fa.html.

Verbrugge, Lois. 1985. "Gender and Health: An Update on Hypotheses and Evidence". *Journal of Health and Social Behaviour* 26: 156–82.

Victoria, Cesar, Bridget Fenn, Jennifer Bryce and Betty Kirkwood. 2005. "Co-coverage of Preventive Interventions and Implications for Child-survival Strategies: Evidence from National Surveys". *Lancet* 366: 1460–66.

Vrooman, Cok, and Stella Hoff. 2013. "The Disadvantaged Among the Dutch: A Survey Approach to the Multidimensional Measurement of Social Exclusion". *Social Indicators Research* 113: 1261–87.

Walker, Alan. 1997. "Introduction: The Strategy of Inequality". In *Britain Divided: The Growth of Social Exclusion in the 1980s and 1990s*, edited by Carol Walker and Alan Walker, 1–16. London: Child Poverty Action Group.

Warr, Peter, Michael Banks and Philip Ullah. 1985. "The Experience of Unemployment Among Black and White Urban Teenagers". *British Journal of Psychology* 76: 75–87.

Warren, Mark, Phillip Thompson and Susan Saegert. 2001. "The Role of Social Capital in Combating Poverty". In *Social Capital and Poor Communities*, edited by Susan Saegert, Phillip Thompson and Mark Warren, 1–30. New York: Russell Sage Foundation.

Whelan, C., B. Nolan and B. Maitre. 2014. "Multidimensional Poverty Measurement in Europe: An Application of the Adjusted Headcount Approach". *Journal of European Social Policy* 24: 183–97.

Wilkinson, Richard. 1996. *Unhealthy Societies: The Affliction of Inequality.* London: Routledge.

World Bank. 2013. *Shifting Gears to Accelerate Shared Prosperity in Latin America and the Caribbean.* Washington, DC: World Bank Publications.

World Health Organization (WHO). 2008. *Primary Health Care: Now More Than Ever.* World Health Report. Geneva: World Health Organization.

World Resources Institute. 2005. *World Resources 2005: The Wealth of the Poor. Managing Ecosystems to Fight Poverty.* Washington, DC: UNDP.

Young, Jock. 1999. *The Exclusive Society: Social Exclusion, Crime and Difference in Late Modernity.* Thousand Oaks, CA: Sage.

INDEX

CPSIA information can be obtained
at www.ICGtesting.com
Printed in the USA
BVHW081911150121
597458BV00001B/78